TELLING AND RETELLING

Indiana Studies in Biblical Literature

Herbert Marks and Robert Polzin,
General Editors

TELLING AND RETELLING

Quotation in Biblical Narrative

GEORGE W. SAVRAN

INDIANA UNIVERSITY PRESS
BLOOMINGTON & INDIANAPOLIS

This book was brought to publication with the assistance of the
Andrew W. Mellon Foundation.

Manufactured in the United States of America

Library of Congress Cataloging-in-Publication Data

Savran, George W.
Telling and retelling.

(Indiana studies in biblical literature)
Bibliography: p.
Includes index.
1. Quotation in the Bible.   2. Bible. O.T.—
Language, style.   3. Bible. O.T.—Criticism,
interpretation, etc.   I. Title.   II. Series.
BS1171.2.S26   1988   220.6′6   85-45315
ISBN 0-253-35928-7

1 2 3 4 5 92 91 90 89 88

To my father, Louis Savran—
May his memory be for a blessing.

CONTENTS

PREFACE

This study is an outgrowth of my interest in the poetics of dialogue in biblical narrative, and it is offered as a small contribution to our understanding of that highly complex issue. The phenomenon of quotation describes the intersection of a number of central aspects of the narrative: It is at once direct speech of the present narrative moment and recollection of prior words. It presents the quoting character as the teller of his own story but also as the subject of the narrator's discourse. Perhaps most important is the way in which quoted direct speech functions as an exegetical exercise, a rereading or respeaking of the past at a later time and in a new context.

An earlier version of this work was accepted as a doctoral dissertation in Near Eastern and Judaic Studies at Brandeis University. Parts of chapters 3 and 4 appeared in another form in *Prooftexts* 5 (1985):1–17. I am indebted to many people for their support and assistance, among whom I can mention only a few. My former advisor, Prof. Nahum M. Sarna, expertly guided my doctoral work and saw my dissertation through to completion, with many helpful suggestions along the way. Prof. Michael Fishbane provided valuable feedback and encouragement throughout the project. His work on inner-biblical Midrash has been one of the more important forces that shaped my thinking about quotation and repetition. Prof. James S. Ackerman, my former colleague at Indiana University, has been unflagging in his enthusiasm. It is no exaggeration to say that without his invaluable help, this study would not have seen the light of day. The entire Department of Religious Studies at IU was very supportive during my years there. Herbert Marks and Robert Polzin were exceptionally generous in their editorial roles and helped me to clarify and strengthen the arguments presented here. Robert Alter and Marc Bregman read the manuscript and provided useful criticism. The people at Indiana University Press merit special thanks for their care and expertise in all stages of the publication process.

Above all, I am grateful beyond words to my wife, Bella, for her patience and support during the writing of this book.

TELLING AND RETELLING

· 1 ·

REPETITION AND QUOTATION IN BIBLICAL NARRATIVE

1.

One of the characteristics of biblical narrative is the frequent repetition of words, phrases, and sentences at points where a brief summarizing remark would suffice. Most often these repetitions are not literal but diverge noticeably from the language and syntax of the original expression, giving rise to a crucial interpretative question: Are such changes in language and syntax to be understood purely as a norm of stylistic variation in biblical Hebrew, with no appreciable shift in meaning? Or do these changes point toward subtle but significant modifications of the meaning of the passage?

Let us begin by examining the views of a number of commentators on the extensive quotation and repetition by Abraham's servant in Genesis 24. Arguing from the position that "the Torah speaks in human language,"[1] Ibn Ezra states:

> It is the custom of the writers of the holy tongue to sometimes explain their words in great detail, and other times to state the matter in an abridged fashion in order that the listener understand the meaning. Know that words are like the body, and the meaning is like the soul, so that a word is only a vessel for the meaning. Therefore it is the custom of sages in every language to preserve the meaning, but not to question a change in the wording as long as the meaning is the same. Let me present some examples: God said to Cain: "You shall be more cursed than the ground. . . . If you till the soil it shall no longer yield its strength to you. You shall become a ceaseless wanderer on the earth" (Gen. 4:11–12), and Cain said, "Since you have banished me this day from the soil . . ." (4:14); who would be foolish enough to think that the meaning [of these phrases] is not identical because the words have been changed? Also, Eliezer [Abraham's servant] said, "Please let me sip" [*hagmî'înî nā'*] in Gen. 24:17, but [later] he said, "And I said, 'Please give me a drink'" [*hašqînî-nā'*, 24:45]. . . . The rule is that in all variant repetitions, like Pharaoh's dream (Gen. 41:1–24) and Nebuchadnezzar (Dan. 2:1–45), and many others like them you will find different words, but the meaning remains the same.[2]

1

In a similar vein David Kimḥi comments on Gen. 24:39 with reference
to the changes in the servant's language in his repetition of the events of
the first part of the story:

> The truth is that he [the servant] organized his speech according to the
> way things really happened, and we cannot give any reasons for the
> numerous omissions and additions. . . . These are only changes in
> wording; the meaning remains the same. This is the way of Scripture
> when it repeats things: The meaning is preserved, but not the [origi-
> nal] wording.[3]

Kimḥi's preference for meaning over wording is in agreement with the
body/soul dichotomy in the theory of repetition proposed by Ibn Ezra.
  A different sort of argument for stylistic variation is offered by Umberto Cassuto, who sees the origin of biblical repetition in the patterns of
epic literature of the ancient Near East, particularly those of Ugarit:

> Ugaritic epic poetry, like all epic poetry, both Eastern and Western, is
> fond of *repetitions*. The listeners are very pleased to hear the poet
> commence a passage that is already familiar to them and beloved of
> them. It is easier for them then to listen to the poet's words, and, so to
> speak, to participate in his narration or song. Consequently it is a
> common feature of epic poetry for whole sections to recur frequently
> in the *ipsissima verba*. Although this is a general characteristic and is not
> confined to the Canaanite epos only, nevertheless it seems to me that
> we ought to pay attention to it, for, since we have already seen that
> biblical narrative prose is to a certain extent a continuation of the
> Canaanite epic tradition, if we now find in it repetitions like those in
> epic poetry, we shall have the right to conclude that in this respect, too,
> it is actually the tradition of the Canaanite epic that is operative. . . .
> Mostly, when the subject is not so technical, as in the case of the
> construction of the Tabernacle (Ex. 25–31, 35–40), or the offerings of
> the leaders (Num. 7:12–83), and it does not require meticulous exacti-
> tude of details, the repetitions in prose are not identical—word for
> word. Prose is intended to be read rather than to be heard, and the
> reader is not as keen as the listener on the repetition of words that he
> already knows by heart. On the contrary, the recurrence of the *ipsissima
> verba* may at times be a burden to him. Hence prose likes, artistically, to
> vary the expressions, or to abridge them, or to change their order,
> when it repeats any subject. Nevertheless, the practice of repetition
> remained in use. . . .
> An interesting example of a theme that occurs four times, with a
> change of phrasing each time, we find in Genesis XXIV, in the story of
> Abraham's servant, the elder of his house, and of his meeting with
> Rebekah. It is first related how the servant prayed to the Lord for a
> sign (vv. 12–14), then how the sign was given to him (vv. 17–21), and
> thereafter how he told Rebekah's family about his prayer (vv. 42–44)
> and the granting of the sign (vv. 45–46). Similar to this is the section
> dealing with Pharaoh's dream (Gen. 41:1–7, 17–24). . . . [4]

Insofar as Cassuto sees these repetitions in Genesis 24 as prosaic manifestations of epic repetition, they have no particular meaning for the story itself.

Diametrically opposed to these views is the position taken by Nehama Leibowitz: "Ibn Ezra and Kimḥi are mistaken in maintaining that 'the text preserves the meaning, but not the precise wording.' They ignore the fact that changing even a single word alters the meaning of the whole."[5] Leibowitz maintains that each word has its own precise meaning in combination with other words:

> We have already seen . . . how a small change in wording contains within it a larger idea. Every addition, every deletion, every change in syntax—whole worlds are hidden within them. The Torah must be read with great care and attentiveness; what it wishes to teach is found not only in its principles, but in each of its words as well. . . . [6]

While this position is a development of the rabbinic notion that every letter in the Torah has a unique significance, Leibowitz offers no theoretical support based on literary or linguistic principles.[7]

A similar attitude toward the function of repetition is taken by Meir Sternberg, who develops a position grounded in the literary style of biblical narrative. Sternberg argues that one of the most noteworthy characteristics of this style is its economy of description. One rarely finds the sort of "gratuitous" details common to most other literatures, e.g., lengthy descriptions of characters or scenes that add color to the story but are not essential for continuing the plot.[8] The absence of such detail about the external makeup of a character often creates gaps of information about his inner motivations as well. This "minimalism" is further compounded by a narrator whose tendency is not to comment directly upon the story and the actors, leaving a great deal to the interpolations and judgments of the reader.[9]

In striking contrast to this reserved style, repetitions provide a surplus of information by rehearsing details that are already known to the reader. The frequency of these apparently superfluous repetitions makes this stylistic lapse all the more glaring; why should the writer be so "stingy" in his descriptions and so "wasteful" with unnecessary repetitions? Therefore, argues Sternberg, such frequent repetitions cannot be an "automatic" response (as Cassuto suggests) but must be a deliberate narrative technique. The notion of absolute semantic equivalence ignores the contextual differences between the original words and their retelling, as well as the discrepancies in perspective and privilege between narrator and character. In fact, each repetition in biblical narrative is individually tailored to fit a certain context and *ipso facto* is potentially meaningful on a number of different levels. These layers of meaning can be unfolded by comparing the differences and similarities between the two, three, or more versions of a reported event with respect to length, wording, point of view, and other contextual variations.

While this theoretical position is well argued, in actual practice Sternberg does not claim that *all* repetitions are meaningful, qualifying his formulations with "sometimes," "often," and the like. While this may be necessary for sensible exegesis, it seriously undermines the larger theory. Moreover, he has been criticized for a lack of precision in his definitions as well as for a lack of consistency. For example, while Sternberg argues that literal repetition is used deliberately in Gen. 6:18 and 7:7 to show Noah's complete submission to the divine command, Yair Hoffmann has pointed out that such a claim runs into trouble in 8:16 and 8:18, where changes in the repetition do occur.[10] Nor is Sternberg's use of the expression "literal repetition" understandable when he claims that Saul, in his oath in 1 Sam. 14:44—"kōh-ya'áśeh 'ělōhîm wěkôh yôsip kî-môt tāmût yônātān" (God do so to me and more also; you shall surely die, Jonathan)—repeats verbatim what he had said in 14:39: "kî ḥay-YHWH hammôšî'a 'et-yiśrā'ēl kî 'im-yešnô běyônātān běnî kî môt yāmût" (For as the Lord lives who saves Israel, though it be in Jonathan my son, he shall surely die).[11] By not establishing the precise boundaries of literal repetition, Sternberg ultimately provides no clear distinction between acceptable stylistic variation and semantic change.[12]

Similar charges of inconsistency can be leveled at the commentators identified with the "style" position, for they too betray their principles in the course of actual exegesis. In Gen. 24:41 Ibn Ezra sees the change from 'ālātî (24:8) to šěbu'ātî as significant;[13] in Gen. 40:23 he explains the phrase "he did not remember" to mean "he didn't mention him [Joseph] to Pharaoh," and the parallel expression "and he forgot him" as a reference to the cupbearer's internal loss of memory.[14] Kimḥi sees the expression "wayyō'kal gam-'ākôl" in Gen. 31:15 as connoting a double portion of Jacob's earnings that Laban has "devoured." In Josh. 2:4 the verb *wattiṣpěnô* indicates that Moses was buried, but the expression *wattiṭměnēm* in 2:6 comes "to show you how he was interred."[15] Cassuto too discovers meaning in variant repetition in Gen. 6:13, in the use of the formula "wayyihěyû běnē pereṣ" in Gen. 46:12, and in his understanding of Aaron's speech in Ex. 32:24.[16] In spite of the theoretical positions taken by these writers, each finds that some changes in repetition consist of more than stylistic variation.

For all the critics we have mentioned, context plays a decisive role in their assessment of the potential change in meaning of a given repetition. Once contextual considerations enter the picture, we move beyond the issue of word-for-word semantic equivalence to address another set of questions: What is the length of the repetition relative to the original report of the event? What is the temporal relationship between the the two, i.e., does the repetition immediately follow the initial event, or has some time elapsed in the interim? Does the repetition occur in the narrative voice or within the speech of a character? Is the source of the repetition a verbal utterance, or the performance of an action, or the depiction of an emotional state, and how does this affect the criteria by which equivalence is determined? Is the repetition expressed by a narrator or character who is aware of the original and is conscious of the fact that he is repeating? Is the repetition part of a larger chain of retellings, a variation on a genre of story or type-scene, or one member of a set of analogies used to depict qualities and relationships, whether between persons or between God and Israel? As these issues are raised it becomes clear that the question of style versus meaning is but a part of a much larger inquiry, namely, what are the functions of repetition itself in biblical narrative?

To be sure, this question is not unique to the Bible, for all literature depends upon repetition for some of its effects. Multiple repetitions of the same word such as are found in biblical *Leitwörter* are as much a part of *King Lear* and the plays of Samuel Beckett as they are of the Binding of Isaac and the Jacob Cycle.[17] Characterization is accomplished not by simple description but by drawing analogies between the repeated words and behaviors of various figures in the text and by judging the constancy of identity in the replication of thoughts and actions in speech, and the reverse. This is equally true for Abraham's faith, Odysseus's cunning, Beowulf's bravery, and Billy Budd's innocence. Recurrent themes and motifs are the stuff that binds together the longer work, be it Genesis or Joyce's *Ulysses,* and that allows the reader to reflect upon the sameness of human experience in the face of constantly changing circumstances. Human consciousness itself is based upon the ability to remember what we repeat and to choose how to repeat, be it destructively as habit, nostalgia, compulsion, or obsession, or constructively as rediscovery, change, and growth.[18]

While the Bible may not be unique in its use of any single repetitive form, both the variety and the concentration of techniques of retelling are unusual. One commonly finds the repetitive sequence of forecasting an action, performing that action, and then telling or retelling of its occurrence. This pattern may occur in full, as with the making of the golden calf in Ex. 32:1–8 or the anointing of Jehu in 2 Kg. 9:1–12. Or it may be found with only the forecast and the performance—"'Let there be light,' and there was light" (Gen. 1:3)—or only the performance and the retelling (1 Sam. 4:1–17), or a number of other permutations and combinations.[19] More than an aspect of style, the pattern underscores the Bible's larger theological concerns in presenting "an account of how divine word—and in more ambiguous ways, often human word as well—becomes historical fact." But at the same time such repetition may serve a more subversive function: "As human actors reshape recurrence in language along the biases of their own intentions or misconceptions, we see how language can be an instrument of masking or deception as well as of revelation."[20]

Even more impressive than sheer quantity is the use of so many different types of repetition in biblical narrative, and their integration within a given story, book, or series of books. The *Leitwort* is a frequently used device that can be repeated within a single narrative pericope (e.g., forms of the verb *B-R-K* [to bless] in Gen. 27:1–45), as well as within larger units (e.g., forms of *B-R-K* and *B-K-R* [firstborn] in Gen. 25–35).[21] Similarly, the repetition of key phrases or sentences is used in developing thematic unity in larger sections, as in the recurrence of the formula "bayyāmîm hāhēm ʾên melek bĕyiśrāʾēl; ʾîš hayyāšār bĕʿênāyw yaʿăśeh" (In those days there was no king in Israel; each person did what was right in his own eyes) toward the end of Judges to emphasize chaotic societal conditions (17:6; 21:25; see also 18:1; 19:1). We also find "repetitive resumptions," by which an editor notes the inclusion of a different type of material into his main story by repeating a verse, or part of a verse, at the beginning and end of the inclusion.[22] The repetition of sequences of activity constitutes another category, as in the thrice-told actions of Saul's messengers (and Saul himself) in 1 Sam. 19:18–24, or those of Elijah, Elisha, and the prophetic disciples in 2 Kg. 2:1–8. A pattern of oracle and fulfillment pervades the Deuteronomic History, whether within the individual chapter (e.g., 2 Kg. 7:1–20), or between separate books, as with Deuteronomy and Joshua, or the editorial expositions in Jud. 2:11–23, 1 Sam. 12, 2 Kg. 17:7–23, and 21:10–15.[23] The description of the behavior of Israel and her judges in Jud. 3–16 as a cyclical movement from apostasy to faithfulness and back again represents yet another kind of repetitive structure. Chiastic patterns, in which words or events are repeated inversely, are used to give shape to individual speeches, as in Num. 11:11–15, to entire episodes, such as Gen. 11:1–9, to cycles of stories, such as Genesis 25–35, and even possibly to whole books, as has been suggested for the Book of Kings.[24] On another level we must take note of the recurrence of themes, such as the victory of the younger sibling over the elder (Gen. 21; 25; 27; 37; 42; 48), the barren wife (Gen. 11:31; 16; 20:18; 25:21; 30:1), and the deception of the foreigner (Gen. 12:10–20; 20; 26; 34), all of which lend unity to the book of Genesis. It has been argued that the "theme" of the entire Pentateuch is the partial fulfillment of the frequently restated promise to the Patriarchs.[25] In some cases two parallel stories of the same event stand in close proximity to each other, e.g., Saul's encounter with David in 1 Samuel 24 and 26.[26]

We also find variant versions of the same story with different actors, as in Elijah's and Elisha's revival of a dead child in 1 Kg. 17:17–24 and 2 Kg. 4:8–37 respectively. One step removed from these categories are type-scenes that repeat conventions of speech and behavior in analogous situations, such as betrothal scenes (Gen. 24:10–61; 29:1–20; Ex. 2:15b–21) and annunciation stories (Gen. 18:1–15; Jud. 13; 1 Sam. 1; 2 Kg. 4:8–37).[27] On a larger scale, the retelling of historiographic elements from Exodus and Numbers in Deuteronomy 1–11 exemplifies the concerns of source criticism with repetition. And on and on.

The interweaving of this great variety of types of repetition and reformulation is one of the most significant sources of the richness of biblical narrative, but it also creates difficulties when we try to address the question of the purpose of repetition in a detailed and thorough manner. Each type of repetition has its own particular conventions and its own identity as a literary device that interacts with other, equally unique forms of repetition in the course of a narrative.[28] In order to understand the phenomenon of repetition as a whole, we must first gain a better understanding of each of these individual genres, in their distinctiveness and in their interrelationship in the narrative. This study addresses this larger goal by examining carefully one particular kind of repetition that has not received the thorough treatment it deserves, namely, the use of quotations in biblical narrative.

2.

The expression "quoted direct speech" describes a type of repetition that is a precisely defined and clearly identifiable subcategory of the more general term "quotation." While the latter is often used to embrace allusions, summaries, and oblique references to other words and phrases, quoted direct speech has a narrower and more specific meaning: A character actually or purportedly speaks certain words in the course of a story; at a later point in the narrative those words are quoted aloud by the same character or by another, with specific reference to the original locution and the original speaker. The quotation may occur within the same pericope as the original speech, in a later chapter, or even in a later book. In texts where both the original locution and the quotation are presented, the quote is termed "verifiable," for the reader can use the original to judge the accuracy of the repetition. When the original speech is not specifically attested in the text, the quotation is considered "unverifiable," and other grounds must be used to determine whether or not it was likely to have been said by its alleged speaker. God's quotation in Gen. 3:17 of the command he originally spoke in 2:16–17 is an example of a verifiable quotation, while David's quotation of Saul's "secret message" in 1 Sam. 21:3 is a case of an unverifiable (and false) quotation. Because of our interest in the question of style versus meaning in repetition, the analysis of verifiable quoted direct speech occupies the greater part of this study, since it affords the reader an opportunity to compare the language of both versions of a particular quotation.

Prior treatments of quotation in the Bible have focused more on prophetic and wisdom literature than on narrative. In a long article entitled "Das Zitat im Prophetenspruch," Hans Walter Wolff presented a systematic discussion of quotation in prophetic literature, with some reference to the Psalms. Wolff distinguished between the prophetic voice, which is by its very nature a "quotation" of the divine word, and the prophet's repetition of "other voices" (*fremde Stimmen*), i.e., human speech drawn from the prophet's experience of the world, which is the focus of his study. He considers quotations in the second person to be most significant (e.g., Jer. 3:23; Hos. 13:10), because of the direct, immediate contact they establish between the prophet and his audience. Wolff's main concern, however, is not the rhetorical strategies of the prophet, but the history of traditions that lie behind the quotations. Many quotations emerge from liturgical settings; Wolff derives the expression "Qûmâ wĕhôšîʿēnû" (arise and save us) in Jer. 2:27 from similar phrases in Pss. 3:8; 12:2; 20:10. The quotations in Isaiah 33 and Hos. 6:1–3 are liturgies unattested elsewhere, as the greatest part of prophetic quotations are equally unverifiable. The frequency of quotation in prophetic judgment speeches such as Is. 3:13ff., Jer. 2:2ff., and Mic. 6:1–8 leads Wolff to conclude that the judicial tradition, together with the cultic-liturgical sphere, was the point of origin for prophetic quotation.[29]

Wolff's work suggests some helpful points of departure for the study of quotation in narrative, such as the question of the authenticity of unverifiable quotations. But his definition of verifiable quotation is too imprecise for our purposes, including many cases that are more properly termed allusions, such as the relationship of "YHWH ʿimmānû" (the Lord is with us) in Jud. 6:13 to "YHWH ʾĕlōhē-ṣĕbāʾôt ʾittĕkem" (May the Lord, the God of Hosts, be with you) in Amos 5:14.[30] Further, in claiming that the source of the above-mentioned quotation in Jer. 2:27 is found in the Psalms, Wolff ignores the fact that the temporal relationship of Jeremiah to the Psalms is very different from that of Jer. 26:18 to Mic. 3:12, where the preexistence of Micah's oracle is firmly established in both historical and literary terms. In prophecy, "before" and "after" exist outside the text, prophetic speech itself being essentially future oriented. Narrative, on the other hand, includes its "was" and "will be" within the confines of the story. Since Jer. 2:27 quotes (or alludes to) a liturgical *tradition* rather than a single, time-bound utterance, the quote is not verifiable in the same sense as Jer. 26:18—which is set within a narrative context.

More recent treatments of quotation have returned to the prophetic literature with a greater interest in the original speakers than in the prophet who quotes them. W. J. Horwitz has suggested that the quotations in Jer. 2:23–25 give an accurate picture of the response of the prophet's audience to his message.[31] Building on the work of A. S. van der Woude, James Crenshaw has advanced the idea that prophetic quotations can present a valuable record of the *vox populi* in Israel, particularly with regard to popular religious beliefs.[32] By examining these quotations Crenshaw uncovers trends in popular religion that, he argues, play an important part in the continuing development of negative attitudes toward prophecy. But the degree to which such quotations can be considered objective depictions free of prophetic bias is highly questionable, and any conclusions drawn on the basis of such an assumption must be treated cautiously.[33] Robert Gordis has also written in some detail about the use of quotations, restricting himself largely to the psalms and wisdom literature, with particular attention to Qohelet.[34] In response to the problem of inconsistency and internal contradiction in that book, Gordis suggests that Qohelet will often quote a conventional wisdom saying and then comment upon it in his own contrary fashion, either with another proverb (e.g., 4:5–6; 9:16, 18) or with his own words (4:9–12; 5:9–10; 7:2; 8:5–6). Frequently these quotations are not introduced as the words of an earlier speaker, but Gordis makes a good case for the existence of such a stylistic phenomenon in both the Bible and Near Eastern literature.[35] The recognition of this convention is a major contribution to the study of the literary function of quotations and has been extremely helpful in understanding Qohelet's rhetorical strategy.

However, Gordis's inability to provide satisfactory criteria for identifying such unmarked quotations poses a serious problem. Gordis accepts as quotations many sentences and phrases that lack any formal attribution to another speaker or tradition:

> The term quotation refers to words which do not reflect the present sentiments of the author of the literary composition in which they are found, but have been introduced by the author to convey the standpoint of another person or situation. These quotations include, but are not limited to, citations of previously existing literature, whether written or oral.[36]

Michael Fox has pointed out that this definition conflates two different types of quotations: (1) those which the speaker appropriates as his own language (quotation by virtue of origin), and (2) those which the speaker ascribes to another voice (quotation by virtue of usage).[37] Quotations of the first sort are more properly understood as instances of "literary borrowing," for the source of the quotation is always outside the work itself, and its effect upon the reader may or may not depend upon the reader's awareness of that source. It is in this sense that the term "quotation" is frequently used in modern literary studies.[38]

Since we are dealing exclusively with quotations that occur in narrative, and indeed with quotations that are also repetitions, only those statements ascribed by the speaker to another voice (Fox's second category) will be admitted as quotations. Because of the temporal constraints of narrative, i.e., the importance of chronological sequence, and the contrasting of earlier and later moments in the story, we impose more stringent rules of formal attribution than does either Gordis or Fox. Not only must we be sure that a given speech is intended by its speaker to be understood as a quotation, but we must also be absolutely certain that the quotation is presented by the narrator as a repetition.

Treatments of quoted direct speech in narrative have been less extensive and less systematic than those in prophecy and wisdom literature, and quotations are often lumped together indiscriminately with other types of repetition. While discussing temporal shifts in biblical narrative, Meir Weiss notes the frequent use of flashbacks to supply important information at key points in the story. While many of these flashbacks are in the narrator's voice (e.g., 1 Sam. 23:6, 28:3b; 2 Sam. 18:18), some are also spoken by the characters (e.g., 1 Sam. 4:10–11, 17; 15:9, 15) in order to bring the past into the present in a dramatic or scenic way. Weiss does not distinguish, however, between a character's retelling in indirect speech and his quotation of prior direct speech.[39] Jacob Licht, in *Storytelling in the Bible,* blurs the equally important distinction between quotation by the character and recapitulation by the narrator.[40] Robert Alter's treatment of repetition in *The Art of Biblical Narrative* brings out many subtleties in the text, but he too does not separate repetitions by the narrator from those by the characters.[41]

Only two critics have written about quoted direct speech in narrative as a phenomenon unto itself. In commenting on the exegetical difficulties created by repetition in Ex. 19:23, Brevard Childs notes that the unique feature of the verse is its actual quotation of an earlier statement, God's command in 19:10–13.[42] He goes on to point out the fairly common occurrence of quotations, mentions a few formal characteristics, and suggests three functions of such citations: (1) to serve as evidence for or against the accuracy of a claim made in the present (e.g., Gen. 20:5 or 2 Sam. 1:16), (2) to establish the validity of a claim made in the past (i.e., the original statement, as in 1 Kg. 1:17), (3) to establish the validity of a claim whose authenticity is determined by indirect evidence (e.g., Num. 11:21). We agree with Childs's observation that such citations occur in a variety of literary and social settings, and that one should resist the temptation to locate their usage within a specific *Sitz-im-Leben*. But Childs has hardly exhausted the possible functions of quoted direct speech with his broad explanation of its uses as evidence. He has not, for example, fully addressed the question of knowledge: the value of any evidence is in direct proportion to how much a character, or a reader, already knows about the truth of a given statement. Indeed, the character and the reader frequently operate on different levels of awareness, with contrasting perceptions. Truth and falseness are highly relative terms in quoted direct speech, and the *degree* to which a quotation supports or undermines a given claim becomes a very important question.

Meir Sternberg has offered the most complete and detailed discussion of the poetics of repetition to date. He points out that in all repetitions not only must one determine whether or not there is a change in meaning in language, but one must also ask whether or not the change is deliberate. Even if all changes are intentional (apart from normal variation in language), as when the omniscient narrator repeats a statement, the characters in the story may or may not be aware of a shift in meaning. Sternberg makes the important distinction between the repetition of originally nonverbal expressions (e.g., actions) and the repetition of earlier direct speech. Narration tends to repeat descriptions of events, persons, and states of mind with some variation, because the repetition itself is also another description of the earlier object. Direct speech, however, is not a description of something else, but a more explicitly defined object in and of itself; as a result, the possibility of verbatim repetition of direct speech is made more likely, as is the possibility of purposeful deviation from the original.[43]

Sternberg's essay has provided many significant points of departure for this study, as it should for subsequent works on specific kinds of repetition. But while he mentions the existence of quotations by characters in the text, Sternberg often does not separate them from other types of repeating done by those characters (e.g., Potiphar's wife in Genesis 39, or Samuel in 1 Sam. 3:9–10), or from the narrator's repetition of direct speech in third-person narration (e.g., "wayyōʾmer ʾĕlōhîm ʿyĕhî-ʾōrʾ" [and God said, "let there be light"] and "wayĕhî-ʾôr" [and there was light] in Gen. 1:3). He notes the difference between narrator-sponsored repetitions (directed at the reader) and character-sponsored retelling (directed at other characters), and suggests an analogous relationship between the two. But he does not extend the implications of the interaction of these two rhetorical frameworks into the realm of quoted direct speech, where the character is placed in a singular position by repeating not just his own speech but the speech of others as well.

3.

Quotations themselves are unique in that they mark a particular intersection of repetition and direct speech. In biblical narrative style, dialogue is used at least as frequently as impersonal narration in indirect speech, if not more so. Instead of relating the story exclusively by third-person narrative "telling," there is a strong propensity toward the use of direct speech for "showing" the attitudes, motivations, and personalities of the characters through their own words. Given the reticence of biblical writers about describing their characters in much detail, direct speech assumes even greater importance. Within the scenic mode typical of much biblical narrative, it is dialogue that adds dramatic presence to the story and encourages confrontation between the characters.[44]

Repetition, by contrast, de-emphasizes the present moment by supplying the perspective of an earlier time. Repetition enriches by providing depth, context, and background, but it causes the original moment to lose its primacy, and the moment of repetition its immediacy. The repetition of dialogue, however, produces a somewhat different effect. The movement into the past is countered by a new present moment of direct speech that both recalls and reformulates. The result may be a complication of reality due to conflicting versions of an event, but more often it is an affirmation of the original statement that helps the story build consistently in a single direction.[45]

When a character repeats dialogue with no explicit reference to the original statement, the extent of his awareness of the repetition is often unclear—e.g., Samuel in 1 Sam. 3:4, 6, 8; Micaiah in 1 Kg. 22:15; or Elisha in 2 Kg. 2:3, 5. In each of these cases, is the repetition part of a stereotyped pattern in which the character is "programmed" to repeat himself? Or does the character intend the repetition to serve some other purpose? While this ambiguity may be interesting, it ultimately prevents the reader from making any decisions about the character's state of mind on the basis of the repetition alone. With quoted direct speech, on the other hand, it is always clear that the repetition is a deliberate act, since the character explicitly refers to the source of his quotation. This embedding of one speech within another creates its own unique juxtaposition of temporal frames. The original statement, which was formerly bound by its own coordinates of time and place, is lifted out and recontextualized as part of a new temporal and spatial configuration. Quoted direct speech is not a description of the past overcome by the present, but a re-presentation of prior speech, which, because it remains in direct speech, retains much more than a memory of its original context.[46]

It is important to distinguish between quotations spoken by characters in the narrative and those "spoken" by the narrator (e.g., Gen. 28:6; 1 Kg. 21:4), which are more accurately termed repetitions. The narrator is always "quoting" the direct speech of his characters when he presents it for the first time; formally speaking, he would have to quote *himself* ("as I said earlier . . .") in a manner alien to his customary narrative voice. The distinction becomes more important when we note that a character who speaks quotations is temporarily cast in the role of narrator. He is granted authority to retell the past by being empowered to repeat the direct speech of another person (or himself) from an earlier time—a privilege that otherwise rests only with the third-person omniscient narrator. Formally speaking, a character's quotation of attributed direct speech separates this "objective" reporting from the purely subjective retelling found in that character's recapitulation formulated in indirect speech. This is not to say that the presence of a quotation renders the entire report objective in the same sense that the narrator is understood to be objective, for the character places the reported speech within his own subjective context. But the deliberate use of another's speech, especially of verifiable quotations where the original is available for inspection, lends a greater degree of objectivity to the character's speech than is usually present.

Narration through quotation by a character in the story is not meant to compete with the impersonal narrator, for the reader must be aware that a character acts and speaks only at the behest of the narrator. Nor does the character's quotation take over the normal narrative function of providing information. In verifiable quoted direct speech, the reader has already heard the original speech that underlies the quotation, and generally receives no new details about the past. But for the other characters within the world of the story, the quoting character does function as just such an authoritative narrator of earlier speech. Moreover, because he reports direct speech in the same manner of discourse as that in which it was originally spoken, the characters in the story usually consider his version to be largely objective. Like the narrator who stands outside the story, this character/narrator uses citations of earlier speeches in combination with his own summarial and descriptive comments to tell a tale, and to tell it in a particular way. Just as the impersonal narrator uses direct speech strategically in his presentation of the past to the reader, so too the character uses quoted direct speech not simply to inform but to present a certain perspective on the past to his listeners within the story.

In order to shed more light on the way quotations function in the story, it is useful to understand some of the conditions of discourse as defined by speech-act philosophers. Responding to the assertion that spoken language is always descriptive of actions that take place outside of it, J. L. Austin demonstrated that in many cases, speaking itself constitutes a performative act and not simply a description of an act. Such speech-acts, as he called them, consist of three parts: (1) the locution, or the words themselves with their particular grammar and syntax; (2) the illocutionary force, i.e., the force or intent with which the locution is spoken, or how the speaker intends his words to act upon the listener— to promise, to plead, etc. The illocutionary force depends greatly upon the context in which the words are uttered, and has an effect upon (3) the perlocutionary force, or the actual effect of the speech-act upon the listener. Stated simply, illocutionary acts set forth intention, and perlocutionary acts register their results.[47]

When a quotation is examined not simply as a description of the past, but as a re-presentation of a verbal act restated in the spoken form in which it originally occurred, then the act of quotation itself must be seen as a speech-act. As such, the quoting character endows the quotation with an illocutionary force, and the response of the listener is a measure of its perlocutionary effect on him. This distinction is valuable when we wish to talk about the intent of a given "quoter" and the function of any given quotation. Sometimes the context is sufficient to determine the intent of the quoter, as in accusations like Josh. 9:22 or Jud. 18:24. But often the reader must also compare the quotation against the original speech for significant discrepancies in meaning that reveal the narrative strategy of the quoting character. Thus, for example, Judah's speech to Joseph in Gen. 44:19–34 is not simply a recounting of the events of chapters 42–43, but a pastiche of quotations with varying degrees of fidelity to their originals, carefully constructed to have a calculated effect upon his audience. The reader who ignores the "sources" of Judah's speech cannot fully understand the logic of his argument.

The issue of knowledge is crucial for any attempt to perceive the intentions of the speaker of the quotation, for it determines the extent to which other characters are aware of how the speaker uses quoted direct speech. When the words in quotation are already known to the reader, he is more likely to be in a position to evaluate the strategy of the quoter. In the many cases in which the quotation presents new information to the character, the latter is at a disadvantage. The reader, however, is always in a position to observe the quoter's narrative strategy, and through that understanding to gain insight into the meaning of the text as a whole.

In each instance of quoted direct speech there are, then, *two* narrators whom the reader must take into account—the quoting character who tells a story to his fellow character, and the narrator who recounts the larger story to his implied audience. It is helpful to differentiate between the two by using the terms "story" and "discourse" as follows: "story" indicates the world inhabited by the characters, the events of the plot, the behavior and motivations of the actors, the words spoken by them as heard by their fellow characters. "Discourse" refers to the means by which the narrator conveys that story and its meaning to the reader.[48] The characters in the text remain unaware of the discourse level, for the biblical narrator always stands outside the story he narrates. The reader, on the other hand, has access to both levels of understanding because, like the narrator, he is not confined by the limits of the story-world. Story can be termed the "what" of literature, and discourse the "way" of telling. What one character speaks to another is a matter of story, but how the narrator arranges the speaker's words to affect the reader falls within the province of discourse.

A diagrammatic representation of the process of communication of quotation on the story level would look like this:[49]

Event	$\rightarrow$	Retold by	$\rightarrow$	Listening
(original speech		quoting		character
by character)		character		

The event may occur within the story or be presumed to have taken place outside the story. In this framework the quoting character acts as a narrator within the story, and the listener may or may not have access to the original. When the discourse level is added, the diagram is expanded at both ends.

Narrator $\rightarrow$	Event	$\rightarrow$ Quotation	$\rightarrow$ Listener	$\rightarrow$ Reader
	(original speech	(by character)	(character)	
	by character)			

Discourse includes everything that is story, and much more. Perspectives upon temporal order and knowledge of circumstances that are hidden from the characters are opened up to the reader by the narrator's discourse. In quoted direct speech the reader has access to both the original speech and its subsequent quoted form, and, through them, to the strategy of the quoting character.

But as much as the reader knows, he is always at a disadvantage with respect to the narrator, who also withholds information, telling the reader "the truth" but not "the whole truth."[50] As a result, the relationship between the speaker of the quote and his listener in the story is analogous to (though not identical with) the relationship between the narrator and the reader:

Quoter   :   Listener   // Narrator   :   Reader

As the characters in the story may not know the original speech from which the speaker quotes, so the reader cannot know the "original" events and words from which the narrator has constructed his text. The analogy, however, can also work to the reader's benefit: the reader's understanding of the quoter's narrative strategy on the story level can help him perceive the intent of the narrator's discourse as directed toward him. Story and discourse are so deeply bound up with each other that any analysis of the role of quoted direct speech must approach the text on both levels of meaning.

Our study seeks to respond to two questions. The first regards style and meaning: Given that quotations are themselves deliberate repetitions, how does change in language affect the meaning of the quotation? The second concerns the literary function of quotation: How does the use of quotation affect the meaning of a character's speech, and the meaning of the text as a whole?

The body of text for this study includes the narrative from Genesis through 2 Kings, which provides a more than ample supply of quotations from textual analysis, and which is sufficient to enable us to make some general observations about biblical narrative style. The sample embraces a wide variety of texts, from those which have a near-mythic status like Genesis 2–3, to those with a historiographical orientation, such as the stories about David in the Succession Narrative in 2 Samuel 9–20 and 1 Kings 1–2.

Chapter 2 describes formal aspects of the use of quotations, i.e., means of introduction; various configurations of original speaker, quoter, and listener; relative frequency and scarcity of quotations in different texts and sources. The general trends of change in language in quoted direct speech will be examined with an eye toward how they touch upon the issue of style versus meaning.

The rest of the work is devoted to the analysis of the functions of quotations on both the level of story and the level of discourse. Chapter 3 is restricted to story analysis, addressing the rhetorical strategies of the quoting character and exploring the impact of the characters' differing levels of awareness on the effectiveness of quoted direct speech. Texts are arranged according to varying degrees of "new" and "old" information, according to the knowledge of the listener. The impact of change in language upon meaning is explored here with reference to specific texts.

Chapter 4 addresses similar questions of strategy on the discourse level, building upon the story analyses of the previous chapter and extending the discussion to include the effects of quoted direct speech upon the reader. We will see how quotations function as a technique of characterization, as an element in plot development, and as a sign of a shift in point of view. The interaction of quotations with other types of repetition will be shown to form coherent structures of meaning, both on the level of the individual pericope and in larger units of narrative as well. Texts in which the narrator quotes a previous speech will also be examined, and unverifiable quotations will be treated in light of the problems of authenticity and ambiguity that are inherent in them.

·2·

FORMAL ASPECTS OF
QUOTED DIRECT SPEECH

In order to be in a position to determine the significance of a particular quotation, it is necessary to examine the conventions that govern the use of quoted direct speech throughout the biblical narrative. Questions of attribution, of frequency and location, and of the style of introduction are relevant as they apply to both verifiable and unverifiable quotations. In addition, we wish to see what general types of changes can be observed in verifiable quotations and how such generalizations affect the exegesis of a given text.

The essential requirements for a statement to be termed a quotation are twofold: (1) the "quoted" words must be claimed to have been spoken prior to the "quoting" statement, and (2) the quoted words must be tagged, i.e., attributed to a specific prior speaker. In most cases the assignation is performed by a character, and not by the narrator; exceptions to this rule will be taken up later. Unlike treatments of quotations within wisdom literature, which admit many untagged passages as quotations on the basis of usage,[1] we are concerned here only with those instances where it is clear that the character knowingly repeats earlier speech. Since we wish to understand the intentions of the character who speaks the quotation, it is necessary to determine whether he is aware that he is quoting, or whether the narrator has assigned him words whose resonances he does not, or cannot, understand.[2]

1.

The question of attribution has a further dimension of great significance: did the original speaker actually say the words ascribed to him by the quoter, in precisely those words or with that specific intention, or is the quote an invention of the present speaker's mind? These variations can be plotted along a continuum that has at one end the perfectly accurate quotation, repeated verbatim with the same tone as the original speaker, and at the other a complete fabrication, in which the attributed words are contrary in content and feeling to the character who is supposed to have spoken them. The former is illustrated by Gen. 38:22, quoting 38:21. As the local people respond to the Adullamite's question with the words "lō' hāyĕtâ bāzeh qĕdēšâ" (There has been no prostitute here), so he faithfully reports their words to Judah. Here the quotation is both verifiable and accurate. For our purposes a quote is termed verifiable only if the original speech is actually present in the text, in direct address, somewhere prior to the quotation itself.

An example from the other end of the continuum is the unverifiable quotation spoken by David to Ahimelech in 1 Sam. 21:3: "The king has ordered me on a mission, and said to me, 'Let no one know anything about this mission on which I send you, about which I have ordered you.'" Saul's alleged command is not found in the text, rendering the quotation unverifiable. It is, in addition, totally false, as the idea of the king entrusting any mission whatsoever to David is in opposition to their hostile relationship at this point in the story. Other unverifiable quotations may in fact be "believable," i.e., the reader can be reasonably certain that the quoted words were likely to have been spoken, either because of the authority of the quoter (e.g., God in Num. 11:20), or because of agreement in attitude between the quotation and that of the alleged speaker. While this chapter includes some data about unverifiable quotations, further discussion of their particular relationship to true and false telling can be found in chapter 4.

Because of our interest in repetition, the major focus of this study is technically verifiable quoted direct speech. These quotations afford the reader the opportunity to compare the two versions of the quoted discourse, to draw specific inferences about the speaker on the basis of that comparison, and to make more general observations about the function of this type of repetition in biblical narrative. All citations refer to verifiable quotations unless they are marked otherwise.

2.

In the narrative sections from Genesis through 2 Kings there are 97 occasions on which a character quotes one or more prior speeches according to the guidelines we have established. Of these 97 instances 70 contain verifiable quotations and 31 have unverifiable quotations. While the majority of speeches quote only one earlier speaker, some quoters repeat two, three, or more originally separate acts of speech, yielding a total of 131 individual quotations, 94 of which are verifiable and 37 unverifiable. These figures do not include the following categories:

(a) Quotations from the book of Deuteronomy, which, because of its particular style (first-person narration), will be treated separately in the Appendix.

(b) "Quotations" repeated by the narrator, who cannot be considered a character in the story, e.g., Gen. 28:6 and 1 Sam. 8:6.

(c) Quotations of YHWH's promise to the patriarchs, such as Ex. 3:16–17, which make reference to a whole tradition of blessings repeated throughout Genesis, rather than to one specific prior speech.[3]

(d) Classes of unverifiable quotations such as visions (1 Kg. 22:20–22), parables (Jud. 9:17ff.), proverbs (2 Sam. 20:18), and rumors (1 Sam. 24:10).[4]

(e) "Anticipatory" quotations, in which a messenger is entrusted with a speech that he then quotes in the name of his lord (e.g., 2 Sam. 11:19ff.), or in which the speaker fears that certain words might be spoken in the future (e.g., Ex. 32:12).

Individual quotations are relatively short, usually confined to a single verse (Ex. 32:22), half a verse (1 Sam. 24:10), a short clause (Jud. 11:17), or even a few words (Jud. 18:24). This is particularly true of unverifiable quoted direct speech (e.g., Gen. 37:17; Num. 11:20; 1 Sam. 9:23), where only 2 Sam. 1:7–9 runs contrary to the rule. In verifiable quotations exceptions are more numerous, though not plentiful.[5] Most speeches also contain only one quotation from a single earlier speaker, but there are some striking departures from the norm. Highly unconventional are the long speeches by Abraham's servant (Gen. 24:34–49) and by Judah (Gen. 44:18–34), which contain, respectively, eight and nine separate quotations. Each character tells an elaborate story in which he quotes himself as well as two or three other parties, presenting us with exceptional examples of narrative "showing."[6] The servant and Judah each portray a few different scenes in their monologues by quoting exchanges of dialogue between the participants: the servant and Abraham in 24:37–41 (three quotes), and the servant and Rebecca at the well in 24:42–47 (five quotes). Judah describes the initial encounter between Joseph and his brothers with five separate quotations in Gen. 44:19–23, and the subsequent dialogue between Jacob and his sons in three quotations in 44:25–29.

Except for the unverifiable account of his encounter with Saul presented by the Amalekite in 2 Sam. 1:7–9 in four quotations, all other quoted direct speech portrayals of two parties in dialogue contain only two quotations: The brothers' report of their meeting with Joseph in Gen. 42:31–34, Aaron's account of the events that led up to the making of the calf in Ex. 32:23–24, Solomon's accusation of Shimei in 1 Kg. 2:42; Ahab's version of his conversation with Naboth in 1 Kg. 21:6. The only unverifiable quotation in this category is the gruesome account of cannibalism during the siege of Samaria, recalled by the anonymous woman in 2 Kg. 6:28–29.

Quotations are not used primarily to tell of the past for its own sake, but to recollect in the service of a present argument. For this reason we find that when the speaker uses two different quotations in the same speech, he more frequently quotes two parties *not* in dialogue with each other, or even two originally separate quotations by the same party now combined into a single speech. In these cases the speaker has the freedom to arrange these quotations to his own best advantage, while still claiming that he is faithfully reporting earlier events. Abimelech's claim of innocence in Gen. 20:5 is buttressed by his quotations of *both* Abraham's and Sarah's descriptions of their kinship as evidence against them. The speaker may appeal to the authority of the past: Jephthah refers to historical traditions from Num. 20:14 and 21:22 as he quotes a single party twice in Jud. 11:17, 19 to buttress his response to the Ammonites' claim against Israel. Samuel's indictment of Israel in 1 Sam. 12:6ff. is rhetorically strengthened by comparing the words of previous generations (1 Sam. 12:10 quoting Jud. 10:10ff.) with the complaint of the people of his own day (12:12 quoting 8:19). In the past, Israel recognized its own sins and cried out to YHWH for salvation, but Samuel's people reject both his and YHWH's leadership. In Gen. 43:7 Jacob's sons try to convince their father that there was no a priori connection between Joseph's initial questions—"Is your father still alive? Do you have a brother?"—and his subsequent demand to actually see Benjamin.[7]

While quoted direct speech can be put to use in myriad ways, the speech situations in which quotations occur tend to fall into two larger groups. The first, which we shall call informational quoted direct speech, uses the quotation to inform the listener of some past events in a manner that may be factually accurate (e.g., Gen. 38:22), modified somewhat to have a calculated effect upon the audience (e.g., Gen. 42:31–34), or entirely false to deceive the listener (e.g., Josh. 9:11). Frequently the quotation is a prelude to a request or a demand by the speaker, often introduced by the adverbial particle ʿattâ to mark the passage from past to present.[8] Thus, for example, after his long speech to Laban with many quotations of past speeches, Abraham's servant finally comes to the point in Gen. 24:49: "And now, if you intend to deal loyally with my master, tell me. . . ." Rebecca finishes quoting Isaac's words to Esau in Gen. 27:7, and, with the word ʿattâ in the following verse, sets forth her plan to Jacob.

The second major classification is confrontational quoted direct speech. Here the quotation is part of the speaker's accusation of the listener, as God's speech to the man in Gen. 3:17: "Because you have listened to your wife's voice, and have eaten from the tree about which I commanded you, 'You shall not eat of it'. . . ." Conversely it may be part of the speaker's efforts at self-justification in the face of an indictment directed at him, as Balaam defends himself before Balak in Num. 23:26: "Did I not speak thus to you saying, 'Whatever YHWH speaks I will do'?". While the passing of judgment (1 Sam. 15:18) and the execution of sentence (1 Kg. 2:42) may utilize a quotation, a judicial setting is not necessarily presupposed by these texts. A detailed discussion of these categories of information and confrontation will be undertaken in the following chapter. At this point let it suffice to say that the use of quoted direct speech imposes no other constraints upon the focus, the length, or the setting of these speeches.

Looking beyond the individual speech to the narrative pericope, we find that most quotations appear only once, but there are occasional exceptions. The triple repetition of the divine prohibition against eating from the tree of knowledge in Gen. 3:1, 3, 17 (quoting 2:16–17), the emphasis upon David's unverifiable oath in 1 Kg. 1:17, 24, 30, and the reiteration of the oracle in 1 Kg. 13:17, 22 (quoting 13:9) highlight the important statement in each of these chapters, as if the story itself revolved around the quotation.[9] In two other instances, the quotation reappears twice in the course of the larger narrative—1 Sam. 10:19 and 12:12 both quote 1 Sam. 8:19, while 1 Sam. 21:12 and 29:5 cite 1 Sam. 18:7—bringing out ongoing themes that help bind the story together: Samuel's (and God's) displeasure with Israel's request for a king is a major current in 1 Samuel 8–12; David's complicated relationship to the Philistines in 1 Samuel 21–30 is reflected in their ironic repetition of a song that celebrates David's victory over them.

Approximately one-quarter of all quotations, verifiable and unverifiable, occur in chapters that display no other examples of quoted direct speech. Another fourth appear two to a chapter, often related to each other in some integral way, though not necessarily within the same speech.[10] We have already mentioned some of the texts containing three quotations—Genesis 3 and 1 Kings 13—to which we now add Gen. 20:5a, 5b (unverifiable), 13 (unverifiable); 42:14, 31, 33–34; and Ex. 32:8, 23, 24. A major theme of these five texts is the truthful presentation of the identity and/or motives of the characters, which may be related to the increased number of quotations in each chapter. This theme is also crucial to those stories with five quotations—2 Sam. 1:7, 8a, 8b, 9, 16 (all unverifiable except the last); 1 Kg. 1:17, 24, 30, 47, 48 (all unverifiable except 1 Kg. 1:47). In the first case, not only is the Amalekite lying to David, but David's own motives for mourning Saul so extravagantly are suspect as well. In 1 Kg. 1, the ambiguity as to whether or not David actually swore to Bathsheba that Solomon would succeed him is carefully developed by the narrator. While one might expect that Genesis 24, with eight quotations, and Gen. 44:18–34, with nine quotations, would carry this theme even further, this is not the case. Such extensive quotation, especially in the context of a single long speech, has a different kind of narrative authority, one that seeks not to hide or misrepresent the past, but to re-present it in a new and equally "truthful" way.

The exceptional amount of quoted direct speech in Judah's long discourse is appropriate to the style of the Joseph story; most of the repetition in Genesis 42–44 is accomplished through quotations—a total of seventeen individual quotations within six separate speeches. There is no comparable concentration of quotations in any longer story or collection of stories, even the Davidic court history. Quoted direct speech can appear in a wide variety of narrative settings, including prophetic legenda (e.g., 1 Kg. 18:11, 14; 2 Kg. 4:28; 5:13), wilderness traditions (e.g., Num. 11:13, 21), Deuteronomic material in Deuteronomy (e.g., 9:12–14; 18:17) and elsewhere (e.g., Josh. 1:13; 14:9), historical traditions about Saul (1 Sam. 9:24; 10:19; 14:28), David (1 Sam. 19:17; 21:12; 2 Sam. 1:16; 18:12), Solomon (1 Kg. 2:42), and subsequent kings as well.[11] There are two quotations in Jeremiah's "trial" scene (Jer. 26:9, 18) even though quoted direct speech does not seem an essentially juridical phenomenon.[12] The frequency or dearth of quotations does not correlate with the particular subject matter of the narrative, given that dialogue and dramatic interaction are present in the story.

In considering the distribution of quoted direct speech among the narrative books, we find that Genesis contains both the highest number of speeches with verifiable quotations (sixteen), as well as the most individual quotations (thirty-three). While the latter figure owes a great deal to the seventeen quotations in Gen. 24 and Gen. 44 alone, there remains a proportionally higher number of quotations spread throughout the book. This particular predilection for the use of quoted direct speech may reflect the exceptional amount of dialogue in the patriarchal narratives. Among the other narrative books, 1 Kings is the closest competitor, with twelve verifiable speeches and fifteen quotations, and an equivalent number of unverifiable quotations (seven). The style of 1 Kings tends toward multiple quotations within a few chapters—five in chapter 1, three in chapter 2, three in chapter 13, etc.—rather than a wider distribution throughout the book. A similar tendency toward grouping is also found in Numbers (ten speeches, ten quotations), where there are four quotes in the Balaam story (Num. 22–24), four in chapter 11, and two more in chapter 14. 1 Samuel, on the other hand, has nearly the same statistics (ten speeches, eleven quotations) but spread out over nine individual chapters. Ultimately, however, the presence or absence of quoted direct speech in a given text does not seem to reflect any historical preference for one style over another.[13]

It is noteworthy that within the narrative in Genesis, Exodus, and Numbers, nearly all verifiable and unverifiable quotations have been ascribed to J, or E or JE by documentary critics. In verifiable quoted direct speech both the original speech and the quotation belong to the same source in all cases. The only quotation from the P source is one in which the *narrator* quotes Isaac in Gen. 28:6 quoting 28:1ff. This lack of attestation may reflect P's tendency to reduce the dramatic to the rhetorical, to minimize dialogue, and to omit those suggestions of personal motivation which are so often the object of quoted direct speech.[14]

<hr/>

3.

<hr/>

There are four basic patterns of discourse in which quotations are spoken. (1) In half of all quotations under consideration, X quotes Y to Z (XYZ), X being the present speaker, or "quoter," Y the quoted, original speaker, and Z the listener. In the majority of XYZ quotations Z was not present to hear Y's original words; as a result, there is a quality of reportage to the quotation, as, for example, when God informs Moses of the people's behavior in Ex. 32:8. But we also find cases of ironic quotation (e.g., 1 Sam. 21:12) as well as outright confrontation, as in 2 Sam. 18:12. Since Joab had already heard David's comments in 18:5, the quotation does not inform him of something he did not already know. It rather serves to dramatize Joab's willful disobedience of David's command, creating a tension that is not released until their confrontation in chapter 19.

Unverifiable quotations taken alone show a somewhat higher proportion of XYZ formulations than do verifiable quotes.[15] While it is difficult to base conclusions on this margin, it is reasonable to say that the concept of verifiability is more suited to XYZ reporting contexts than to confrontational situations. There is simply more force to an accusation or a self-justification whose "proof" is attested in the text than to one whose authority must be decided on the basis of context. Outright lies in unverifiable quotations always use the XYZ format, for obvious reasons: Josh. 9:11; 1 Sam. 19:17; 21:3; 2 Sam. 1:7–9; 16:3; 1 Kg. 13:18; 2 Kg. 5:22.

(2) One-quarter of the cases involve X quoting X to Y (XXY), where X is the speaker quoting his own words from an earlier point in the narrative, and Y is the present listener. These texts may also reflect a reporting situation if Y was not present when X originally spoke those words. For example, in 1 Kg. 21:6 Ahab tells Jezebel what he had said to Naboth; in Gen. 44:32 Judah quotes to Joseph the pledge he had made to their father concerning Benjamin. But in the majority of cases the quote is

already known to the hearer, resulting in a powerful sense of confrontation. The speaker quotes his original statement to prove the correctness of his claims (e.g., 2 Kgs. 4:28), and often the errant quality of Y's words or actions as well (e.g., Gen. 3:17).

(3) A more heightened degree of confrontation is found in the twenty-four cases in which X quotes Y to Y (XYY), where X is the speaker, and Y is both the original speaker (quoted) and the present listener. An example of this type would be Abimelech's challenge to Isaac in Gen. 26:9a: "How could you say, 'She is my sister'?" While there are a few instances in which this configuration is used for recapitulating the story (e.g., Gen. 44:19, 21) or mollifying an angry God (Ex. 33:12; Num. 14:18), most occurrences of XYY present X demanding to know how or why Y could have said the things that he did (e.g., Josh. 9:22; Jud. 18:4).

(4) The fourth pattern is utilized in the relatively small number of cases in which the narrator himself repeats a discourse previously spoken by one of the characters, as in Jud. 21:18 or 1 Kg. 12:12. Strictly speaking, these instances should be defined as repetitions rather than quotations, since the narrator is always at a remove from the characters in the stories. These cases invoke neither the aspect of reportage nor those of accusation or self-justification, for the narrator is "speaking" only to the reader, who is already aware of the details being repeated. Although repetition and recapitulation are very common in biblical narrative, only rarely does the narrator repeat direct speech. Most of his repeating is done via indirect discourse and narration, leaving dialogue as the province of the characters alone. The recalling of events or words by a character within the story creates the more dramatic effect of "showing" the action through the character's eyes, rather than "telling" of these matters in the narrative voice. From this perspective the narrator seems to sabotage his own art with inappropriate repetitions.

In certain instances, such as the repetition in 2 Kg. 7:18–19, the narrator's quotation may reflect an emphasis upon the idea of prophecy and fulfillment, which is in fact characteristic of the Book of Kings. But in other texts this technique is more frequently used by the narrator to comment upon the character who hears, rather than upon the one who speaks the quotation. Thus the repetition of the people's demand for a king in 1 Sam. 8:6, followed by God's statement that "they have not rejected you, only me," highlights Samuel's private feelings of resentment. In 1 Kg. 21:4, the repetition of Naboth's refusal to sell his vineyard is used to explain Ahab's anger and disappointment. What was expressed by Naboth as a religious oath, "ḥālîlâ lî mēYHWH mittittî" (the Lord forbid that I should give . . .), becomes in Ahab's eyes Naboth's personal rejection of the king's offer, "lō' 'ettēn lĕkā" (*I* will not give you . . .).

4.

A noticeable number of quotations involve divine speech, which includes God's quotations both of himself (Gen. 3:17; 1 Kg. 13:22) and of humans (Gen. 18:13; Ex. 32:8), as well as more numerous quotations by humans of words from YHWH or his angelic messengers.[16] Is there anything particularly distinguishing about this speech—is YHWH a more faithful quoter than humans are? Conversely, do humans quote YHWH's words with greater fidelity to the original than is found in ordinary quoted direct speech? To these possibilities we must respond in the negative. God's two quotations of himself follow their originals closely, but not extraordinarily so. Both cases are shortened, in keeping with the usual standards of quoted direct speech (see below), and in 1 Kg. 13:22 God takes at least as much liberty with variation as does the man of God, in his quotation of the same message in 13:17. God quotes Sarah more freely in Gen. 18:13, while still being essentially truthful; in Num. 11:20 he even cites an unverifiable quotation.[17]

In response to the second question, quotations of God are generally treated as authoritative statements (who would dare misquote YHWH?), just as divine speech itself is accepted by the narrator as true and authentic. When spoken by humans these quotations are also generally accurate, but again, not to an exceptional degree. Shortening of quotations is common (Ex. 33:12a; Num. 14:18), as is a fair amount of paraphrasis (Num. 11:21; 32:11–12; 2 Kg. 9:36–37), and, in one case, a short addition (1 Sam. 15:18). Nor is divine speech beyond misappropriation; one need only mention the serpent's deceptive quote in Gen. 3:1 or the old prophet's false oracle in 1 Kg. 13:18 (unverifiable) to see the power and the effect of any quotation of the divine word.

5.

All the quotations under discussion are tagged by the speaker with a verbal component that indicates its "spokenness." The verbs we will discuss here are those used by the speaker to introduce the quotation, not those employed by the narrator to introduce the speaker. By far the most common verb of presentation is a form of the root ʾ-*M-R* (to say) in either a finite or infinitival construction. As a finite verb it is used in the perfect tense, either the unprefixed perfect (*ʾāmar,* etc.) or the converted imperfect (*wayyōʾmer,* etc.), the latter being more common. The infinitive always occurs in the form *lēʾmōr* (to say, saying), as is common in biblical direct discourse, preceded by a finite verb. Finite forms of ʾ-*M-R* occur in more than 50 percent of all cases of quoted direct speech, but only rarely is it found together with the infinitive *lēʾmōr*.[18] Rather, *lēʾmōr* is reserved for use in conjunction with finite forms of a variety of other verbs of introduction: *D-B-R* ("to speak," e.g., Gen. 27:7; 42:14), *Š-L-Ḥ* ("to send," Num. 22:10; Jud. 11:17), *Ṣ-W-H* ("to command," Gen. 3:17; Josh. 1:13), *ʿ-N-H* ("to sing," 1 Sam. 21:12; 29:5), *B-K-H* ("to cry," Num. 11:13, 18, 21), etc. In only five cases is the verb *ʾ-M-R* completely absent from the introduction of the quotation in any form.[19]

While the root *ʾ-M-R* functions as an indicator of direct speech, other finite verbs that, together with *lēʾmōr*, introduce quotations, may be important in describing the nature or purpose of the quotation, or the tone of voice in which it is spoken. On the most obvious level, the root *Š-B-ʿ* in the *hipʿil* (e.g., Gen. 24:37; 50:5) and in the *nipʿal* (e.g., Ex. 32:13; 33:1) defines the quoted words as part of a sworn oath. The verb *Š-L-Ḥ* is used to introduce communications sent by messenger. The speaker may change the verb of introduction from the original verb of speaking in order to produce a pejorative tone and to heighten the condemnation of the character who is being quoted. This technique is apparent in Pharaoh's substitution of the verb *Ṣ-ʿ-Q* (to cry out) in place of *ʾ-M-R*, to describe the complaints of the Israelites in Ex. 5:8. It can also be seen when Joshua uses the verb *R-M-H* (to deceive) to confront the Gibeonites in Josh. 9:22, and again when Gideon employs the verb *Ḥ-R-P* (to mock) to condemn the people of Succoth for not supporting him against Zevah and Salmunna in Jud. 8:15. In each case the quoter repeats the original statement with only minimal changes; it is the new verb of introduction that recontextualizes and reinterprets their words.

The great majority of cases of quoted direct speech are introduced by verbs in the *paʿal* form, as would be expected in a phenomenon that involves the quotation of words previously spoken at an earlier point in the narrative. But in a small number of cases, a participial form is used to introduce the quotation. These instances should be understood in the durative present tense,[20] as if the quoter still has the quoted words ringing in his ears when he repeats them. Their function is not so much to remind the reader, or speaker, of what has been said, but rather to reemphasize those words in the present moment of the quotation. For example, in 1 Kg. 18:11, and again in 18:14, Obadiah confronts Elijah with the precise words he had spoken just previously in v. 8: "wĕʿattâ ʾattâ ʾōmēr lēk ʾĕmōr laʾdōnêkā hinnēh Ēlîyyāhû" (And now you say, "Go, say to your master, 'Here is Elijah'"). The use of the introductory form *ʾattâ ʾōmēr* in both vv. 11 and 14 adds to the immediacy of his criticism of Elijah for the prophet's suggestion that Obadiah was not willing to put his life on the line for the sake of Elijah and YHWH. The fact that the quotation follows closely upon Elijah's original discourse adds still further to this urgency. The purpose, and the result, of such a confrontation is to elicit from Elijah an oath (v. 15), programmatically parallel to the oath stated by Obadiah (v. 10); just as Obadiah did not forsake the prophets of YHWH, so Elijah will not betray Obadiah. In a similar fashion, in Ex. 33:12a Moses uses a participial introduction to confront God with the impossibility of performing the task laid upon him without divine assistance (33:15) and to exact a promise of continual divine presence throughout the journey. In both cases the participial form emphasizes the dialogical encounter between quoter and quoted.

Another occurrence of the durative is found in Ex. 5:8, where Pharaoh says, "ʿal-kēn hēm ṣōʿăqîm" (that is why they cry out), as if Moses and Aaron were still clamoring outside Pharaoh's door at that very moment. In 5:17 he again introduces the quotation with a participle (ʾōmĕrîm) to stress that the ongoing demand of the Israelites to worship their God in the desert is the real reason behind their complaint of v. 15. In both cases a stative form, *nirpîm,* precedes the quote, as if to say, "It is because you *are* slacking off that you *are* saying, 'Let us go and sacrifice to the Lord,'" even though Pharaoh's quote refers to what they had said in the past. By claiming that the Israelites' complaint is ongoing, Pharaoh defends the continuation of his harsh "no straw" policy. On the basis of these examples it is reasonable to conclude that the use of a participial introduction reflects a deliberate attempt by the speaker to heighten the drama of the conflict.

An equally small number of texts use *yipʿal* verbal forms to introduce quotations, in ways that also draw attention to the present moment. In 1 Sam. 21:12 and 29:5, the song celebrating David's victory over the Philistines is introduced as though the women are still singing the song for him, in order to stress to Achish that David remains a threat to his people.[21] In Num. 11:13, Moses' use of the phrase "kî-yibkû ʿālay" (when they complain to me) to introduce the quotation gives the impression that the people are continually crying to him for meat, making his problem all the more urgent. Sometimes the *yipʿal* has a subjunctive, or potential force, even though the act referred to has already taken place. In Jud. 18:24 Micah quotes the words of the Danites spoken to him in v. 23 with a sense of outrage that, after their crimes against him, they could dare to ask *ma-lāk* (colloquially, "What's bothering you?"). In Gen. 43:7, a quote is introduced by a verb in the *yipʿal* because the quotation reflects a moment that, from some earlier point in time, was construed as future, even though that moment is now in the past.[22] "How could we have known that he would say, 'Bring your brother here'?" Jacob's sons try to explain to their father that they can retell the past but cannot rewrite it, for they are but characters in a story fashioned by someone else.

6.

In order to address the question of meaning in variation that was raised in the previous chapter, we must first identify the norms and conventions of such modifications. We will therefore outline the types of change in language that occur in verifiable quoted direct speech between the original speech and its subsequent quotation. To what degree is repetition in quotation "literal" and to what degree is it paraphrastic?

As with other types of repetition in the Bible, verbatim repetition of the original speech, with no omissions or additions whatsoever, is an infrequent occurrence. There are only ten instances of this type of quoted direct speech: Gen. 20:5; 26:9; 38:22; 44:25; Ex. 32:8; 1 Sam. 21:12; 29:5; 1 Kg. 18:11, 14; 22:18. Each of these discourses is very short (from two to seven words), increasing the statistical probability of literal repetition. In half the cases there are clear indications of oral traditions behind the quotations that may have stabilized their language. This is most apparent in the oral character of David's victory song (1 Sam. 21:12 and 29:9 quoting 18:7),[23] as well as the people's proclamation in Ex. 32:8 quoting 32:4: "ʾelleh ʾĕlōhêkā yiśrāʾēl ʾăśer heʿĕlûkā mēʾereṣ miṣrāyîm" (These are your gods, O Israel, who brought you up out of the land of Egypt). It is also likely that the story tradition of the wife/sister in Genesis may have fixed the phrase *ʾăḥōtî hîʾ* (She is my sister), which is spoken and quoted in Gen. 20:5 and 26:9 and quoted unverifiably in Gen. 12:19.[24]

All of the remaining eighty-four quotations manifest some type of change in language, which we have divided into three categories: shortening, lengthening, and paraphrase. "Shortening" refers simply to the omission of words, phrases, and clauses, just as "lengthening" indicates the addition of these elements to the quotation. The term "paraphrase" broadly describes changes in the actual words used, as well as the rearrangement of syntactic order in the quotation. These changes are often not exclusive of one another, and in some cases it is difficult to determine where shortening and lengthening leave off and paraphrase begins. Furthermore, many quotations will exhibit two or even all three types of change; one clause may be lengthened or omitted altogether. Nevertheless, it is possible to make some general statements about each of these categories.[25]

Shortening

The overwhelming tendency of the narrator is to abridge the material repeated in quoted direct speech. At least three-quarters of the remaining quotations are shortened, sometimes by the omission of a few words

(Gen. 26:9) or, more frequently, by the removal of whole clauses, as in Gen. 3:17:

Quotation	*Original Speech*
Gen. 3:17	Gen. 2:16–17
"which I commanded you saying,	And the Lord God commanded the man, saying: "From every tree in the garden you may eat. But from the tree of the knowledge of good and evil, You
'You shall not eat from it.' "	shall not eat from it; For on the day you eat from it you will surely die."

Quotation	*Original Speech*
Gen. 26:9b	Gen. 26:7
And Isaac said to him: "Because I said,	For he [Isaac] was afraid to say 'my wife'
'Lest I die because of her.' "	"Lest the local people kill me because of Rebecca, because she is very beautiful."

There is a slight preference for retaining the initial clause of the original speech, but by and large the position of the phrase in the speech does not determine whether or not it will reappear in the quotation. This decision often reflects a utilitarian approach to repetition; the listener is told only what he needs to know to continue the plot, and the reader is not bogged down by extensive and slavish repetition, as is common to ancient Near Eastern epic poetry.[26] Sections of what originally appeared as direct discourse may be repeated as free indirect speech, e.g., Gen. 24:48, where Abraham's servant recounts to Laban the prayer he had spoken directly to God in 24:27. The swearing of an oath in direct speech is abridged in the retelling by the simple formula "X adjured me . . ." (the root *Š-B-ʿ* in the *hipʿil*) followed by the oath itself in quotation (Gen. 24:37; 50:5).

Synonymous words or phrases that added depth to the original speech but convey no new information are excised:[27]

Gen. 42:33 quoting 42:19:
From: wĕʾattem lĕkû hābîʾû šeber raʿăbôn bātêkem.
(And as for you, go, bring provisions for your starving households.)
To: wĕʾet raʿăbôn bātêkem qĕḥû wālēkû.
(Take [food] for your starving households and go.)

Gen. 44:32 quoting 43:9:

From:
'im-lō' hăbî'ōtîw 'ēlekā wĕhiṣṣagtîw lĕpānêkā wĕḥāṭā'tî lĕkā kol
hayyāmîm
(If I do not bring him to you and set him before you,
I will be eternally guilty before you.

To:
'im-lō' 'ăbî'ennû 'ēlekā wĕḥāṭā'tî lĕ'ăbî kol hayyāmîm
(If I do not bring him to you,
I will be eternally guilty before my father.)

This follows also for phrases that are repeated in the original discourse:

Jud. 13:7 quoting 13:3–5:

From:	wĕhārît wĕyōladt ben	You will conceive and bear a son.
	. . . .	. . . Indeed you have conceived
	kî hinnāk hārâ wĕyôladt bēn	and will bear a son.
To:	hinnāk hārâ wĕyôladt bēn	Indeed you have conceived
		and will bear a son.

Double verbs, or verbal chains, are shortened:

Gen. 24:39 quoting 24:5:

From: 'ûlay-lō' tō'beh hā'iššâ lāleket 'aḥăray
(Perhaps the woman will not agree to follow me.)
To: 'ûlay lō' tēlēk hā'iššâ 'aḥărāy
(Perhaps the woman will not follow me.)

Ex. 32:23 quoting 32:1:

From:	qûm 'ăśēh lānû 'ĕlōhîm	(Arise, make us a god)
To:	'ăśēh lānû 'ĕlōhîm	(Make us a god)

It is not surprising that pronouns, emphatic or otherwise, as well as an occasional proper name may be omitted, but even the divine name and epithets of YHWH may be shortened in quotation. In Gen. 24:40, Abraham's expression "YHWH 'ĕlōhê haššāmayîm" (The Lord, God of the heavens—24:7) becomes simply *YHWH,* and the doubling of the divine name in Ex. 34:6 is repeated with only a single Tetragrammaton in Num. 14:18.[28] Given the almost normative occurrence of shortening in quoted direct speech, it can be difficult to determine whether or not the omission of certain details in quoted repetition is rhetorically significant. For example, Num. 14:18 consistently deletes synonymous phrases from the original speech in Ex. 34:6–7, perhaps for nothing more than stylistic convention. But Moses' omission of the phrase "nōṣēr ḥesed lā' ălāpîm" (keeping steadfast love for thousands [of generations]) may carry with it a deliberate change in meaning; since the phrase refers only to the innocent, Moses would be insulting God if he pretended that these words should apply to Israel at that moment of intercession.[29] Similarly, as we saw above in Jud. 13:7, when Manoah's wife quotes to him the instructions of the angel from 13:3–5, some clauses are omitted because they are repetitive or unnecessary for either the reader or Manoah. But the removal of any reference to the prohibition against cutting the boy's hair highlights Manoah's ignorance in Judges 13, which serves as a prolepsis of his son's lack of awareness of Delilah's true intentions in Jud. 16:4ff.[30]

These cases, and others like them, demonstrate the absence of any "automatic" connection between shortened quoted direct speech and simple stylistic convention on the one hand, and deliberate change in meaning on the other. The frequency of shortening in quoted direct speech cannot be ignored, but the context of the quotation in the story must be the final arbiter. Only after we have examined the whole of the Samson story and determined its meaning can the possible functions of such omissions become clear. In a story that is ironic throughout, the dismissal of such an ironic portrayal of the hero's father would undercut the effectiveness of the characterization of Samson himself. If the omission of certain details in quoted direct speech supports or coincides with a major theme of that narrative, then the possibility of deliberate abridgment for strategic purposes exists and should be explored. On a general level it would be unwise to claim more than this; the determining factor lies in the degree to which the suggested reading emerges from the context of the story in a convincing way.

Lengthening

In contrast to the great number of shortened quotations, the extent of lengthening in quoted direct speech tends to be quite limited, both in the number of texts that exhibit additions and in the extent of those additions. A total of eighteen quotations are expanded in some manner, by adding a parallel synonymous phrase, as in Gen. 24:40, or by expanding a verbal chain, as in Gen. 44:23, 26. Only once is a clause repeated twice in quoted direct speech (Gen. 24:41) or lengthened by an extensive introduction or conclusion (Gen. 31:11–13; 42:34). In no instances are pronouns or names, divine or otherwise, added to the text or expanded upon. In a few quotations the expansion serves to underscore the point being made by the speaker. In Jud. 8:15 Gideon quotes the people of Succoth's rejection of the appeal of his "exhausted" men—"'ănāšêkā hayyĕ 'ēpîm"—just prior to punishing them. In his quote of God's command to destroy the Amalekites in 1 Sam. 15:18, Samuel describes them with the term *haḥaṭṭā'îm* (the sinful ones); by making their wickedness more pronounced, he strengthens his case against Saul for not destroying them utterly. But in the majority of cases these additions are limited to a word or two that have no effect on the meaning of the quotation.

The fact that only some of these additions are meaningful changes reinforces our point about style and meaning in shortened quoted direct speech. Since lengthening occurs so seldom, one might hypothesize that each expansion must indicate a shift in meaning from the original speech. While this is true for Jud. 8:15 and 1 Sam. 15:8, such changes in meaning are no more automatically determined by the scarcity of lengthened quoted direct speech than are all omissions of detail in shortened quotations to be understood as stylistic variation (with no attendant change in meaning), simply by dint of their frequency. For example, in Num. 24:13, Balaam's addition of the word *millibbî* (of my own mind) adds nothing to the meaning of the verse when compared with 22:18, because his intentions—to justify his own behavior—are so similar in both statements. On the other hand, the woman's addition of the phrase "*wĕlō' tiggĕ'û bô*" (and you shall not touch it) in Gen. 3:3 becomes significant in light of the serpent's continued argument in 3:4–5 and her subsequent contact with the fruit of the tree in 3:6. In both cases the significance of the additions cannot be assessed in isolation from the surrounding verses. While there are conventions of lengthening in quoted direct speech, it is the context of the quotation that is the ultimate basis of such determinations.[31]

Paraphrase

The most frequent changes found in quoted direct speech are paraphrastic in nature, given that most lengthened and/or shortened quotations exhibit changes in language as well as in length.[32] These range from the simplest kinds of morphological variations in verbal forms, to the interchange of synonymous words and phrases, to complete changes in language and syntax. The first category includes transformations from the imperfect to the converted perfect (Num. 22:11) and vice versa (Gen. 50:5), or from perfect to converted imperfect (Num. 22:10) and the reverse (2 Sam. 1:16), changes in conjugation (Ex. 32:24), tense (Gen. 43:9), person (Gen. 24:44), and number (2 Sam. 4:10). These changes represent only stylistic variation, with no particular change in meaning. Some of the changes are a necessary result of the new context into which the quotation is placed. For example, the use of the plural *tō'kēlû* in Gen. 3:1 and 3:3 adjusts the original command in 2:17 to the presence of a second party. A similar logic may involve a shift in person;

in Gen. 42:10–11, 13; 44:19–32 the brothers employ polite usage when speaking to Joseph, but report their words to Jacob in the first person. But these adjustments do not signal an attempt by the quoter or the narrator to alter the meaning of the original speech in quotation.

The use of synonymous words or short phrases in direct substitution one for another is quite common in paraphrased quoted direct speech and extends to all parts of speech. In some cases this practice may signal a change in emphasis, if not in meaning as well, within the quotation. Jacob's sons tell him that Simeon was "left" with Joseph in Gen. 42:33 ("hannîḥû 'ittî"), making the force of their words very different from Joseph's actual demand that Simeon be imprisoned ("yē'āsēr bĕbêt miš-markem," 42:19). When Isaac is called to task for his deception of Abimelech in Gen. 26:9, he tactfully rephrases his actual thoughts, which showed his mistrust of the locals (26:7, "pen yahargūnî 'anšē hammā-qôm," "Lest the people of this place kill me"), into a less offensive quotation that describes his fears in an indefinite, even passive way (26:9, "pen 'āmût 'ālêhā," "Lest I die because of her").

But for every instance of meaningful substitution, there are many more that are purely stylistic:

Gen. 24:37 quoting 24:3:

From: *bĕqirbô* (in his midst)   To: *bĕ'arṣô* (in his land)

Gen. 24:43 quoting 24:14:

From: *hanna'ărā* (the maiden)   To: *hā'almâ* (the young woman)

1 Kg. 12:10 quoting 12:4:

From: *hiqšâ* (he made difficult)   To: *hikbîd* (he made heavy)

Num. 24:13 quoting 23:26:

From: *'e'ĕśeh* (I will do)   To: *'ădabbēr* (I will speak)

With respect to the last example, the roots *D-B-R* (to speak) and *'-Ś-H* (to do) alternate throughout the Balaam story in similar contexts (cf. 22:20, 23), perhaps because all of Balaam's "doing" is centered on "speaking." Even in a situation such as this, where there is a demonstrable lexical difference between the two words, the context renders them virtually equivalent.

As paraphrastic language within a quotation becomes more extensive, categories of change become less and less distinct. The syntax of sentences may be completely rearranged, shortening quotations as well as rephrasing them, sometimes to the extent that the verifiability of the quotation is called into question.[33] This problem is most noticeable in the Joseph story, where a number of quotations differ significantly in language and syntax and, to a lesser degree, in the information that is conveyed. In addition, these are set within multiple retellings of the same or similar events. The initial encounter between Joseph and his brothers in Gen. 42:7–20 is repeated first by the brothers in 42:29ff.; another, somewhat conflicting version is referred to in 43:1–10; and a third telling, with closer connections to the second, is undertaken by Judah in 44:18–34. To present one specific example, in 43:3–5 Judah, speaking to his father, quotes Joseph (twice) as having said: "lō'-tir'û pānay biltî 'ăḥîkem 'ittĕkem" (You shall not see my face unless your brother is with you). While the sentiment is accurate, nowhere earlier in the story does the text present Joseph expressing himself precisely in this fashion. How is the reader to understand this quote—as an extensive paraphrase of Joseph's words in 42:18–20 (and therefore verifiable)? As a fanciful embellishment on Judah's part to impress upon his father the gravity of the situation (and therefore unverifiable)? Or perhaps as remarks made by Joseph to which the reader was not privy (also unverifiable, but "believable")? Similar complications arise with respect to the relationship of 43:7 and 42:31–32 to 42:11, 13, as well as the connection between Judah's long discourse (44:18–34) and the events and speeches of both chapters 42 and 43.

While it is generally true that the greater the amount of paraphrased language, the greater the difference in meaning between the original speech and the quotation, this axiom is not without exception. 1 Sam. 11:12 approximates the sentiment of 1 Sam. 10:27 quite closely, despite a complete change in language. In 2 Sam. 4:10, the words David attributes to the messenger from 2 Sam. 1 bear little resemblance to his actual words in 1:4ff., but certainly the message—"Behold, Saul is dead"—is accurate. From another perspective, we note that in Gen. 3:1 the serpent's quote of God's words is composed of two clauses, both of which are actually present in 2:17, even if the serpent's inversion of their order and the addition of the negative particle *lō'* endow them with a significantly different meaning.[34] These are unusual situations, to be sure, but they demonstrate once again the point we have made regarding other types of change in quoted direct speech. A certain amount of paraphrase is to be expected in quotations, but there is no absolute correlation between the type and extent of the paraphrase and any change in meaning of the quoted words. One must therefore examine not only the words with which a speaker quotes his source, but also the context, the tone of voice, and the purpose of the repetition. It is to these questions that we turn in the following chapter.

We conclude with the following observations:

(a) About 70 percent of all quotations in the narrative sample of Genesis–2 Kings are verifiable, and 30 percent are unverifiable. Nearly all verifiable quotations are relatively accurate repetitions of the content of

the earlier speech, and two-thirds of the unverifiable quotations are believable, i.e., likely to have been spoken. Quoted direct speech generally
does not involve outright prevarication, the exceptions being mostly unverifiable quotations. Rather, it is concerned with the varying degrees of
truthful representation in reporting prior speech. The fact that verifiable quotations outnumber unverifiable quotes by more than two to one
may reflect the interest of the narrative in that gray area between the
truth and the lie.

(b) God is treated by the narrator as "one of the characters" in matters
related to quoted direct speech. His quoting voice displays no less variety
in repetition than do human voices, nor are his words immutable when
placed in the mouths of other speakers. At the same time, the narrator
does have a special attitude toward God regarding his understanding of
quotations, granting God an omniscience equivalent to his own that
allows God, like the reader, to compare the quotation with the original in
all cases.

(c) In terms of change in repetition, both conciseness and variation in
language are high priorities in quoted direct speech. Quotations rarely
appear in a form identical to their source, or with substantial additions
tacked on by the quoter. But the significance of these changes (and the
significance of verbatim repetition) can be assessed only in light of the
context in which the quotation is placed.

·3·

THE FUNCTION OF THE
QUOTATION:
STORY ANALYSIS

As we remarked in chapter 1, the discussion of narrative texts must address two interrelated elements: (1) the *story* told by the narrator, which includes the characters, the events of the plot, and the physical and emotional elements of their world; (2) the *discourse* of the narrator, which is his means of realization of that world: his mode of language, his point of view in telling the story, and his method of investing the story with meaning beyond the plot itself and conveying its significance to the reader. This distinction is of particular relevance to our topic because quoted direct speech involves a temporary transfer of the role of narrator to the quoting character. This role change is most obvious in a text like Genesis 24, where, in vv. 34–48, Abraham's servant retells through quotations the events that have occurred in vv. 2–17, but it is true of shorter quotations as well. The character, in turn, uses the quotation(s) in the service of a larger plan: Abraham's servant tries to get Laban to agree to his daughter's marriage to Isaac (24:49); Aaron attempts to justify his own failure to Moses (Ex. 32:23–24); Joshua uses the Gibeonites' words as evidence against them (Josh. 9:22). In taking over the role of narrator, the character likewise engages in the traditional narrative tasks of characterization, organization of the plot (of the quotation), and representation of point of view. When a quotation is verifiable, the reader is in a position to evaluate the speaker's intentions by comparing the original speech with its quoted form and its new content. Thus, when we look at a "quoter," we are examining a narrator at work addressing another audience (the character), and we can scrutinize that speaker's words to understand the rhetorical strategies he uses to argue his case before that audience in the story. The interaction between the speaking character and the listening character—i.e., the illocutionary force of the quotation as directed by one character toward another, and its perlocutionary effect upon that listener—we designate as a *story* level dynamic of quoted direct speech, because both the quoter and his audience remain within the confines of the story. The analysis of this story level of quoted direct speech is the subject of this chapter. The ways in which the narrator deploys character, event, and speech to address the reader who stands outside the story will be the subject of *discourse* analysis in chapter 4.

As noted earlier, three types of quotations are possible within the story:[1] (1) X, the speaker, quotes Y, another speaker, to Z, a listener (XYZ); (2) X, the speaker, quotes Y, who spoke earlier, to Y, now a listener (XYY); (3) X, the speaker, quotes X (himself), to Y, a listener (XXY). In all cases X functions as a narrator, retelling an earlier event or speech in his own edited fashion. In the situation XYZ, the listener (Z) is unlikely to have been aware of this information prior to the quotation, but in the configurations XYY and XXY the opposite tends to hold true. There are, however, enough exceptions to these rules that it will be more useful to divide the texts into the categories of new information and old information, according to the degree of knowledge of the listener. In order to examine the rhetorical aims of the speaker, it is essential to know whether his words are directed at an ignorant, or innocent, listener who could be deceived more easily, or at a more knowledgeable one who would, in a sense, keep the quoter "honest."

Under these rubrics of new and old information two other major elements will guide the discussion. The *tone* in which the quotation is spoken helps to determine the illocutionary force and its function in the story. Since the biblical narrator generally introduces quotations with only the verb '-*M-R* (to say), eschewing a more descriptive verb or an adverbal modifier, tone must be discerned from the context into which the quotation is placed, the awareness of the listener, and the presence or absence of deliberate irony in the speaker's words.[2] The categories that we will use range from a neutral tone for the transfer of information with no bias on the speaker's part, to less straightforward, pseudo-informational intentions, to confrontational quotations made in the service of accusation or self-justification. The tone of a given quotation reveals some aspects of the intentions of the speaker in a general way but does not disclose his strategy of speech in a more particular sense.

The other central element is *time,* for quotation is a temporal art that involves the juxtaposition of an earlier moment with a later one. Two aspects of time must be taken into account: (1) narrative time, or time of reading. We will distinguish between quotations whose source is found within the pericope and those whose origin is outside, either in an earlier chapter of the same story or in an entirely different story or book. (2) Narrated time, or time of action in the story, where the amount of time between the original statement and its subsequent quotation can affect a character's knowledge of even his own words.[3]

In this chapter we will discuss issues of relative states of knowledge, the tone of the speaker, and the temporal relationship between the quotation and its source, as they function in verifiable quoted direct speech on the level of story alone. Using the above-mentioned criteria we will analyze verifiable quotations in order to see the range of possible modes of use in biblical narrative. Some texts will be discussed at greater length to show the working out of these functions within the story. While the separation of story and discourse analyses may be initially frustrating to the exegete (and to the reader), it will ultimately enable us to perceive different levels of meaning in these texts more clearly.

1. New Information

We begin with texts in which the speaker is presenting information previously unknown to his listener. All of these quotations function as reportage, but we can distinguish between quotes that convey facts naïvely, often in answer to a question, and those quotes which are part of more complex responses.

Neutral Delivery

In a relatively small number of cases, the information in the quotation is conveyed in a manner so neutral as to make X a mere conduit from the earlier speaker Y to the present listener Z. This neutrality can be manifested in literal or near-literal repetition, particularly when the quoter speaks in response to a request by the listener. We noted above that Gen. 38:22 is an example of literal repetition, where the Adullamite repeats to Judah precisely what the townspeople had told him in the previous verse: "No prostitute has been here." The literalness of the quote, its close proximity to the original speech, and the lack of ulterior motives on the quoter's part emphasize the purely informational quality of the Adullamite's speech. While the narrator may have some purpose in emphasizing to the reader the absence of a cult prostitute,[4] this quotation functions in the story in much the same way as a simple summary. 1 Kg. 13:17 contains a similarly neutral quotation of 1 Kg. 13:9, though here the repetition entails a few relatively minor changes in language. While the subsequent requotation of the phrase in 13:22 functions as an explanation of his fate, in v. 17 the man of God is simply explaining to the old prophet why he cannot accept his invitation. Similarly neutral quotes are found in 1 Sam. 14:28 quoting 14:24 and in 1 Kg. 1:47 quoting 1:36–37. The latter case in particular has a noticeable amount of shortening and paraphrase, but Jonathan ben Abiathar's report of the anointing of Solomon is essentially correct in all its non-speech aspects as well. A worthy man may serve as a faithful messenger, though not necessarily as the bearer of good news (1:42).

Strategic Delivery

Far more common are those situations in which speaker X tries to use quoted direct speech in a strategic manner to control Y's or Z's responses. Since X speaks not simply as a messenger but as an aggressive character in the story, he establishes himself as an authoritative narrator in a more significant sense and is in a better position to influence the perceptions of his listener. All the texts in this section also follow the pattern XYZ, but the point in time when Y originally spoke those words varies greatly and thus may impinge upon the listener's awareness. Accordingly, the discussion will begin with those quotations which are most distant in time from their sources.

In Jud. 11:12–27 Jephthah sends a long diplomatic letter to the king of Ammon recounting the history of Israel's passage through the Transjordanian lands in the period following the Exodus. In v. 17 he quotes the text of an earlier message from Israel to the king of Edom, which is found in Num. 20:17. In v. 19, he quotes a similar request from Israel to Sihon, the Amorite king, found in Num. 21:21 (and Deut. 2:26). In both cases the quotations are considerably shorter than the versions in Numbers. Jephthah uses these quotes as a means of characterization, showing the consistency of Israel's policy toward its neighbors even before they *were* neighbors. The quote regarding the Edomites and the mention of the Moabites in vv. 17–18, are meant to demonstrate to the king of Ammon Israel's respect for traditional land boundaries, and the quote regarding Sihon serves to give notice of Israel's readiness to fight when provoked. Moreover, Sihon's land is claimed as Israel's *own* possession by YHWH, just as Chemosh parcels out land to his peoples.[5]

Jephthah's quotations are obvious cases of quotations of historical precedent, a term that, in this context, can span as much as the above-mentioned period of 200–300 years of narrated time between the original speech and its reappearance in quotation. Similarly, in Jer. 26:18, the elders of the land cite an oracle from Mic. 3:12, presumably spoken at least a century before, as a legal precedent in Jeremiah's defense. But it is not absolutely necessary for quotations from outside the chapter to reflect the passage of generations. Significantly less time elapses between the original singing of the song about David and Saul in 1 Sam. 18:7, "hikkâ šā'ûl ba'ălāpāw/ wĕdāwid bĕribăbōtāyw" (Saul has slain his thousands, and David his ten thousands), and its repetition in 1 Sam. 21:12, where a compromised David has no recourse but to feign madness in order to escape capture by Achish. One senses that the irony the reader perceives is not lost on David either. In 1 Kg. 2:8 David recalls (also with some irony) an oath he swore to Shimei ben Gerah years before in 2 Sam. 19:24. While David originally promised to safeguard his life, he now quotes the oath as part of his instructions to Solomon to dispose of Shimei himself.[6]

Although each narrative draws its own time boundaries around itself, historical precedent quotations break down this closed temporal framework to address a broader context. Most frequently, the quoter seeks to validate his present position in light of the past, as in Josh. 1:13 quoting Deut. 3:18, or in Jephthah's quotations in Jud. 11:17, 19 mentioned above. But the quotation may also serve to contrast moments within the life of single character, as illustrated by the above examples from the life of David.

In the great majority of examples of quoted direct speech, source and quotation are contained within the same narrative, in situations of "old" and "new" information alike. Given the terse style of biblical narrative, the presence and proximity of two parallel versions encourages a much closer examination of their similarities and differences. If, in the original speech, the reader concentrated on the content of the message being transmitted, in the quotation he looks more closely at the *speaker,* the way of telling, and the reason behind the retelling.[7] The quoted material is set within the context of a request, X wishing to obtain concessions from Z, as demonstrated by the following text.

In Gen. 27:7, Rebecca repeats to Jacob a part of Isaac's speech to Esau (vv. 1–4). Her hopes of gaining Isaac's blessing for Jacob depend entirely upon Jacob's willing participation in a scheme of deception. In order to gain his cooperation she must spark his jealousy and desire without arousing too many of his fears. Her use of quotation moves toward this end in at least three ways. By quoting direct speech—as opposed to indirect speech or summary—Rebecca achieves a more "objective" narrative status in Jacob's eyes and awakens Jacob's envy of his brother as his *own* response to the "reported facts." Second, her use of the participle *mĕdabbēr* in referring to Isaac's words emphasizes the urgency of Jacob's situation—he must act now or forever lose his chance. The narrator underscores this immediacy to the reader with his own use of the participial form *šōmaʿat* as well as the infinitival form *bĕdabbēr*, referring respectively to Rebecca's listening and Jacob's speaking in v. 5.[8] Third, Rebecca shortens and paraphrases Isaac's words about hunting (27:3) to deflect an anticipated negative reaction by Jacob, were he to hear the whole of Isaac's speech. In Rebecca's version, all of verse 3 is omitted, with the exception of the final phrase, which is reformulated as follows:

Gen. 27:3	Gen. 27:7
Isaac to Esau	*Rebecca to Jacob*

śā'-nā' kēlêkā telyĕkā wĕqašteka
wĕṣē' haśśādeh
wĕṣûdâ lî ṣāyidh (Ketib: *ṣydh*)   hābî'â lî ṣayid
(Take your weapons, your quiver,
  and your bow, and go out to the
  field, and hunt game for me.)   (Bring me *sayid.*)

As a verb, the root Ṣ-W-D always refers to hunting, but the noun *ṣayid* standing alone can have a more general connotation of prepared food, as in Josh. 9:5, 14.[9] In the scenes between Esau and Isaac verbal forms of Ṣ-W-D are conspicuous (27:3, 5, 30, 32), but in the encounter between Jacob and Isaac in vv. 18–30, only the nominal form appears. When Jacob refers to *ṣêdî* in v. 19, he means simply the food he brought with him. This is not to say that he is unaware of the double meaning of the word in vv. 19 and 25, or to deny that he is deliberately lying to his father. But Rebecca's reformulation of v. 3 has shifted the focus of Jacob's concern away from hunting (which he is not prepared to do). His initial objection to his mother in vv. 11–12 makes no mention of his inability to hunt, centering instead on his fear of being unmasked in this deception, a fear more easily calmed by his mother's promise to assume responsibility if the scheme backfires. In this sense Rebecca's quotation also reorganizes the "plot," or sequence of events, of Isaac's words to fit her plan for Jacob.

Another example of the use of quotation to arouse emotion in order to win over the listener is found in Ex. 32:8, where God cites the people's declaration of 32:4 verbatim: " 'ēlleh 'ĕlōhekā yiśrā'ēl 'ăšer he'ĕlûkā mē'ereṣ miṣrāyîm" (These are your gods, O Israel, who brought you out of the land of Egypt). The quote is part of God's request for Moses to "let Him be" to destroy the people and start over again with Moses alone. The paradox of Israel's actual liberator addressing Moses as the one who brought up Israel from Egypt (32:7) and quoting the people praising another, *false* image of a redeemer from Egypt (32:8), sets up the central issue of the ensuing argument: When Israel is irresponsible, who will be responsible for Israel? The direct quote emphasizes the "objective" presentation by God as reporter. The consecutive speeches by God in vv. 8 and 9 may indicate an intended pause between the verses, a deliberate attempt to let Moses weigh the evidence before God gives his own interpretation and suggestion for the future.[10] Moses' counterargument in vv. 11ff. fights quotation with quotation; after rebutting the intent of v. 7 by addressing God as Israel's actual redeemer, he sets forth a hypothetical anticipatory quotation of Egypt's reaction to the destruction of Israel in the desert: "Let not the Egyptians say, 'It was with evil intent that He delivered them . . .'" (32:12). Everything God had worked for in gaining recognition from Pharaoh and Egypt would be lost. Moses follows hard upon this with another quotation, this time a genuine one of God's own past promise to the patriarchs of progeny and eternal possession of the land (32:13). The juxtaposition of the words of the Egyptians with those of God, of hypothetical speech with verifiable quotation, sets up a contrast in point of view on the Exodus that proves extremely compelling to God. In the end, Moses turns out to be more effective in his use of quotations than God himself.[11]

In a similar testament to the effectiveness of quotation, in Gen. 50:5 Joseph appeals to Pharaoh to allow him to bury his father in Canaan on the basis of an oath sworn in 47:29–31. While the actual swearing in 47:31 may have had more to do with Jacob's doubts about Joseph's willingness to leave the comfort of Egypt, Joseph uses it in 50:5 to persuade Pharaoh to let him go and perform his filial obligations.[12] Further modifications in the wording of the quotation made by Joseph would seem to indicate that Pharaoh had to be treated delicately in this matter. Certainly Jacob's entreaties not to be buried in Egypt—"'al-nā' tiqbĕrēnî bĕmiṣrāyîm" (Do not bury me in Egypt), and "ûnśā'tanî mimmiṣrāyîm" (Carry me out of Egypt)—would have been highly offensive to a royal court that had been so hospitable to its foreign guests. The ancestral, religious aspect of Jacob's phrase "wĕšākabtî 'im-'ăbōtay" (Let me lie with my fathers) is rendered by Joseph as "bĕqibrî 'ăšer kārîtî lî bĕ'ereṣ kĕna'an" (In the tomb which I dug out for myself in the land of Canaan); it is now Jacob's *own* gravesite in another country. It has been suggested that Pharaoh might have been more amenable to the idea of a personally "prepared" gravesite, much the way that an Egyptian might stock his own burial place with all his requirements for the hereafter.[13] Finally, Joseph deletes the phrase "if I have found favor in your eyes" from within the quotation and uses it instead as part of his own entreaty to Pharaoh in 50:4. What was successful from father to son now succeeds from servant to master.

Gen. 50:5 has affinities with two other texts in which quoted direct speech is used as part of a strategy of convincing the leader of a group to release one of its members to go to another land. In Gen. 42:31–34 Jacob's sons return to tell him all the details of their encounter with "the man" in Egypt and request that Benjamin be allowed to accompany them on a return trip. They are aware that the request will be hard on Jacob, and their "verbatim" report reflects the beginning of their efforts to persuade him. They omit from their account the most frightening aspects of their adventures—that they were imprisoned for three days (42:17), that Simeon remains in jail (42:19), that a death threat hangs

over them (v. 20). As they showed respect to Joseph in Egypt, referring
to him as their lord, to themselves as his servants, and to their father
simply as "a certain man" (*'îš 'eḥād*, 42:10, 11, 13), now Jacob is honored
as their father and Joseph is called "the man" (*hā'îš*, 42:30, 33). Further,
they represent themselves as having performed better in their argument
with Joseph than they actually did. From 42:9 onwards we see them
constantly kept off balance; Joseph accuses them of lying no fewer than
five times (42:9, 12, 14, 15, 20), causing them to blurt out information
about home and family in their desperate attempts to vindicate themselves. In sharp contrast to this, vv. 29–34 mention only one accusation
by Joseph, and one response. Certainly some of this shortening is due to
the routine attenuation of repeated sections common to quoted direct
speech and to other forms of recapitulation, but in this case eight originally discrete acts of speech are recombined into three. As the brothers
recapitulate their words to "the man," their single speech in 42:31 is a
well-organized rational response to what seems to be a lunatic demand
by the Egyptian lord.[14] The brothers have Joseph end his speech on a
positive note, focusing upon Simeon's release and on their general freedom to move about the land.[15] In v. 35 we expect to find the typical
request section beginning with *wĕʿattâ*, in which the speaker, having
appealed to the authority of the past, now makes his own future-oriented
request. The brothers omit this step, choosing to let Joseph's words alone
convey the necessity of Benjamin's descent to Egypt. In so doing they
reemphasize that it is not they but "the man" who demands this difficult
sacrifice.

This is one of the few quotations attached to a request in which the
speaker is not successful in winning over his audience (cf. also Ex. 32:8;
1 Kg. 20:5), and it is instructive to explore some of the reasons for this
failure. In one sense Jacob's negative reaction in 42:36 is not surprising, if
only because of his special attachment to Benjamin. But given the
brothers' skillful editorial reconstruction, we might have expected something less than an unconditional refusal. In fact, Jacob responds strangely
in a number of ways. He does not react immediately to the brothers'
speech but waits until the discovery of the money in the sacks has taken
place in v. 35. When he does respond, he shows much less concern for
Simeon than might be anticipated, placing him in the same absent, irre-
trievable category as Joseph—*'ênennû*—"he is no longer." Some critics
explain his reactions by appealing to documentary theory or to editorial
glossing, but neither of these possibilities gives an adequate understanding of the text as it now stands.[16] We maintain that, despite the brothers'
careful reconstruction of events in 42:29–34, whatever success they
achieved in persuading their father was undercut drastically by the discovery of the money in the sacks in 42:35. Jacob's immediate reference to

Joseph's absence in 42:36 and his use of the same word for Simeon's fate suggest a comparison with the report the brothers made to Jacob in Gen. 37:32. In that instance Jacob accepted their version of the events so completely that the narrator has Jacob spontaneously conclude "ṭārōp ṭōrap yôsēp" (Joseph is surely ripped to pieces) in 37:33, using the very words the brothers planned to use to explain Joseph's disappearance in 37:20 but never spoke aloud.[17] In chapter 42, the discovery of the money causes Jacob to doubt the veracity of their present account and even to suspect foul play toward Simeon on their part.[18] The interplay of ironies is remarkably dense, as Jacob, ignorant of the true circumstances of Joseph's disappearance, suspects the brothers of perpetrating an identical crime upon Simeon and fears a similar fate for Benjamin. As in Egypt, the brothers find themselves accused of far more than they expected (how could he have found out about Joseph?) and are thrown off balance once again by "the man" in control. Reuben's offer in 42:37 is the final betrayal; at a time when his father is concerned with the continuation of the line and the survival of the next generation, Reuben's offer to kill his own sons only excites Jacob's worst fears about the future.[19] Whatever chance might have remained for negotiation is quashed by Jacob's final statement in v. 38: "lō'-yērēd běnî 'immākem"—"*My* son will not go down with you."

Genesis 24 shares some aspects of theme and language with both Genesis 42 and Genesis 50. Once again quoted direct speech is used by a protagonist seeking to persuade the head of a family (or the figure in power) to allow one of its members to go off to a foreign land. As in Gen. 47:29–31, the agent is sworn to loyalty with a form of the root *Š-B-ʿ*, and the phrase "śîm-nā' yādĕkā taḥat yĕrēkî" (Place your hand under my thigh—24:2). In both cases the request includes an explicit negative injunction about remaining on alien soil; the command to prevent Isaac from going to Haran is even repeated twice by Abraham in 24:6, 8. In the retelling of the event, both Joseph and the servant summarize the oath-taking with similar phrases:

24:37: "wayyašbiʿēnî 'ădōnî lēʾmōr" (My master adjured me).
50:5: "'ābî hišbîʿānî lēʾmōr" (My father adjured me).

Both speakers are also tactful enough to omit the negative judgments about their host countries. As in Gen. 42, the future of the family's prosperity is at stake, and the only tool the agent has at his disposal is his ability to construct a convincing argument from words already spoken, promises already made. All three narratives present crises in the continuation of the line: The future of the covenant depends upon Isaac's having the proper wife through whom the blessing will be passed on. Jacob must release Benjamin to the brothers in order to survive the famine, as well as to recover Joseph and restore the unity of the family. Joseph, for his part, must bury his father in Canaan to foreshadow the future return of Israel to the land.

Genesis 24 is unique in the amount of quoted direct speech it contains. There are ten separate speech-acts in vv. 2–27, all of which are repeated by the servant in one long monologue (vv. 34–39). In only one other case does a character establish himself so centrally as narrator by the use of quoted direct speech (Judah in 44:19–34). This controlling voice is all the more remarkable in light of the servant's anonymity and his relative passivity; he narrates at such length not to bring out *his* role in shaping events, but to demonstrate that ineluctable divine providence which has pointed everything toward Rebecca as the chosen woman. These two paradoxical factors—the servant's narrative authority and the centrality of divine providential authority—constitute the axis upon which the story rotates. As in most biblical narratives, providential expectations are realized only by human initiative within a realm where there are always choices to be made.

There is little doubt but that the servant believes the series of events to be divinely guided—at the well he himself heard Rebecca repeat aloud and act according to what he had silently prescribed in v. 14. Nor should we doubt the sincerity of his thanks to God in vv. 26–27. But it is a much more difficult thing to convince those who stand outside the servant's consciousness of the inevitability of what transpired there. As narrator of the retelling, the servant controls the story, yet he must tell a story that emphasizes his own *lack* of power and God's controlling hand.[20] While critics have pointed out the absence of any "heroic activity," of the sort found in other well and betrothal stories,[21] no one has viewed this lack in light of the important active/passive dichotomy we are describing. In Gen. 29:1–20 and Ex. 2:15–21, Jacob and Moses respectively are physically active in impressing their future wives, because the woman's love is at stake, and because both intend to live with the wife's family. But in Genesis 24 such activity would be inappropriate, for the servant is not really a suitor, and it is not the girl who must be impressed; only her family will decide whether or not she will go off with the servant.

The servant accomplishes his task by means of a variety of subtle changes introduced into his retelling of the story in vv. 34–49,[22] and it will be helpful to view these differences as reflexes of the active/passive axis. On one hand, the servant omits or de-emphasizes those elements which might detract from the providential model. It is not simply tact that leads the servant to omit Abraham's negative judgments about bringing Isaac back "there" (vv. 6, 8); the servant must present an argument in which human choice (especially Abraham's) is minimized, though not altogether removed. But even as he emphasizes the unmistakable divine stamp upon the choice of Rebecca, he places final responsibility upon the family: "wĕ'im lō' yittĕnû lāk" (And if *they* will not give her to you . . .—v. 41). This phrase is framed by a double mention of the oath to which the servant is bound, perhaps to impress upon Laban the gravity of his responsibility. The servant flatters the family by changing Abraham's instructions to go to his *môledet* (birthplace)—a physical location; instead, he uses the words *bēt 'āb* (father's house) and *mišpāḥâ* (family), emphasizing familial and tribal connections.[23] In the servant's version Rebecca is given gifts immediately after she says she is from the family of Nahor,[24] though the actual course of events implies that a woman from any family could have met the requirements set forth by Abraham. If there were any other girls around the well, the servant makes no mention of them in the retelling.[25]

Modifications in the servant's description of God serve a similar purpose. YHWH is no longer " 'ĕlōhê haššāmayîm" or " 'ĕlōhê hā'āreṣ" (vv. 3, 7), but " 'ĕlōhê 'ădōnî 'abrāhām," "the God of my master Abraham" (vv. 12, 27, 42, 48). Omitted are all references to Abraham's special relation to YHWH as the one who took him out of his father's house and promised him land and progeny. Such items might insult Laban, who does not wish to leave his land; more important, they smack of possible "arrangements" made between God and Abraham to take away another family member. This would ascribe to Abraham too much control, and too little to Laban; YHWH works behind the scenes, the servant intimates, in ways *equally* unknown to both parties. Also omitted are any of the servant's earlier references to the *ḥesed* relationship between Abraham and God (vv. 12, 14, 27), which also might strike a conspiratorial chord in Laban's mind. In place of these the servant uses the vague formula "YHWH 'ăšer-hithallaktî lĕpānāyw" (The Lord, before whom I walk, v. 40), which describes only Abraham's behavior toward YHWH, and not the converse. In v. 48 however, the servant stops quoting, choosing to narrate in free indirect speech the prayer he spoke aloud in v. 27. While it is important for the servant to indicate his own amazement at what has just transpired, he does not need to overemphasize his piety by quoting his actual words. At this point the servant changes the description of YHWH from the God "who led me to the house of my master's kinsman" to "who led me on the right way *to take my master's kinsman's daughter for his son.*" As the events at the well led directly to Laban's door, so the retelling of those events leads inescapably to the servant's conclusion. The change from quoted direct speech to narration allows the relative clause that describes God's activity in the past (*'ăšer hinḥanî . . .*) to lead directly into the present situation, the "request" portion of the speech introduced by *wĕ'attâ* in v. 49. In place of his earlier description of God who maintained his *ḥesed* with Abraham, the servant now defines

YHWH as the one who touches the life of Laban's family as well. In v. 49 he proposes a new relationship of *ḥesed weʾĕmet* between Abraham and Laban. The servant began his speech in v. 35 with a fairly detailed description of the wealth with which God had blessed his master. When he suggests to Laban in v. 49 that he "deal" with Abraham because of the power of his God, he does so after having shown Laban physical proof of the rewards that have come from that relationship. If anything is surprising in this chapter, it is the speed with which Laban agrees unconditionally to the marriage; this, we suggest, is a tribute to the success of the servant's rhetorical strategy.

A related aspect of the servant's argument can be seen in the order in which he describes the gift-giving incident at the well. In 24:22 the servant gives Rebecca jewelry before he asks her name, while in the retelling in v. 47 the gifts are proffered only after she reveals her identity. In the initial event, the servant may have been thrown off balance by the coincidence of events, or was trying to ingratiate himself to the girl, or was simply offering payment for services rendered.[26] In the repetition, however, a clearer strategy emerges. The reversal of the order clearly serves to flatter Laban by saying, in effect, that her mention of the family name occasioned the gift-giving. But in a deeper sense it also sets up the expectation of reward for the person who will again give the correct answer. Laban's material interests have been aroused by what the servant has brought with him, by his earlier description of Abraham's wealth, and by the presents to Rebecca mentioned again in v. 47. The servant subtly induces Laban to agree to the marriage (the "correct answer") *in order* to get the rewards—the gifts he gives to Laban in v. 53. From this perspective it might be expected that the servant would give Laban his present as soon as he consented in v. 51. But in keeping with the servant's emphasis on divine control, Laban himself is never thanked, nor does he receive his "rewards" immediately, for that would undercut the larger thrust of the servant's argument by reducing this agreement to the status of a business transaction. Instead, the servant's praise of God in v. 52 serves as a sign of approval to Laban, to reinforce the idea that he will receive his gifts for his recognition of the power of divine providence, rather than in exchange for the girl herself. We should note that the servant does not eat or drink until he has gotten the desired response, structurally recapitulating his behavior at the well. Earlier, in spite of what was likely a deep thirst after a long trip, he waited for the woman who would give the right answer to his question before he drank. By refusing Laban's food in 24:33, he has avoided being in his debt in any way and has subtly increased his pressure on Laban to respond affirmatively. As a result, the eating and drinking in 24:54 confirm to Laban the correctness of his decision and serve as an appropriate conclusion to this part of the story.

Quotations of Thoughts

Biblical narrative contains a number of examples in which a character gives voice to his unspoken thoughts from an earlier point in time. Most often these "quotations" take the form of unverifiable direct speech; only rarely does the narrator present both the earlier thought and its quoted repetition. In general, biblical narrative style does not dwell on interior states or psychological evaluation, preferring to let the reader draw conclusions on the basis of a character's external speech and actions. Internal description is usually conveyed in summarial fashion ("he knew," "they feared," "he loved," etc.) or by the narrator's use of free indirect speech and description, as in Gen. 29:25, 37:4, or 2 Sam. 13:15. When these thoughts are reported more articulately, the narrator often combines them with his own observations about the speaker's motives or the consequences of his thoughts, as in 1 Sam. 18:20–21.[27] Rarer still are thoughts of characters presented as actual speeches thought aloud, along the lines of soliloquy or interior monologue.[28]

As infrequently and as briefly as the narrator grants these inside views to the reader, his characters are far more reticent about recalling out loud their earlier thoughts, perhaps because such "evidence" is so utterly subjective. The strategic function of such quotations is to explain the point of view of the speaker at an earlier time in an attempt to make his audience sympathize with his feelings both then and at the present moment. In Gen. 20:11 Abraham tries to excuse his behavior by appealing to his earlier fears for Sarah's safety, but the narrator has made no attempt to support Abraham's claim to these thoughts. In a parallel story in Gen. 26 Isaac's actual thoughts are given in v. 7: "pen-yahargūnî ʾanšē hammāqôm ʿal ribqā kî-ṭôbat marʾeh hîʾ" (Lest the local people kill me on Rebecca's account, for she is beautiful); his quotation of these thoughts is also presented in v. 9: "kî ʾāmartî pen-ʾāmût ʿālêhā" (For I said: "Lest I die on her account"). Such an attempt at self-justification seems dubious to Abimelech simply on the basis of its content. Perhaps more important, a character can claim to have thought anything at all, and no other character can possibly refute him. As such, the value of such thoughts as proof of anything is intrinsically limited. It must further be remembered that this is not a comparison between two verbalized speeches. The depiction of thought as direct speech is more a convention of style than a verisimilar representation of the way thoughts really exist in the mind. While a character might be expected to give a reasonably faithful reproduction of words he spoke earlier in the story, fidelity to what one actually thought is nearly impossible to attain, at least in biblical narrative style.[29] As a result the reader cannot use these recalled thoughts to draw the same kinds of inferences about the speaker as he can from public speech-acts (though he can still draw some conclusions). Such evidentiary ambiguity severely limits the function of internal quotations and may account for the scarcity of verifiable quoted direct speech thoughts.

The other example of this category manifests a more complex version of the movement from thought to speech. In Gen. 24:14 the servant "speaks" silently to God his own future words to the girl as well as the response necessary to pass his test. In 24:17–19 a version of these words is spoken aloud for the first time by both characters. When the servant retells his story, he repeats his thoughts (vv. 43–44) and the actual events (vv. 45–46). In accordance with what we noted above, the narrator apparently has no qualms about using different words for the thought and speech of the same person, reflecting the basic difference between the two modes of expression. The servant "thinks," "haṭṭî-nā' kaddēk" (incline your jug) in v. 14 but actually says, "hagmî'înî nā'" (let me drink) in v. 17. Once spoken aloud, the remaining repetitions have greater similarity to one another:

> 24:17 "hagmî'înî nā' mĕ'aṭ-mayîm mikkaddēk"
> 24:43 "hašqînî-nā' mĕ'aṭ-mayîm mikkaddēk"
> 24:45 "hašqînî-nā'"

The particularly close identity between vv. 43 and 45 adds to the servant's overall strategy, showing that events occur (and words are spoken) precisely as they were anticipated. Rebecca's words, both anticipated and spoken, are alike throughout:

> 24:14   "šĕtēh wĕgam-gĕmallêkā 'ašqeh"
> 24:18–19 "šĕtēh ... gam ligmallêkā 'eš'āb"
> 24:44   "šĕtēh wĕgam ligmallêkā 'eš'āb"
> 24:46   "šĕtēh wĕgam-gemallêkā 'ašqeh"

The close correspondence between thought and word is to be expected here, since it is precisely by her repetition of the servant's words that the girl reveals the providential aspect of the story. There is also a difference in the servant's state of mind in the two halves of the story. In the first section, the narrator conveys some of the suspense felt by the servant. In v. 18 the girl speaks the appropriate phrase about giving him water ("šĕtēh"), but she finishes with the servant before returning to complete the test by saying that she will also attend to his camels (v. 19—"gam ligmallêkā 'eš'āb"). In the retelling, such suspense would be superfluous; rather, confirmation of a choice already made is necessary in order for the servant's strategy to succeed. In v. 45 the servant abbreviates the request outlined in v. 43 and presents the girl's answer immediately afterward, omitting any reference to his own astonishment (v. 21), which might detract from his credibility before Rebecca's family.

It is unfortunate that there are so few cases of quoted direct speech in which a character presents, in essence, his thoughts about his thoughts, but self-consciousness is hardly a major facet of biblical characterization. Still, much of the fascination of biblical characters lies in the relative impenetrability of their personae in conjunction with activities, events, and a style of narration that invites, if not demands, interpretation of their motives.[30]

At this point it will be useful to pause and reflect upon what we have seen about quotations of new information. While the dynamics of each text are different, all quoting characters make use of a number of narrative techniques traditionally ascribed to the narrator. First, the speaker can use quoted direct speech to present a revised version of the original words and events, frequently displaying changes in the organization of the plot. This practice can be seen in the tale told by Abraham's servant in Gen. 24:34–49, or in Rebecca's quotation of Isaac's words in Gen. 27:7, though the purpose of the reorganization is different in each case. Second, the speaker may use quotation to characterize one or more of his subjects, as in Jephthah's depiction of Israel in Jud. 11:17, 19, or Jacob's sons' recapitulation of their meeting with Joseph in Gen. 42:29–34. Most frequently, the quotation of a third party (XYZ) marks a shift in point of view, as in the ironic quotation of David's victory song in 1 Sam. 21:12, or in Joseph's presentation before Pharaoh of Jacob's request to be buried in Canaan (Gen. 50:5). It is also interesting to note that, in cases where new information is contained in the quotation, the speaker tends to approximate closely the language of the original discourse. This is not to say that in so doing he assigns no illocutionary function to his words. But the relative "honesty" of the quoter, that is, the degree to which similar language implies a similar message, is an issue that merits further scrutiny.

2. "Old" Information

In this section the discussion will proceed along the same lines, but in the following cases the listener already knows the content of the quotation addressed to him. We will pursue the question of the speaker's motives as reflected in the tone of quotation, moving from the informational and pseudo-informational to the deceptive, and finally to texts of confrontation. Within each category texts will be classified along a temporal axis, from longer to shorter distances in narrative and narrated time between the original discourse and its reappearance in quotation.

Repetition as Reminder

It is not entirely precise to carry over the term "informational" from the previous section, as the ideas or facts expressed in quoted direct speech were previously made known to the hearer in all the texts to be discussed here. But there is a significant gap between active and passive knowledge; in more than a few cases repetition serves primarily to *remind* the hearer (and the reader) of what he or she may have been told but may not remember, whether because of time or circumstance. In some cases of quoted direct speech the speaker has no rhetorical tricks up his sleeve in quoting but is simply "retrieving" information for his audience, as in the earlier section on neutral tone. This is particularly true for texts in which a long period of narrated time has elapsed between the speech and the narrative present. In Josh. 1:13 Joshua quotes to the tribes of Gad and Reuben the promise made to them by Moses in Deut. 3:18–20, in order to gain their cooperation for the impending entry into the land.[31] Similarly, Caleb in Josh. 14:9 "reminds" Joshua of the promise Moses made in Deut. 1:36—at least one generation earlier—in order to claim the area of Hebron as his inheritance.[32] In both cases the speaker encounters no resistance from his listener, only immediate accession to his demands. This is typical of the promise-fulfillment style of the Deuteronomic History in relation to the Book of Deuteronomy.[33]

In other instances, the "reminder" is directed at God—not at any hypothetical forgetfulness on his part, but specifically in response to divine wrath, and in this context the quotation does function strategically for the speaker. In his attempt to assuage God's anger after the people's negative response to the report of the spies, Moses, in Num. 14:18, quotes God's own description of his merciful nature stated in Ex. 34:6–7. The quote in Num. 14:18 omits a number of words and phrases present in the original discourse, all of which are essentially synonymous amplifications whose absence does little to change the meaning of the passage.[34] In its original literary context the description was spoken by God as part of a statement of forgiveness toward Israel, and in Num. 14:18 Moses tries to recapture some of that merciful quality in calling God "by name," and by recalling the moment of re-covenanting in Exodus 34. Moses appeals to a level of relationship between God and man that transcends momentary anger, recalling the promise made in the past (14:16) and looking toward its fulfillment in the future (14:19). In order to insure that future, Moses utilizes a rhetorical pattern similar to that of Ex. 32:11–14. In both texts his argument revolves around the quotation of a promise made by God at an earlier point (in Ex. 32:13 the reference is to the promise to the patriarchs). This quote is set up by appealing to God's "egotism"—his concern for his reputation outside Israel. In Ex.

32:12 Moses depicted Egypt saying terrible things about God's intentions; in Num. 14:17 he attributes to the surrounding nations a similar hypothetical speech that impugns God's power to deliver his people and implies that he killed them off in the desert to hide the evidence of his own failure.[35] Further, in both cases the reference to the promise is a response to God's proposal (Ex. 32:10, Num. 14:12) to "substitute Moses for Abraham" by explicitly restating the promise made in Gen. 12:2.[36] Yet in each instance, Moses' strategy is slightly different; whereas in Exodus 32, he tries to evoke God's sense of responsibility for his people, in Numbers 14 he appeals to God's nature—patience, fairness, mercy. Despite the similarities between the chapters, Moses' argument is much less effective in Numbers 14. He succeeds in averting an immediate disaster, but the promise is given an ironically literal twist for the desert generation; now it is *only* their descendents who will enter the land.

Ex. 32:13 raises other questions because it does not refer back to a lone speech-act spoken at one specific moment in the past, but rather quotes some elements of the tradition of the promise to the patriarchs. From a literary standpoint, God did not speak those words to each of the patriarchs in the same sense that he spoke, in Ex. 34:6–7, the quote repeated in Num. 14:18. Each of the constituent elements of this formulation have their counterparts in more than one patriarchal promise. "Your seed shall be as the stars of heaven" is found in Gen. 15:15, 22:17, and 26:4. This simile of countlessness cannot be divorced from other kindred phrases such as "the sand of the sea" (Gen. 22:17; 32:12) and "the dust of the earth" (Gen. 13:16; 28:14). Indeed, almost too numerous to mention are the many occasions on which God promises the land to the patriarchs' descendents.[37] An attempt to recover a single textual source for the quotation in Ex. 32:13 misses the literary importance of the presence of the tradition. The very multiplicity of sources, the similar but nonidentical formulations, and the collective object of the promise, "Abraham, Isaac, and Jacob" stress the ongoing nature of the pledge, its ability to bridge generations and transcend individual relationships. Since the speaker of the promise is God, the reliability of the source is never in doubt; only the time of its fulfillment is left unspecified. Because the promise is such a basic datum of the Pentateuchal narrative, and because it can be formulated authoritatively in so many different ways, its appearances in quoted direct speech tell the reader less about the quoter than about the original speaker and his original intentions. In this sense quotations of the promise are most often equivalent to restatements of its essential claim, even when the speaker is human (Gen. 24:7, 32:10, 48:34; Num. 10:29). The frequent use and reuse of promise expressions in the Pentateuch undercut the temporal/ spatial juxtaposition that is central to quoted direct speech. The quotation loses much of the uniqueness of being set in a new context because the promise itself is made (and remade) in so many different contexts. In this case more than in any other, quotation approaches simple repetition, but its "divine" status saves it from becoming repetitious.[38]

At the same time, the diverse ways of expressing what is essentially the same blessing reflect upon the special status of YHWH as a speaker in the narrative. Divine speech has its own, self-referential standards of verifiability because of the peculiar nature of the bond between the narrator and the figure of God. Statements originating from God are as authoritative as those made by the narrator himself, even though in a literary sense, the narrator "controls" God.[39]

Thus far we have seen quoted direct speech used to emphasize either the fulfillment of a past idea in the present (e.g., Josh. 1:13), or the reaffirmation of an earlier promise. A third function of quotations from outside the pericope is a comparative one. The temporal and spatial distance between the original discourse and the quotation allows the speaker to draw an analogy between the situation of the original speech and the present circumstances that the quoter now addresses. The purpose of such analogies is to aid the speaker in promoting a point of view that goes beyond the immediate situation and examines the issue from a larger historical or historiographic perspective. In Num. 32:10–15, faced with the potential defection of the tribes of Reuben and Gad prior to the conquest, Moses "reminds" them that the sentence passed upon the desert generation was the direct result of a similar effort to dishearten the people in Num. 13–14. In 32:12 he contrasts their fate with the rewards that Joshua and Caleb will reap as a result of their obedience and faithfulness. The quotation is drawn from a combination of the two speeches in Num. 14:21–24 and 14:28–35, and its exemplary function is spelled out in 32:20–24.

Another type of analogy between past and present is seen in the warning against disobedience spoken by Samuel in 1 Sam. 12:12, quoting the people's demands for a king in 8:5, 19–20. Samuel places his condemnation of their request in the context of their historical involvement with sin against YHWH. Until now, the people cried out to God for deliverance (vv. 8, 10—*wayyiz'āqû*) and God responded by sending the appropriate leadership in the form of a judge (12:8, 11—*wayyišlaḥ YHWH*). Despite their sins of idolatry, these previous generations are adjudged to be more worthy; at least they confessed contritely and accepted whatever help God sent, as Samuel brings out with a quotation from Jud. 10:10, 15. When Samuel quotes the people of his own generation in 1 Sam. 12:12, their behavior is set off against the background of the distant past as well as the more recent events of chapter 8. Not only do these people not confess their guilt, but they are so willful as to ask a member of that same chain of judges for a change in the type of leadership as well. As the people chose (*ʾăšer bĕḥartem*) foreign gods in Jud. 10:14, Samuel now condemns them for "the king whom you have chosen" (*ʾăšer bĕḥartem*— 12:13), an equal if not greater crime in his eyes. This interpretation of the people's request by Samuel ignores the entire problem of the failure of Samuel's own sons, which was the occasion for the request in 8:1ff. But as in other places in 1 Samuel, it is difficult to distinguish Samuel's resentment of his personal loss of status from the theological challenge implicit in the people's demand.[40]

The last two examples in this category involve David, once as speaker, and once as the object of speech. In 2 Sam. 4:10, he quotes the words of the messenger who brought the news of Saul's death in 2 Sam. 1:4ff. David is addressing Ba'anah and Rechab, two Benjaminites who have brought him the head of Saul's son Ishboshet, with the expectation of some reward from the now unchallenged king. David cites his reaction to the earlier *mĕbaśśēr* as relevant to the present situation, adding to his image as a king who reacts violently to "bad" news.[41] His execution of Ba'anah and Rechab completes the analogy to 2 Samuel 1. David praises Ishboshet but takes care not to raise the now-dead heir to a status equivalent to his father Saul.[42] Whatever David's true feelings may be, his words are directed at two audiences: the accused murderers themselves and the people loyal to Saul's family, who would naturally suspect David of having engineered the deed himself. D. M. Gunn describes the true ambiguity of the situation:

> On the one hand there is something appealing in his (David's) refusal to countenance the violence done to his rival; we are reminded of David's relationship with Saul in I Sam. 24 and 26 (cf. also II Sam. 1). This focuses our attention on the remarkable fact that David, despite his obvious position of power, has made absolutely no attempt to seize by force the throne of Israel. . . . On the other hand, David's role is not entirely passive. It remains the case that the gift of the head is extraordinarily convenient. . . . David is far from being averse to the thought of gaining the kingdom. Indeed, there is more than a hint of a public relations exercise in his dramatic despatch of the bringers of the gift. . . .[43]

David is again placed in an awkward situation in 1 Sam. 29:5, as the Philistine officers repeat to Achish king of Gath the song first heard in 1 Sam. 18:7: "Saul has slain his thousands/David his tens of thousands." Earlier, in 21:12, Achish's own servants had quoted the same refrain to warn him of the potential danger of David. In a similar way the Philistine chiefs use the song to persuade Achish not to allow David to fight at Mt. Gilboa. Each time this song appears it clashes with its context in an ironic fashion. In 18:8–9 Saul "interprets" the song in a jealous manner, which leads to his attempt on David's life. In 21:12 the warrior praised in the song must degrade himself by acting deranged in order to escape the Philistines, even though he holds Goliath's sword. In 29:5 his very success in battle becomes an argument against his going to war. Even though David earned his reputation (and his song) fighting the Philistines, Achish wholeheartedly believes that David is loyal to him and not to Saul. Perhaps we are meant to understand this situation as similar to 27:1–12, where Achish is completely taken in by David's ploy, but the text leaves the truth of the matter embarrassingly unclear.[44]

There are relatively few instances of quoted direct speech of old information used for pseudo-informational purposes within the individual narrative pericope. When the distance in narrated and narrative time between statement and quotation is decreased, the notion of "reminding" invoked above does not seem to apply in the same way. Here the mimetic aspect of quoted direct speech respects the psychological reality of human emotions, and reminding is used primarily to restore perspective to an angry or shocked individual. This is not unlike Moses' efforts in Ex. 32:13 and Num. 14:18, but in these cases the injured party is human, and very little time passes between the original speech and the quotation. In 2 Kg. 5:11–12, Naaman expresses outrage at the lack of hocus-pocus in Elisha's instructions to bathe in the Jordan River to cure his leprosy. In v. 13 his servants mollify him by emphasizing the minimal effort required to try Elisha's suggestion—so minimal that Elisha's message is reduced from nine words in the original (v. 10) to two in the quotation. In 2 Sam. 13:32, Jonadab ben Shimeah tries to calm a grieving David by telling him that only Amnon, not all his sons, was killed by Absalom. Jonadab does this by first quoting the false message—"All the king's sons are dead"—in order to refute it with the truth: "Only Amnon is dead."[45]

Since the speaker is presenting old information to his listener, it might be anticipated that quoted direct speech would function more as stylistic variation than as rhetorical strategy. 1 Kg. 12:1–17, for example, contains a great deal of repetition in all types of direct speech. Rehoboam asks the same questions of both sets of his advisors in vv. 6 and 9; the people's complaint of v. 4 is quoted twice in vv. 9 and 10. Rehoboam's postponement in v. 5 is quoted by the narrator in v. 12, and the advice of the *yĕlādîm* (younger advisors) in v. 11 is repeated (verbatim!) by Rehoboam in v. 14. But even here, in a text where summary seems unknown, context still determines the potential significance of variations in quoted direct speech, and these quotations do have strategic importance on the story level.

The complaint of the people from the North, delivered to Rehoboam in Shechem on the occasion of his coronation (12:4), is quoted twice in 12:9–10. The initial request has two parts: a historical prologue, which locates the source of the problem with Solomon—v. 4a, "'ābîkā hiqšâ 'et-ʿullēnû" (Your father made our yoke heavy)—followed by a request of the new king to ease the heavy load of taxation and corvée labor. The story involves two groups of advisors, the *zĕqēnîm* (older advisors), who counsel temporary appeasement (v. 7), and the *yĕlādîm*, who champion a hard-line position (vv. 10–11). When Rehoboam quotes the people's words to the *yĕlādîm* in v. 9, he omits the historical prologue and begins with an abbreviated version of the request section. But when the *yĕlādîm* respond in v. 10, they preface their answer by quoting the *first* part of the people's statement virtually word for word.[46] While an attractive chiasm is thus formed between vv. 4, 9, and 10, there is something more than artful design here, which sheds light upon Rehoboam's unfortunate decision to follow his younger advisors.

The narrator offers a theological explanation of Rehoboam's folly in 12:15: the split of the kingdom was divinely ordained as a punishment for Solomon's sins. But subtler human influences upon the young king can also be discerned. Rehoboam was forty-one years of age at his coronation (14:21) and was certainly aware of the oppressive nature of his father's economic policies. He was also under pressure to grant some sort of relief, or release, concomitant with his ascent to the throne.[47]

The question Rehoboam puts to the younger advisors in 12:9 is oriented toward the present moment of crisis, as reflected in his beginning the quotation with the request portion—"lighten our yoke"—and his omission of the historical introduction. But the reaffirmation of a strong central authority at the beginning of the new reign is foremost in the minds of the *yĕlādîm*, whether for personal ambition or for lack of experience in diplomacy.[48] To help persuade Rehoboam, they play upon the new king's insecurity, and the son's desire to surpass the father—"Say to this people: 'My little finger is thicker than my father's loins'" (v. 10). What Solomon did to oppress the North was minimal compared with what Rehoboam has in mind—or, rather, what the *yĕlādîm* have in mind. The suggestion of generational friction is supported by the elder advisors' connection with Solomon (v. 6) and, conversely, the peer relationship between Rehoboam and the *yĕlādîm* (v. 8). Quite intentionally, therefore, the *yĕlādîm* quote the first part of the people's statement— "*Your father* made our yoke heavy"—playing down the people's request and setting the stage for their harsh advice. Whereas the people implied in 12:4 that Rehoboam could be better than his father by lightening their burden, the *yĕlādîm* use their words in quoted direct speech to criticize the son vis-à-vis Solomon. The *zĕqēnîm* were aware of the moderate nature of the people's request, and their advice in v. 7 is based on the people's continued promise to serve the king.[49] But both Rehoboam and the *yĕlādîm* omit any reference to the people's loyalty in their quotations, emphasizing instead the challenge to royal authority as the central issue. Whatever the possibilities may have been for keeping the kingdom together, the new advisors do their best to escalate the challenge from threat to action.[50]

The long speech that Judah delivers to Joseph in Gen. 44:19–34 deserves special consideration for a number of reasons. In terms of overall length and quantity of quotations (sixteen verses, nine quotations), it resembles the speech of Abraham's servant in Gen. 24:34–49. Unlike that speech however, this one is addressed directly to Joseph, with Judah quoting Joseph's *own* words back to him in 44:19, 21, and 23, interspersed with the brothers' responses. It is one thing to recall or to remind the listener of a few details, but the quotation of a lengthy dialogue whose content is already known to the listener is unprecedented. In addition, Judah reveals new information to Joseph in 44:25–33, placing this text in a category of its own, "mixed old and new information." But this information about Jacob and Benjamin is not as fresh to Joseph's ears as Judah supposes, for Joseph is in the curious position of knowing more than the speaker thinks he knows. The element of deception involved in Joseph's interaction with his brothers is nowhere more powerful than in the respective perceptions of the words Judah attributes to Jacob in 44:27–29, as we will see below. While Judah is not conscious of this difference, Joseph's awareness of it creates another level of meaning for the quotation on the story level.

Further complications arise from the fact that Judah's speech recapitulates actions and words from the previous two chapters, and some of this dialogue is quoted here for the second or third time. Joseph's demand to bring Benjamin to Egypt (44:21, 23) was first spoken in 42:20, then quoted by the brothers speaking to Jacob in 42:33. The information about Jacob's and Benjamin's existence (44:20) was first disclosed to Joseph by the brothers in 42:13, quoted to Jacob in 42:32, and again to Joseph in 44:20. The phenomenon of multiple occurrences of a quotation is not unique to this text, but some of the language used by Judah differs substantially from that of the original discourse as well as that of the earlier quotation. Jacob is an "aging father" and Benjamin the "child of his old age" in 44:20, while in 42:11, 14 Jacob is simply "one man" and Benjamin is "the youngest." In 44:19 Judah begins his speech with the statement: "My lord asked his servants, saying, 'Have you a father or a brother,'" which he also quotes in 43:7, but no such question is actually present in the speeches of chapter 42. Similar problems emerge from the brothers' reactions as quoted in 44:22, and from Joseph's response in 44:23. The latter is also quoted twice (43:3, 5) but can only be inferred from 42:18ff.; the former must be classified as an unverifiable quotation. Further, there is noticeable variation in the degree of fidelity to the original speech in adjacent quotations. While 44:25 quotes 43:2 verbatim, the brothers' response in 43:3–5 is quoted by Judah in substantially paraphrased form (44:26). Even though the speech Judah attributes to Jacob in 44:27–29 may have its roots in Jacob's comments in 42:36, 38, the quotation is at least partially unverifiable, leaving open the possibility that Judah may have created these words from his own imagination.[51]

One approach to the problem has been to ascribe the differences between Judah's speech and the events of chapter 42 either to a mixture of parallel J and E sources or to "Reuben" and "Judah" editions.[52] But such "solutions" do not really help our understanding of the text as it was redacted and which, at some point in its history, was considered a unified story. Recent arguments for the unity of the Joseph story have demonstrated the continuity of theme, plot, language, and character very convincingly, and it is from this presupposition that we will proceed.[53] We will let Judah bear full responsibility for the words he speaks and, given the importance of this speech, attempt to understand significant changes from his source material in terms of Judah's overriding strategy—to persuade Joseph to release Benjamin.

Like Abraham's servant in Gen. 24, Judah embodies the paradoxical situation of an ostensibly authoritative, controlling narrator who is powerless to act on his own behalf. He is granted authority insofar as he is allowed by Joseph and by the narrator to reshape the whole story, to change actions and dialogue, even to the point of placing words in Joseph's mouth that he never said, without Joseph crying fraud.[54] At the same time, this narrative control of the past contrasts starkly with his inability to do anything *but* speak. As if to heighten this inferior status, Judah calls Joseph *'ādôn* (lord) seven times, likens him to Pharaoh, and refers to himself, his brothers, and even Jacob as Joseph's servants no less than thirteen times. In Gen. 24 the servant brought out his own powerlessness in order to emphasize divine providence; here Judah uses subservience to argue *for* his own servitude—his final plea in 44:33 is to allow Judah to *serve* Joseph in Benjamin's stead.

The argument of Judah's speech is twofold: to demonstrate how and why he has come to be responsible for Benjamin, and through that to arouse *Joseph's* sense of responsibility for Jacob as well. In the service of this argument Judah omits the accusation of spying (42:9, 30) and the subsequent imprisonment of Simeon (42:19, 33), opening instead with a direct focus upon father and son. His quote in v. 20 shows the brothers stressing the close bond between the two, concerned about danger to their "old father" and the only remaining child of his old age. The verse is inspired more by Jacob's remarks in 42:38 than by the brothers' original language in 42:11, 13. We demonstrated above how the brothers in

42:29–34 restructured their encounter with Joseph to portray themselves before Jacob in a more favorable light. In 44:20–23 Judah continues in this vein, contrasting the responsible, loving family with the heartless and uncaring Joseph. Despite Joseph's full awareness of the bond between Jacob and Benjamin, and in spite of a justified protest by the brothers in 44:22, Joseph still demands Benjamin's presence in Egypt in v. 23, for no reason other than his own personal satisfaction.[55] Judah's omission of the spy story also supports this dimension of his argument by removing the reason behind Joseph's original demand in 42:18–20 and suggesting in its place more capricious, or selfish motivations.[56]

In addition, Judah depicts a change from group responsibility (or the lack of it) in the past to one-for-one accountability in his contract to act as pledge for Benjamin's return. Jacob has entrusted Benjamin, his "only son," to Judah, and only Judah can act on his behalf. Judah quotes Jacob saying that they (the brothers) "will bring down my hoary head in grief to Sheol" (v. 29), but Judah then declares in his own voice that he alone is liable. In quoting the actual pledge agreement, Judah assures Joseph that his obligation is both legally and psychologically binding upon him. Given the subservient tone of the discourse we might expect Judah simply to beg for mercy before Joseph, requesting Benjamin's release on the basis of Jacob's emotional attachment to Benjamin and the potentially disastrous consequences. Instead, Judah requests that he be allowed to live up to the terms of the pledge, to serve Joseph in Benjamin's place; only then does he ask that Benjamin be allowed to leave with his brothers. His closing line stresses his own feelings, that his fear of seeing evil come upon his father is far worse than any servitude could ever be. Judah does not blame himself, for this would run counter to his argument. But contrary to his own prior irresponsibility, and to a tradition of buck-passing that extends back to Adam and Eve, Judah takes his charge seriously by putting his own life on the line for his brother and father.[57]

Concomitant with this display of familial concern is Judah's corollary, that Joseph must show a corresponding sensitivity to Jacob's situation. The extensive focus on the absent Jacob—'āb is used fourteen times in the speech—and the repeated mention of Jacob's dependence upon Benjamin are greatly out of proportion to the amount of recognition this theme receives in the actual events of the story. While Judah may not understand why Joseph is so interested in his father, he cannot have missed Joseph's concern for the well-being of their father in 43:27 or the blessing and fivefold portion he bestowed upon Benjamin in 43:29–34. Whether or not Joseph actually asked the question as formulated in 44:19 is less important than Judah's assumption that it is a reasonable question for Joseph to have asked, and his correct estimation of its influence upon Joseph. By beginning his speech with the quotation, "My lord asked his servants saying, 'Do you have a father or a brother?' " Judah has effectively cited Joseph's interest in Benjamin as the cause of the present crisis.[58] As the speech continues, Judah has his brothers describe their missing sibling as decidedly dead—*mēt* (44:20)—as opposed to the less precise *'ênennû* (not present, vanished) used in 42:13, 32, 36. While Judah does this simply to sharpen the focus upon Benjamin as the only surviving son of Rachel, his use of *'ênennû* with respect to Benjamin in 44:26, 30, 34 creates an unintentional irony, which is certainly not lost on Joseph.

When we examine Judah's speech from the angle of his attempt to convince Joseph of the latter's responsibility, the double-edged character of the quotations becomes apparent. As mentioned above, the brothers' objections in 44:22 not only demonstrate their familial loyalty but implicitly criticize Joseph's complete indifference to these concerns. By pointing out the effect of Benjamin's departure upon Jacob, twice through quotations (44:22, 27, 29) and twice more in his own words (44:31, 34), Judah reveals to Joseph the devastating implications of his selfish demands. The true beauty of Judah's remarks lies in his ability to affirm explicitly his own responsibility while effectively "blaming" Joseph for his father's anticipated death.[59] As Judah has become personally liable for Benjamin, so the obligation to prevent Jacob's death rests on Joseph's shoulders alone. Judah's use of deferential language such as *'ebed* and *'ādôn* also emphasizes the master's responsibility to his servants, extending to Jacob as well (44:24, 27, 30, 31). Yet in spite of his frequent use of these expressions, Judah does not grovel before Joseph; in the final lines of his speech he appeals to Joseph on the basis of legal responsibility (44:32–33) and, in v. 34, in terms of the nonservile, profoundly human caring for his father.[60]

Judah's version of events includes not only omissions but also a significant rearrangement of speeches, which adds rhetorical weight to his argument. While Judah leaves out Jacob's initial refusal to release Benjamin (42:38), he has drawn upon other details and formulations from 42:36, 38 in the speech he assigns to Jacob in 44:27–29. Most noteworthy are the theme of Joseph's disappearance, the fear of Benjamin being "taken" (*L-Q-Ḥ*) by the brothers, and the nearly identical use of the phrase: "ûqārā'hû 'āsôn . . . wĕhôradtem 'et-śêbātî bĕyāgôn šĕ'ôlâ (If disaster befalls him, you will bring down my gray head in sorrow to Sheol). In Judah's speech these words are no longer part of Jacob's refusal to part with Benjamin (42:38) but signify Jacob's pessimistic agreement to the brothers' demand (44:26). The relationship between Judah's guarantee and Jacob's accession to his promise is also restructured. In the original story, Judah's offer of personal security for Benjamin precedes such agreement, indeed makes it possible (43:8–10). But in Judah's speech this pledge is the final quotation, the last detail he recalls from the past. The reason for these changes is bound up with the movement of Judah's narrative from past (19–29) to present (30–34). As one brother died (44:20, *wĕ'āḥîw mēt*) and intensified Jacob's affection for the other, the disappearance of the second will lead to the father's death (44:31, *wāmēt*). Jacob's speech is relocated because Judah wishes to draw as close a connection as possible between Jacob's fears for Benjamin (v. 29) and the anticipated realization of those fears in v. 31: "wĕhôrîdû 'ăbādêkā 'et-śêbat 'abdĕkā 'ābînû bĕyāgôn šĕ'ōlâ" (Your servants will have brought down the gray hairs of your servant our father in sorrow to Sheol). The quotation of Judah's promise to his father appears here because the present-oriented context of this part of the speech (*wĕ'attâ*, vv. 30, 33) serves to reaffirm his commitment in an immediate sense. Not only did Judah make a promise to his father, but now he demonstrates that he intends to keep it. This shift in temporal orientation is so noticeable because, after the extensive amount of simple retelling Judah has done in vv. 19–29, the reader does not expect any more quotes after v. 30. Having established the emotional and familial climate, and having aroused Joseph's sympathy, Judah's mention of his pledge offers Joseph a respectable, even legal alternative to the grim scenario he has predicted.

It is not possible to determine whether Judah was trying to persuade Joseph to pardon Benjamin, or if he simply hoped that his request for substitution would be honored. But we can make some observations on how Joseph might have perceived certain statements in a manner not intended by Judah. Joseph's privileged knowledge vis-à-vis Judah points up an important dynamic in quoted direct speech, which we will term deceptive knowledge. In certain texts, the listener is in the exceptional position of knowing more than the speaker thinks he does, thereby being able to evaluate the speaker's words from a perspective completely unknown to the speaker. In this case Joseph's perspective is entirely congruent with the shape of Judah's argument, amplifying and reinforcing its illocutionary focus. First, the realization that he might be causing harm to Jacob must be devastating to Joseph, as if, while trying to prove something about power and responsibility to his brothers, he might bring about the death of his own father.[61] Next, he learns that on some level Jacob holds the brothers liable for his disappearance: "If you take this one from me as well . . ." (44:29)—a detail that must be somewhat satisfying. Further, he learns that Benjamin is now a *yeled zĕqunîm*, a favored child of Jacob's old age, as was Joseph (37:3), but his father still remembers him and considers him special (44:27–28). Judah also says a number of things that are not true, and that only Joseph knows to be false. He is not dead, nor was he torn by beasts (v. 28), nor is Benjamin the only remaining son of Rachel (v. 20). Judah's unwitting statement of the "facts" of his death aids in moving Joseph to reveal his true identity—partly to set the record straight, but mostly to correct the imbalance of emotion that threatens Jacob's life.

The success of Judah's strategy is reflected not only in the immediacy with which Joseph reveals his identity in 45:3, but also in the choice of language in which the disclosure is couched. Joseph's first question to his brothers (45:3) reveals his great anxiety about Jacob's life: " 'ănî yôsēp; ha'ôd 'ābî ḥāy" (I am Joseph. Is my father yet alive?). When the brothers need convincing, he asks them to approach him (N-G-Š, 45:4), as Judah did in 44:18, and explains the situation in "responsible" terms: The brothers were not truly to blame, for it was all part of a divine plan. The charge he gives to his brothers in 45:13 is a response to the fears expressed above by Judah: "wĕhôradtem 'et-'ābî hēnnâ," "You shall bring down my father hither," to Egypt, and not to Sheol, to live, not to die.[62]

But of greater importance is the fact that it is *Judah* who has pledged his life for Benjamin and who has delivered this speech. One must remember his central role in the events of chapter 37: "Twenty-two years earlier, Judah engineered the selling of Joseph into slavery; now he is prepared to offer himself as a slave so that the other son of Rachel can be set free."[63]

Deceptive Quotation

In certain situations a quotation may be repeated by a speaker who is unaware of the fact that his listener already knows some or all of the information contained in the quotation. We have just seen how prior knowledge affected Joseph's perception of Judah's words, and possibly his actions as well. In this particular case Joseph did not request that information, and his secret knowledge reinforced Judah's argument. This could be termed, therefore, a deception of silence on Joseph's part. In some texts, however, the listener actively requests "old" information from the unknowing speaker, initiating a more deliberate deception that the reader is invited to examine.

The quoted direct speech in Gen. 3:1, 3 is a paradigm of this category because its form and content are so closely related. At its core it is a story of the birth of awareness of superior knowledge, and of the deceptions that arise from such awareness. While the extent of the serpent's knowledge is not made explicit, his exceptional designation as clever, or cunning ('ārûm), and his remarks in vv. 4–5 indicate an advanced state of understanding relative to his fellow characters. The question he puts to the woman in 3:1 is a deliberate misstatement that cannot be answered in one word. His reformulation of 2:16–17 can imply that God has forbidden one or more trees (true), and/or that he has prohibited all trees (false).[64] The ambiguity is enriched by the fact that while every word in the serpent's quote is faithful to the language of 2:16–17, its component phrases are recontextualized to distort the original meaning. On one level the serpent's phrase "lō' tō'kēlû" opposes the divine command " 'ăkōl tō'kēl" in 2:16, but his quotation also takes advantage of the presence of both positive and negative injunctions in God's speech, and reverses the reference of negativity from "the tree of the knowledge of good and evil" to "all the trees of the garden":

YHWH—2:16–17	Serpent—3:1
"mikkol ʿēṣ-haggān"	"lōʾ tōʾkĕlû"
(From any/every tree in the garden)	(You shall not eat)
" ʾākōl tōʾkēl"	
(you shall surely eat)	
"ûmēʿēṣ haddaʿat ṭôb wārāʿ "	
(But from the tree of the knowledge of good and evil)	
"lōʾ tōʾkal mimmennû"	"mikkol ʾēṣ haggān"
(you shall not eat of it)	(from any/every tree in the garden)

In addition, the omission of God's gift of all the trees in 2:16 attributes an arbitrariness to the commandment. The effect of the misquotation is to force the woman to repeat the injunction anew, and the serpent's choice of quoted direct speech over indirect speech compels the woman to respond in kind in order to support her claim. Whether or not her zeal to correct him leads her to place the additional stringency of "wĕlōʾ tiggĕʿû bô" (nor shall you touch it) on the commandment, the serpent has accomplished his purpose. By forcing her to talk about the forbidden tree, he has created an opening for his more radical argument in vv. 4–5.[65]

Toward the end of David's career, in 1 Kings 1, an extraordinary example of deceptive quotation is directed at David by Nathan and Bathsheba in their efforts to get the declining king to ensure the succession of Solomon over Adonijah. In vv. 13 and 17 a quotation is ascribed to David in which he vows that Solomon will succeed him. The quote is unverifiable and quite possibly wholly invented by Nathan, for nowhere in 2 Samuel does David make such a promise to Bathsheba. Moreover, the emphasis on David's age and impotence in 1 Kg. 1:1, 4, 15 adds to the impression that he can be manipulated by those around him. The question need not be resolved for the purpose of our discussion; the literary quality of the story only benefits from this ambiguity. Because of the "reminding" function inherent in some quotations from earlier points in time, we should understand David's "forgetfulness," whether real or contrived, to be the target of their ploy. David must be convinced that he swore this oath and, more important, that he must act immediately to fulfill its conditions. Given the king's overwhelming passivity in 1 Kg. 1:1–10, this will be no mean feat, even if the oath is genuine.[66]

Nathan's plan has two parts: Bathsheba will remind David of his oath, and Nathan will make a well-timed entrance to back up her claim before David has a chance to respond. Nathan suggests that she phrase her remarks as interrogatives; the quotation of the oath should be set within a rhetorical question, and her subsequent remarks should ask for a response to the query "maddûᶜa mālak ădōnîyyāhû"—"Why is Adonijah king?" (v. 13). However, in the execution of the speech, Bathsheba displays her own variations. The oath is quoted in v. 17 as simple fact but is preceded by the claim that it was sworn "by the Lord your God," to emphasize the seriousness of possible violations.[67] Bathsheba then moves to the present, underscoring the fact that even *now* (*wĕᶜattâ . . . wĕᶜattâ*, 1:18) the king is unaware of what goes on around him, namely Adonijah's feast and the defections of Abiathar and Joab. David is reminded of his public responsibilities—"The eyes of all Israel are upon you"—and of his personal debts as well—"My son Solomon and myself will be regarded as traitors" (v. 22).

At this point Nathan enters and speaks before the king replies, and it is his words that finally move David to take action. Here the deceptive quotation is used to full advantage, exploiting the "innocence" of the speaker with the calculated effect of an incorrect quotation upon the listener. Because no interrogative prefix is attached to ᶜattâ in v. 24, it is not certain if it is to be understood as a question—"Did you say,' . . . '" (*AV, RSV*)—or as a conclusion—"You must have said,' . . . '" (*NJPS Prophets, NEB*). Nor is it clear whether Nathan's tone is one of innocence, of insult, or of criticism toward the king. Using a strategy not unlike that of the serpent beguiling the woman in Gen. 3:1–3, Nathan succeeds in getting David to "correct" him. But since more than acknowledgment of his words is required, Nathan stresses that not only Joab but *all* the officers of the military are in attendance at this party, described in "a little vignette of Adonijah's company eating and drinking and shouting 'Long live King Adonijah', a scene calculated to rouse the ire of the still reigning king."[68] Nathan concludes with a question (true to his instructions to Bathsheba in v. 13) that emphasizes his own loyalty to the king and his (feigned) hurt at not having been consulted in this apparent decision. When David finally gives his answer in vv. 29–31, the imprint of Nathan's successful strategy is apparent in the form of his response. Not only does David acknowledge his earlier oath as quoted by Nathan and Bathsheba, but he requotes those words in the context of a new oath that binds him to fulfill its conditions "this very day."

Examples of deceptive quotations are scarce, there being few deceptive questions of any type in biblical narrative. Apart from the texts discussed above, in only five instances does a speaker ask a question whose answer he already knows: Gen. 3:9–10, 4:9, 42:7; 2 Sam. 20:9; 2 Kg. 5:25. In spite of the fact that deception is a major theme in many biblical stories, most questions are either honest inquiries or rhetorical formulations in which the speaker's knowledge is not hidden from the listener.

Confrontational Quotation

Quotations with which the speaker accuses another or defends himself display radical change in the tone of speaking. Whereas pseudo-informational and deceptive quotations are used in contexts that involve subtle planning and complex strategies, confrontational quoted direct speech is more straightforward about its intentions, and the predominant tone is hostile or defensive. The majority of quotations appear in XXY or XYY formulations, the patterns of direct address. There is, moreover, a powerful sense of urgency in these speeches; accusations occur soon after the events and words that provoke them, and they occasion equally quick responses. One indication of this urgency is the use of participial and *yip'al* forms in the verb of introduction in more than one-quarter of the cases, such as Gen. 43:7; Ex. 5:8, 17; Num. 11:13. (Informational quotations are always introduced by *pa'al* forms). In some cases the illusion of immediate confrontation is deliberately created—as if the speaker quotes the words as soon as he first hears them—even though a longer period of time has actually elapsed (e.g., 1 Sam. 11:12 quoting 10:27). When the narrated time between the original speech and the quotation is of a longer duration, the narrative time may be shortened considerably in order to create the necessary sense of confrontation. In 1 Kg. 2:42 quoting 2:37–39, three years have elapsed between Solomon and Shimei's conversation and its repetition, and in 1 Kg. 20:28 quoting 20:23, a number of months have passed, but in both cases the passage of time is marked by only a few words in the two intervening verses.

The discussion will proceed according to the nature of the relationship between the speaker and the listener: Is the person quoting to defend him/herself against some charge? Or is the speaker using quotation in order to make an accusation against his audience? A second criterion is the relative positions of power between speaker and listener, and how this reflects upon the results obtained by the speaker's rhetorical techniques.

Self-Justification

In this first category of confrontational quotations, quoted direct speech is used by an accused party attempting to vindicate himself or seeking to justify his previous behavior. Since the quotation is always a response to the initiative of the accusing party, the speaker's strategy is dictated by the charges leveled against him. The content of the quotation is meant to refute the allegation, or at least serve as evidence that the offended party was forewarned and should have been forearmed. In most cases the speaker quotes his own words (XXY) as a testament to his own innocence. His defense is usually phrased in the interrogative mood, beginning with the particle *hălô'* and the *verbum dicendi* in the perfect, first-person singular.[69] In Gen. 42:22 Reuben responds to the self-indictment of his brothers by quoting the good intentions he voiced in 37:21–22 in defense of his own behavior: "Did I not say to you, 'Do not sin against the boy'?" Similarly Balaam defends himself against Balak's charges twice in Num. 23:26 and 24:12–13 by quoting his earlier (and oft repeated) caveat that he would speak only what YHWH tells him (22:18, 38; 23:12). As noted above, there is no elaborate rhetorical structure or strategy to be uncovered in this type of quotation. Since it is essentially defensive in nature, the speaker does not try to persuade the accuser of anything but his lack of culpability.

Accusation

The term accusation describes a situation in which a speaker acts on his own initiative to attempt to redress an imbalance in the scales of justice, or, from his perspective, an injustice done to him. This second category is more complex than the previous one, in terms of both rhetorical strategies and various subgroupings that appear. The primary distinction to be made here is between the challenge to authority by an individual who is essentially powerless, and the exercise of that authority by a human leader or by God.

In Jud. 18:24 Micah places his quotation of the surprised Danites within a speech that upbraids them for the fatuousness of their comments as well as for the criminality of their actions. Similarly, in 1 Kg. 18:11, 14 Obadiah twice quotes Elijah's simple demand to be presented before Ahab (18:8) in order to point out how dangerous the request really is. In both cases the speakers protest a lack of perception and sensitivity, and both quote their sources literally.[70] The weaker of two parties uses the words of the stronger to voice his complaint. Once again we find no hidden strategies; Obadiah wants assurances from Elijah (which he receives in 18:15), and Micah wants to recover his stolen idols and hijacked priest (which he does not). In both cases the speaker uses the quotation to help establish his point of view on the issue at hand.

Quotations as part of challenges to authority occur between man and God as well. In Ex. 33:12a quoting 33:1, Moses uses a style of argumentation similar to that of Ex. 32:11–12 and Num. 14:13–19, employing a careful combination of quotation and repetition. In 33:1 God again refers to Israel as Moses' responsibility ("The people which *you* have brought up"), but when Moses responds in v. 12, his quotation uses the neutral designation *hā'ām hazzeh*—"this people." Instead of stressing God's covenantal responsibility to Israel through the patriarchs as he did in Ex. 32:13 (and as God does in 33:1), he appeals first on the grounds of his own personal relationship with God. Strikingly, this was the very basis of God's unsuccessful appeal to Moses in 32:10! Only at the end of his speech in 33:13 does Moses identify "this people" as "*your* people," picking up on language from the beginning of his petition: "ûr'ēh kî 'ammekā haggôy hazzeh." When God replies in 33:14 that only Moses is so favored ("wahănihōtî lāk"), Moses makes his personal identification with the people more explicit—"'al-ta'ălēnû"—"do not bring *us* up"—and in v. 16 he states it even more clearly: if Moses has truly "found favor in God's eyes" (4 times in v. 12–16), then God must favor the people as well. Moses refers to himself as an integral part of the group twice in 33:16—"'ănî wĕ'ammekā" (I and your people); God must go "with *us*, so that *we* may be distinguished." In the end, God's positive response in 33:17 affirms that Moses has indeed "found favor in my eyes," as have the people as well.[71]

A more complex challenge to divine authority is found in Num. 11:13, where Moses quotes one part of the people's complaint voiced in 11:4–6, in an effort to persuade God to alleviate Moses' impossible situation: "Where am I to get meat to give all this people, when they whine before me and say 'Give us meat to eat'?" Although the words of the people are quoted, it is Moses who challenges God. The words of the quotation per se are not objectionable in Moses' eyes; it is the difficulty of fulfilling them that leads him to complain to God. More than any other narrative we have considered, our discussion of this chapter is complicated by the question of the unity of the story, as elements of two originally separate stories have been juxtaposed within a single narrative unit. The account of the quail is presented in vv. 4–10, 13, 18–24a, 31–34, while vv. 11–12, 14–17, 24b–30 tell of the bestowing of the spirit upon the elders.[72] The quotation in v. 13, among other devices, helps to bring the two strains together, but it does not eradicate the problem of continuity in the resulting plot. Depending upon whether or not one accepts the unity of the chapter, two different readings of Moses' quotation present themselves. If we read only the quail story (4–10, 13, 18–24a, 31–34), Moses emerges primarily as the people's advocate; the phrase "ûb'ênê mōšeh rā'" in v. 10 would refer to Moses' disapproval of God's anger at the people. In the quotation in v. 13 he omits any reference to the people's expressed desire to return to Egypt (vv. 5–6)—by far the most offensive statement in God's eyes—and focuses instead upon the logistics of feeding. God partially rejects this approach in vv. 18–20, granting the request for meat but turning it into a punishment. In order to refute Moses, God himself quotes the people's complaint in 11:18, ascribing to Israel more explicitly rebellious language, which reflects their sentiments more accurately than Moses' quote: "kî-ṭôb lānû bĕmiṣrāyîm" (We were better off in Egypt), and again in v. 20, "lāmâ zeh yāṣā'nû mimmiṣrāyîm" (Why did we ever leave Egypt?). In this reading, God's actions are directed more at the people's rebellion than at Moses' difficulties.

If, on the other hand, we read Num. 11:4–34 as a unified story, Moses' use of quoted direct speech in v. 13 is part of his larger complaint in vv. 11–15 about the difficulties of solitary leadership. Moses' patience is tried by impossible requests such as "Give us meat"; his words are more histrionic ("kill me, I beg you"), more self-concerned than in the previous reading. Moses complains of being a "single parent" in v. 12, a nursemaid to God's children, and God responds in vv. 18–20 by rebuking Moses as well as Israel. Moses is told he is not alone in this venture, and that the good parent will both provide and punish. Moses' skeptical response to this pronouncement in 11:21 quotes God's words from 11:8, and he again voices his distress about his solitary position in the face of the announcement of punishment for the people. He makes no attempt to turn aside God's anger at the people, fearing instead that his own credibility as a leader will be undermined by God's "irresponsible" promise. In this sense Jobling is correct when he suggests that "the sending of the quail is a demonstration of Yahweh's power to *Moses.*" Leadership rests ultimately in God's hands, and Moses is out of line in ascribing too much control to himself. In this reading Moses' disbelief in v. 21 mirrors the people's lack of trust throughout the chapter.[73]

Given the peculiar characteristics of this text, we cannot say that one of these explications is preferable to the other. To insist upon the first reading is to ignore the careful joining of the stories. On the other hand, it would be dishonest to discount the presence of elements that have little to do with the main story (whichever that may be), and that disturb any reconstruction of the narrative logic of the story.[74] There are, however, important themes shared by both readings, which will be discussed below.

The final text to be mentioned in this category of challenges to authority is complex for different reasons. In 2 Kg. 4:28 the Shunammite woman comes to Elisha after the death of her son and accuses him with the very words she spoke when he first promised her a child in v. 16: "Do not deceive me."[75] In v. 16 the words indicate little more than her own incredulity about this suddenly decreed pregnancy, not unlike Sarah's reaction in Gen. 18:12, if somewhat less derisive. At this point she does not fear that the child will die at an early age, but, like Sarah, she cannot believe that the birth itself will ever come to pass.[76] But in 4:28, after the birth, there is a significant shift in point of view about her earlier words, giving them a different connotation in the quotation. It is not clear whether she seeks to gain Elisha's help to revive the child, or if she is simply accusing him of not living up to his word, justifying her position by saying "I told you so." The words tumble from her mouth with all the anger and pain that she has held back since the child died in v. 20, through her brief conversation with her husband (vv. 20–23) and the ironic greeting by Elisha in v. 26: "Is the child well?" to which she replies, "It is well." The polite style of v. 16 has disappeared in v. 28, and the quotation has an immediate effect upon the prophet. Her opening phrase, "'al-'ădōnî 'îš hā'ĕlōhîm" (No, my lord, man of God) is omitted, and the self-deprecating expression *šiphātekā* (your maidservant) is replaced by the simple pronominal form *'ōtî*. This change is in keeping with the physical posture of the woman in 4:27, holding tight to Elisha's legs as she speaks. Whereas the man of God issued the commands in the first part of the story (4:12–16), now the woman demands that Elisha fulfill the responsibility to her contained in her earlier words, and implicit in the gift of the child. We will return to this episode in our discussion of discourse strategy to examine this hiddenness in greater detail.

When the relationship of weaker to stronger is reversed, the person in authority uses the quotation to attest to the guilt of the accused party. The quotations are taken directly from the words of the accused, apart from a few texts in which a divine prohibition is quoted to establish the basis of guilt (e.g., 1 Sam. 15:18). Most frequently, the punishment that proceeds from the situation is intrinsically connected to the quotation. For example, in 1 Kg. 2:42 Solomon quotes to Shimei not just the oath he swore about remaining in Jerusalem, but also the previously stated penalty for breach of promise:

> "Did I not adjure you by the Lord and warn you:
> 'On the day you leave to go to any other place,
> know well that you will die';
> And you said to me: 'This is good; I accept.'"

While quoted direct speech accusations presuppose a judicial background, they do not represent legal cases actually tried in court with judge and witnesses, in the manner of 1 Kg. 21:9–13. They are closer in spirit to those prophetic judgments against individuals or against the nation, in which unverifiable quotations are placed in evidence by the prophet, but which convene no court other than that on high.[77]

In some instances of quoted direct speech, God acts as judge, jury, and executioner of the offending party. Gen. 3:17 is clear and direct in its condemnation of the man, quoting only the divine standard that was transgressed, and not the words of the man himself. Given the earlier (mis)use of the quotation by the serpent and the woman in 3:1 and 3:3, the words that introduce God's quotation in 3:17—"because you have listened to your wife's voice"—imply a deliberate correction of that earlier voice by means of the present, more literal, citation. God's use of the root *Ṣ-W-H* (to command) as the verb of introduction is a critique of the earlier use of *'-M-R* by the woman and the snake as the *verbum dicendi* in

3:1, 3. Other texts that fall within this subgroup include Num. 11:18 quoting 11:4–6; 1 Kg. 13:22 quoting 13:9; and 1 Kg. 20:28 quoting 20:23.

In most accusations, the recognized political authority (e.g., Joshua, Gideon, David, Solomon) or God's spokesman (Samuel) quotes the words of the accused party prior to punishment. For example, in Jud. 8:15 quoting 8:6, the speaker (Gideon) calls for immediate retributive justice on the basis of the offending quotation. Even when the quotation is placed within an interrogative sentence inquiring about the reasons behind the commission of the alleged misdeed or misstatement, the speaker has little interest in the motivations of the accused. Thus in Josh. 9:22–23 Joshua inquires into the motives behind the Gibeonites' deception of Israel, but he passes sentence on them before they are given a chance to respond. When they do reply in v. 24, their pious statements about their fear of YHWH have no effect whatsoever upon their situation. Similarly, in 1 Sam. 15:18 Samuel asks Saul to explain his disobedience to the divine command, but the king's fate has already been decided in v. 11. Despite the interrogative form of the quotation, its rhetorical purpose is to bring the accused's own words as evidence against him.

This is not to say that the biblical story is uninterested in the motivations of its characters. On the contrary, such information is made available through the character's words and actions, and the reader is constantly invited to evaluate those attitudes. But once an accusation has been made, rarely does the motive of the accused actually affect the decision to execute justice. God's punishment of the man and the woman in Genesis 3, or of Cain in Genesis 4, is not mitigated by their excuses any more than Saul's self-defense and confession in 1 Sam. 15:20–25 change God's mind. On the functional level, then, questions of motivation containing quoted direct speech are essentially rhetorical questions, and the accusations themselves are not complicated by hidden motives or strategies.

But occasionally, the accuser uses quotation for more covert purposes as well. In 2 Sam. 1:16 David addresses the Amalekite messenger *after* he has already been executed in 1:15. To whom, then, is David really speaking? Given David's previous association with the Philistines in 1 Samuel 27 and 29, there must have been some concern in Israel that he might have been involved in Saul's death in some way, even though the text goes out of its way to place him in another conflict (with the Amalekites!) in 1 Samuel 30 at the same time as the battle at Mt. Gilboa. The first explicit mention of this doubt is voiced by those factions who suspected David's collusion in the deaths of Abner and Ishbaal in 2 Sam. 3–4, but these sentiments must have developed earlier, as David set out to cull support for his rival cause in 1 Sam. 22.[78] It is toward these quarters within Israel that David directs his remarks. In 2 Sam. 1:16 he attributes to the messenger the use of the highly charged epithet "mĕšîaḥ YHWH" (the anointed of the Lord) to describe Saul (see also 1 Sam. 24:6, 26:9), whereas the Amalekite simply said, "waʾămōtĕtēhû" (And I slew him) in 1:10. What was first explained as a casualty of the battlefield is now decried as a crime against God's anointed. While the mourning for Saul and Jonathan is elaborate and lengthy, this does not necessarily imply insincerity on David's part, only that one so politically astute would anticipate his enemies' attacks and take steps to forestall them.

A more insidious use of quoted direct speech as accusation occurs in Pharaoh's quotation of Moses' and Aaron's words in Ex. 5:8, 17. Not only does Pharaoh use the quotation to deflect attention from his own actions, but he also turns the newly formed coalition of Moses, Aaron, and the Israelites against itself. The words Moses and Aaron speak in 5:3—"Let us go, we pray, a three days' journey into the wilderness to sacrifice to the Lord our God"—derive from God's command to Moses in 3:18. Pharaoh cites their demand twice, first to the Egyptian taskmasters in 5:8 (XYZ) and then to the Israelite overseers in 5:17 (XYY). In both cases the quote is "proof" of his claim that the Israelites are slacking off, which in turn justifies his elimination of the "gift" of straw used in brickmaking while requiring the same daily quota of bricks. If the logic of such an equation seems rather strained, it is because Pharaoh *wants* the Israelites to be infuriated and frustrated by his strategy, and wants them to blame Moses and Aaron for this new misfortune. By creating a system in which Israelite slaves work for Israelite overseers, who are in turn responsible to Egyptian taskmasters, Pharaoh can maintain hostility between the various segments of the Hebrew slave population. Compelled to produce the same number of bricks, the Israelite overseers can only demand more from their own people. While the overseers sided with the Egyptian taskmasters in vv. 6–13, they are turned upon by the Egyptians in the following verse. When they protest to Pharaoh, they are insulted and rejected with the very words by which Moses and Aaron hoped to win their freedom. Although Pharaoh excluded them from punishment in 5:8 ("Therefore *they* cry out"), he lumps them together with the rebellious slaves in 5:17: "Therefore *you* say, 'Let us go that we may worship to God.'" When they vent their anger upon Moses and Aaron in vv. 20–21, their speech reflects the reversal of the program forecast in vv. 1–3. The sword (ḥereb) that Moses feared in 5:3 has been unwittingly placed in Pharaoh's hands by the prophet himself (v. 21). Pharaoh's strategy is so successful that not only do the Israelites repudiate Moses and his message, but Moses himself questions God's reliability in vv. 22–23.[79]

There are three unusual accusations that merit special attention. In two of these texts quoted direct speech is used to establish the guilt of the original speaker, but the quoter does not prescribe any specific punishment to go along with his accusations. In Gen. 18:13 God responds to Sarah's laughter of 18:12 by quoting to Abraham her personal words of disbelief and rebuking her suggestion that something might be "too wondrous for YHWH." It is very odd to find X quoting Y to Z when Y is both present and the subject of the accusation. Rashi explains this unusual construct by positing that God's intent is to reprove Sarah, but Abraham's presence demands that the quote be changed to disparage only herself and not her husband, "in the interest of peace." More disturbing is the presence of a hostile accusation in a text that promises a favorable future to Sarah and Abraham. On a larger contextual level, the emphasis on the root Ṣ-Ḥ-Q in 18:12–15 points ahead to the birth of *Yiṣḥaq* (this is a "laughable" pregnancy). But within the boundaries of 18:1–15 Sarah's skepticism is given a strong negative coloration, especially when compared with a similar response by Abraham in 17:17–19.

The second text displays a similar tension between approval and disapproval, the negative element again being supplied by a quotation. In the context of Saul's election at Mizpah (1 Sam. 10:19) Samuel quotes the people's request for a king made in 8:19–20. While 10:17–27 was formerly considered to be part of the anti-kingship source found in 1 Samuel 7–8 and 12, it is now understood as a conflation of two originally separate stories of Saul's selection, one by lot (10:20–21a), and another by stature (21b–24), neither of which is intrinsically anti-monarchic.[80] Indeed, Samuel's positive response in v. 24 would seem to indicate his approval of Saul on some level. In looking at the pericope as a redacted whole, Samuel's words in vv. 17–19 cast a negative pall over these otherwise optimistic events. The speech is structured along the lines of the prophetic oracle of judgment: call to attention (17), messenger formula (18a), recitation of YHWH's saving acts (18b), and the accusation (19a), into which the quotation of 8:19–20 is placed "in evidence." Absent, strikingly, is the judgment that generally follows such accusations both in prophetic speech and in narrative quoted direct speech situations.[81] Thus, in the redacted version of 10:17–27, the story of the choosing of Saul occurs precisely at the formal point where we expect judgment to be pronounced. The implication is clear: Despite Samuel's overt praise of Saul in 10:24, kingship *itself* is to be Israel's punishment.[82]

Within the larger narrative of Saul's rise and fall, Samuel's hostile attitude becomes somewhat more understandable to the reader. But a powerful tension between acclamatory and derogatory tendencies permeates the story of 10:17–27. Although the larger context reduces the need to harmonize these elements within the story, it does not do away with it altogether. The resulting picture of Samuel is one of profound ambivalence toward Saul, whose downfall he works to bring about in 1 Samuel 13–15, but whom he mourns deeply in 15:35, 16:1.

In Num. 14:31 quoting 14:3, the quotation is placed in the context of a pronouncement upon the people in vv. 28–35: "And your children, about whom you said, 'They will become a prey.'" Unlike all the prior examples, the quotation is not brought as evidence against the people or as a justification for a particular form of punishment. Instead, its purpose is to mock the fears of the people and to bring out the irony inherent in the reversal of their situation. The concern the people had voiced about the welfare of their wives and their children in 14:2–3 is silenced in an unexpected way, as God promises to take care of the children by disposing of the parents. The irony in this case is not simply for the reader but is pointedly directed at the Israelites themselves as part of their punishment. Such conscious irony is also present in other examples of quoted direct speech, e.g., Zebul's quote to Ga'al ben Ebed in Jud. 9:38, and Pharaoh's quote to the Israelite overseers in Ex. 5:17. But in all these texts the irony is secondary to the accusation. Only in Num. 14:31 is the ironic effect raised to the level of the primary intention of the speaker.

The schematization developed in this chapter is intended to describe only the primary function of each quotation on the story level. We do not mean this categorization to imply that each case of quoted direct speech has only one function. On the contrary, many informational quotations have secondary and tertiary accusatory or self-justifying effects, just as these last two intentions may both be present in the same speech. For example, although the information about Saul's oath is presented neutrally in 1 Sam. 14:28, it nonetheless serves to accuse Jonathan in the context of the story. Likewise, both God and Samuel indict Israel on the basis of the facts that they quote in Ex. 32:8 and 1 Sam. 12:12 respectively. Isaac tries to justify his actions in Gen. 26:9b, as does David in 1 Kg. 2:8, using quotations we have classified as "informational." In certain accusatory quotations the speaker also "reminds" his listener of his obligations, as Moses does in his challenge to God in Ex. 33:12. It is not at all unreasonable to describe the persons passing judgment in Ex. 5:8, 17, Jud. 8:15, 2 Sam. 1:16, and 1 Kg. 2:42 as simultaneously defending their own executive actions by appealing to the quotations they cite. This list is hardly exhaustive but illustrates that quoted direct speech can and does operate on a number of different levels within the story.

This examination of quotations on the level of story reveals two complementary tendencies:

1. In most texts the use of quoted direct speech by a character is more than a rhetorical flourish or a form of gratuitous repetition of earlier

details. In the great majority of cases, old information is repeated for clear accusatory or defensive purposes, or, when the tone is less hostile, to appease the listener or refresh his memory. Even in texts where old information is repeated in quotation for what seem to be only stylistic reasons, such as 1 Kg. 12:9–10, the quotation has been revealed to have a significant function or functions within the argument of the speaker. The quotation may be used for purposes of plot organization, characterization, the expression of a point of view, or some combination of these strategies. Moreover, regarding the presentation of new information, in only a few texts is the information told to the listener without being part of such an argument or lacking some personal bias on the part of the speaker (e.g., Gen. 38:22; 1 Kg. 13:17). The functionality of quoted direct speech within the character's narrative program makes it very likely that changes in his language in quotation will support that program and must therefore be evaluated in terms of the way the speaker has recontextualized them.

2. At the same time, despite the self-interest of the quoting party, the great majority of cases of quoted direct speech are fairly similar to their original formulations. No character ever protests that he has been quoted incorrectly, even when his earlier words are repeated directly to him. In quotations of new information, this fidelity is even more striking, given the speaker's opportunity to distort the truth in light of the naïveté of his listener. Pseudo-informational quoted direct speech includes both relatively accurate quotations used for persuasion (e.g., Gen. 27:7, 50:5), as well as more selective repetitions used for self-justification (Gen. 26:9, 42:31–34). But in no instance do we find the type of outright prevarication that appears in unverifiable quotations such as Josh. 9:11, 1 Sam. 19:17, or 21:3. Even in a deceptive quotation like Gen. 3:1, the language of the quote mimics the words of 2:16–17. But a text like the garden story serves as a reminder that the faithful reproduction of language and fidelity in meaning are related but not equivalent to each other. The context into which the speaker inserts the quotation determines the meaning of the quote, and changes in language can be understood only against the background of that location.

At this point, the question of the relationship between these two tendencies must be addressed. Is it not strange that, given the opportunity for deception, the quoter does not take advantage of his superior position, at least in quotations involving new information? It must be remembered that the model for the quoting character is not a limited or unreliable narrative but the omniscient narrator of the biblical narrative. The authority of this narrator derives not from his greater knowledge but from the fact that he "speaks for" or represents a God who is seen as the ultimate source of meaning and understanding.[83] As the primacy of that

God is absolute in the Bible, so too is the reader meant to accept the trustworthiness of that narrator. He may be challenged or critiqued on historical or historiographic grounds, but his literary/theological position is unassailable. The effect of this narrative model upon the image of the quoting character is that, despite his humanness as a character, he functions less according to the ideal of human verisimilitude than as a scaled-down model of the third-person omniscient narrator who empowers him to speak. The next chapter will explore the relationship of that impersonal narrator to the character who presents the quotation, and to the reader who perceives both story and discourse.

·4·

THE FUNCTION OF THE QUOTATION: DISCOURSE ANALYSIS

We earlier defined discourse as the narrator's communications with his implied audience. In biblical narrative such contacts do not take the form of asides addressed directly to the reader but must be perceived through the story, and through the means by which the story is told. Any of the variety of components and techniques of narration that are apparent to the reader, from narrative structure, convention and repetition, direct or indirect commentary on the characters, shifts in point of view, to a host of subcategories, are eligible to be elements of discourse, if it can be shown how they contribute to the telling of the story and the transmission of its meaning to the reader. The focus of this chapter is how quoted direct speech participates in this communicative process, as demonstrated by a select group of texts.

Because the narrator prefers to let his characters speak for him, there is a marked preference for direct speech in biblical narrative.[1] From the standpoint of objectivity such speech is considered far more reliable by the reader because it is free of the kind of narrative inference or bias that inevitably accompanies indirect speech or summary. If direct discourse is "objective," then quoted direct speech would seem to be doubly immune to interference from the narrator, since he is twice-distanced from the spoken speech quoted by another. This adds to the effectiveness of characterizations accomplished through quoted direct speech because the reader's judgments seem to proceed directly from his observation of the quoter's use of speech, and the character appears to be independent of the narrator or of narrative commentary.

Despite this illusion, the reality is otherwise. The narrator has complete control of his characters, deciding what words they will speak, and when they will speak them, whether in normal direct discourse or in quoted direct speech. He determines not only what will be spoken, but when it will be repeated, to whom, and under what circumstances. In this broader perspective everything that is story becomes, for the reader, part of the discourse of the narrator. As the previous chapter focused upon the strategy of the quoter with regard to his audience within the text, the treatment of discourse that follows is an analogous exploration of the narrator's use of quotations with respect to his implied audience outside the story.[2]

Occasionally some of the aspects of discourse are also perceptible within the story, as when both reader and character(s) share the same level of understanding about another character. For example, both the reader and Joseph become aware of the maturity of Judah through his speech in Gen. 44:19–34.[3] But even in this case the shared perspective is only momentary, for the reader knows more about both characters than either knows about the other. As a result of his privileged position outside the story, the reader can be aware of ironies, conflicts, and ultimate objectives to which the characters have no access. In this sense story and discourse can work together in many texts, like the Joseph story, to produce striking contrasts in knowledge between reader and character, contrasts that may be used for a variety of purposes: constructing ironic portraits, emphasizing theological concepts such as divine providence, or even calling attention to the limitations of the reader's knowledge.

When the various categories employed in the previous chapter are applied to discourse analysis, some interesting correspondences can be seen. First, regarding the audience's knowledge of the quotation, all the information found in verifiable quotations is "old" to the reader. But, as we saw earlier, such knowledge is far from omniscience, and the narrator uses quoted direct speech to give a particular slant to these details in the service of his presentation. Second, in terms of the triad of original speaker–quoter–listener (XYZ), the narrator is always the source of both the quotation and the quoter, since it is he who animates the characters. The audience is always the reader, resulting in the following configuration: X (the narrator) quotes X (his own words placed in the mouth of a character) to Y (the reader).

Most important, the traditional tasks of plot development, characterization, and point of view revert to the narrator.[4] In the microcosm of the story, the characters (both quoter and listener) are limited to a diachronic understanding of time, moving from the prior speech to the present moment of quotation. But the narrator's discourse can be read synchronically as well, the reader moving back and forth across time, comparing not just the words of the quotation but also the sequences of events in which they are embedded. Regarding characterization, in the previous chapter it was shown how the speaker uses quoted direct speech to depict the character whose words are being repeated. The quoter usually describes Y or Z through the character's own speech; even when he quotes his own words, he portrays himself at an earlier point in time. But in discourse analysis, the narrator uses the quotation as a means of characterizing the *quoter* as he speaks the quotation, at the present moment of narration.

The presentation of point of view on two levels can be understood in an analogous fashion. The character in the story uses quoted direct speech to offer his own perspective on the words he quotes. In discourse analysis we step back further to see the narrator's perspective on that point of view, allowing the reader a stereoscopic vision.[5] The character and the narrator may agree in their evaluation of a scene, as in the accusation in Gen. 3:17; the reader concurs with God that the man has transgressed the command stated in Gen. 2:16–17. But the two perspectives may just as easily stand in opposition to each other, as in the unverifiable quotation in Josh. 9:11. The Gibeonites' claim to have traveled a great distance is temporarily accepted by Joshua, although it is clear to the reader that they are lying. The result is an ironic juxtaposition of conflicting viewpoints, which is revealed to Joshua only when the deception is uncovered in 9:16.

Like "justification," "accusation," and other categories discussed in the previous chapter, depiction of character and change in point of view are not necessarily exclusive of each other as discourse functions. Our analysis of 2 Kg. 4:8–37, for example, has been placed under the rubric of formal structures for reasons that will become obvious below, but aspects of character and point of view are also dealt with therein; similar combinations will emerge in the discussions of other texts as well. These studies should be seen not as definitive but as illustrative descriptions of various discourse functions, which will present some models for the analysis of other texts as well.

These narrative functions serve as the organizing principle for this chapter. The first section examines the use of quotation to depict character, including a discussion of divine omniscience as an aspect of God's character. Next, in a discussion of plot, we explore how quoted direct speech functions in the development of the story line with attention to the formal structure of the narrative. The third unit takes up a group of quotations that are repeated by the narrator to indicate a shift in the point of view of narration, and the final section deals with the particular discourse problems created by unverifiable quotations.

1.

It is a commonplace in the discussion of biblical narrative style that narrated descriptions of the psychological attitudes of its actors are scarce, and that one must interpolate such matters from the external words and deeds of the individual.[6] While direct speech is always a useful indicator of these attitudes, verifiable quoted direct speech is of particular value. Since the reader has already gleaned the necessary information the first time the words were spoken, he is free to focus upon the *speaker* of the quotation rather than the details of his message. In cases where there is little or no variation from the original speech, the quotation can establish the reliability of the messenger in the reader's eyes, as in Gen. 38:22, 1 Kg. 1:47, and 13:17. In the first two examples, this determination is of only passing significance, as the messenger figures play no further part in the story. In 1 Kg. 13:17, however, the reliability of the man of God from Judah is first established, then immediately undercut by his obedience to the false, unverifiable oracle quoted by the old prophet from Bethel in 13:18. But, in a surprising move, the old prophet then speaks a *genuine* oracle from YHWH, condemning the man of God for his disobedience and quoting the original oracle again in v. 22. Not only is the "reliable" man of God proven untrustworthy, but the lying prophet from Bethel ends up with the true word of God. The effect of these reversals is to dramatize vividly one of the major problems of biblical prophecy: If a prophet can speak *both* true and false oracles, how can prophecy itself be a reliable means of revelation?[7]

Characterization is most often accomplished by having the quoter change the language of his original speech in a significant and revealing way. Not only does the narrator in Gen. 3:1 tell us that the serpent is crafty, but he shows us as well by means of his use of a deceptive quotation. David's ascription of the statement "'ānōkî mōtattî 'et-měšîaḥ YHWH" (I slew the anointed of the Lord) to the messenger who claims to have killed Saul is intended to justify his execution of the Amalekite. But taken together with David's extravagant praise of, and mourning for, the deceased king, the quote reveals something of his ambition and his political savvy. At the very end of David's life, in his final speech to Solomon in 1 Kg. 2:2–9, he instructs his son how to consolidate his power and settle some old scores at the same time. When, in 2:8, he quotes his oath of clemency to Shimei ben Gera (2 Sam. 19:24), he changes the emphasis from a general promise—"lō' tāmût" (You will not die)—to a more specific limitation on David's personal behavior—"'im-'āmîtěkā beḥāreb" (*I* will not put you to death by the sword). The implication is that once David is dead, Solomon will be free to act against Shimei. Solomon displays his own "wisdom" in this regard by binding Shimei himself to an oath (2:37–38) restricting him from traveling to his ancestral holdings in Bahurim, and specifying the death penalty for disobedience.[8]

In all the preceding examples, it is probable that the character himself is aware of the change introduced by the quotation, that these characterizations exist both on the level of story (the character's intention) and on the level of discourse. As such, the speaker of the quote is never the object of irony, as he in some sense shares in the privileged knowledge of the narrator and the reader. In the following example, however, characterization takes place primarily at the discourse level; because the quoter is unaware of the significance of the change in the quotation, his own words comment ironically on his own character. In 1 Kg. 21:6 Ahab responds to his wife's question about his depressed mood by quoting his conversation with Naboth in vv. 2–3. His own words are retold with considerable accuracy, but his quotation of Naboth contains a significant variation. In Ahab's eyes Naboth's land is simply a *kerem*—mere property, as he refers to it both in his original overture in v. 2 and in the quotation in v. 6. Naboth, on the other hand, uses the phrase "naḥălat 'ăbōtay" (my ancestral holdings), stressing the familial-religious aspect of maintaining ownership of the land. Ahab's insensitivity to these religious restraints is shown further by the replacement of Naboth's oath, "ḥālîlâ lî mēYHWH" (the Lord forbid me), with a simple negative assertion, "lō'-'ettēn" (I will not sell)—changing Naboth's refusal into an act of personal willfulness. The placement of the indirect object immediately after the verb ("lō'-'ettēn lěkā") in v. 6 shows how Ahab takes this as a personal rebuff: "Perhaps I would sell to someone else, but not to you."[9]

Ahab's passivity makes it unlikely that he introduced these changes with any more intent than expressing his frustrations to his wife. The quotation aids in condemning Ahab not only by highlighting his disdain for Naboth's traditional values but also by showing the great discrepancy between his feelings and his actions. The fact that Ahab does not act on his anger and invoke his royal power to confiscate the vineyard at first seems to speak on his behalf; he may resent Naboth's position, but he still respects the validity of the law and the limits of kingship. But as he stands by while Jezebel abuses his power of the throne, this hypothesis is proven false. His passivity is no longer a sign of self-restraint but of silent partnership, and his unquestioning response to Jezebel's announcement in v. 16 is to proceed immediately to claim the vineyard. Elijah's accusation in 21:19 voices the connection between complicity and passivity by accusing Ahab himself, not Jezebel, of Naboth's murder.[10]

Quoted direct speech is also used to portray character by contrasting quotations by two different figures in the same text. We previously discussed Joseph's quotation in Gen. 50:5 of his father's request to be buried in Canaan, presented in such a way as to ensure Pharaoh's agreement. Joseph's speech witnesses once again to his understanding of how to speak to Pharaoh, and to his sense of responsibility to his father. But now that Jacob is dead, the brothers fear recriminations from Joseph and quote to him a command allegedly spoken to them by Jacob sometime earlier (50:17), prohibiting the taking of revenge. As there is no record of such a statement earlier in the story, the quotation must be classified as unverifiable; is it, however, "believable"?

The nature of the comment, together with the stated motivations of the brothers in 50:15, points to the conclusion that this statement has been fabricated by the brothers.[11] Jacob had no reason to suspect Joseph of insincerity; nor is it clear that he was ever aware of the brothers' mistreatment of Joseph. The brothers' reaction is reminiscent of their previous self-indictment in 42:21. Their guilt for their earlier crime turns into the kind of anxiety that fosters this uninspired ruse, as they try to take advantage of Joseph's devotion to their father. Fearing to speak directly with Joseph, they prefer a messenger as a go-between; for all the reconciliation that has taken place, the contrast between Joseph and his brothers is very clear. In 50:5 Joseph discharged an obligation to his father at the risk of Pharaoh's disapproval; his brothers, on the other hand, invent an "obligation" that dishonors Jacob's memory as much as it does Joseph's intentions. In 50:6 Pharaoh recognizes filial devotion and accedes to it; in vv. 18–19 Joseph sees lying self-interest for what it is but rises above it and looks at the past from a broader perspective. The chapter closes with the command to fulfill another familial obligation, as Joseph has the "children of Israel" (his brothers?) swear to bring his bones out of Egypt. What Joseph did for his father, Israel must now do for him.

A similar fraternal comparison is made between Moses and Aaron in Exodus 32. We remarked above on Moses' brilliant rhetorical style in 32:11–14 in relationship to God's use of quoted direct speech in 32:8. Whereas Moses' speech is very effective in controlling God's anger, Aaron's speech in 32:22–24 has no mollifying effect on Moses. In fact, it could be said that nowhere else does a speaker use quoted direct speech quite so unsuccessfully. The reader is already aware of Aaron's failings from the events of 32:1–6, but the style of his quotations reinforces his unreliability as both leader and narrator. His negative bias toward the people, stated before he begins quoting—"You know that this people is bent on evil" (v. 22)—damages in advance any claim to objectivity that the quotation might have lent to his report. The first quotation in 32:23 is a near-perfect account of the people's words in 32:1. But his replication of his own words in v. 24 is much less precise, lacking the degree of specificity found in v. 2 and omitting his command that the people should bring their gold to him. The reader, of course, expects the opposite—the speaker should be able to reconstruct his own words and actions with greater fidelity than those of another person. Thus when, in 32:24b, Aaron makes no mention of his role in crafting the molten image described in v. 4, nor of his proclamation in v. 5, "ḥag laYHWH māḥār"

(Tomorrow shall be a feast to the Lord), the accuracy with which he quoted the people in v. 23 becomes even more damaging evidence against himself.[12] Since such stylistic testimony is out of all proportion to the absence of any critique or punishment of Aaron by Moses, we agree with Childs' suggestion that the narrator's real concern

> ... did not lie with Aaron himself. Rather Aaron's whole behavior both in his original weakness and subsequent defense, serves merely to highlight by contrast the role of the true mediator. Aaron saw the people "bent on evil"; Moses defended them before God's hot anger (vs. 11); Aaron exonerated himself from all active involvement; Moses put his own life on the line for Israel's sake. Aaron was too weak to restrain the people; Moses was strong enough to restrain even God.[13]

A different kind of characterization involving quoted direct speech appears in the Samson cycle, where Samson's ignorance in Jud. 14:1–16:31 is likened to his father's lack of awareness in 13:1–25. In this case the comparison results not so much from the characters' interaction with each other as from their analogous behavior in two separate stories. Of particular note is the rare occurrence of a change in the quotation that is insignificant on the story level (i.e., it means nothing to the characters) but that intimates something important to the reader.

In Jud. 13:7 Manoah's wife quotes to him a deficient version of the words spoken to her by the divine messenger in 13:5:

Jud. 13:5

{a} kî hinnāk hārâ wĕyōladt bēn
{b} ûmôrâ lōʾ-yaʿăleh ʿal-rōʾšô
{c} kî-nĕzîr ʾĕlōhîm yihĕyeh hannaʿar min-habbāṭen
{d} wĕhûʾ yāḥēl lĕhôšîyaʿ ʾet-yiśrāʾel miyyad pĕlištîm

{a} Behold, you are pregnant and will bear a son.
{b} No razor shall go upon his head,
{c} for he will be a Nazirite to God from the womb;
{d} and he will begin to deliver Israel from the hand of the Philistines.

In her repetition she retains clauses {a} and {c} intact but paraphrases {d} ("ʿad-yôm môtô," until the day of his death) and omits {b} entirely. These changes are not inconsiderable, given that clause {b} contains information that is crucial to the boy's Nazirite identity, and {d} is no less important in predicting his role in society.[14] Manoah's wife has no visible motive for quoting the words to her husband, other than passing on significant information that is necessary for the continuation of the plot. Given her guileless character and the subsequent unimportance of Samson's parents in the rest of the cycle, it is improbable that Manoah was deliberately deceived by his wife. The narrator, however, does have reasons for keeping Manoah in the dark, or rather, for depicting him as a character with gaps in his understanding. Throughout chapter 13, Manoah is presented as something of a fool. Skeptical of his wife's report, he demands to talk to the messenger himself (v. 8), but he gets no more information than what his wife told him in v. 7. To each of his four questions—vv. 11, 12, 15, 17—he receives only vague answers.[15] While the reader and Manoah's wife correctly perceive the divine nature of the visitor, Manoah himself remains unaware of this (13:16, "kî lō'-yāda' mānôaḥ," For Manoah did not know) until the angel's mysterious disappearance in the flame in v. 20. When the angel does not return Manoah finally understands (13:21, "'āz yāda' mānôaḥ"), but he draws the wrong conclusions (v. 22), and it is left to his wife to correct his misperceptions in v. 23. Despite the fact that she is identified only as "Manoah's wife," she is the one with greater knowledge throughout, and the one who bestows a name on the child.

An analogous situation obtains in Jud. 16:4ff., where Samson is subject to the control of his present consort, Delilah. Though he seems to be the figure of authority, it is she who actually dominates, first by her seductiveness, and then by her private arrangement with the Philistines. While Samson may know more than his father about his untrimmed hair, at the crucial moment he is unable to keep its secret. His failure is in his lack of awareness (16:20, "wĕhû' lō' yāda' "), not of the presence of the divine but of the realization that God has actually "departed" from him. The overall parallel between the two characters is strengthened by a mixture of symmetries and asymmetries. In both cases four questions are asked, and evasive responses are given, but Manoah is the questioner in chapter 13, and Samson the respondent in 16:4ff. The degree of both men's knowledge is controlled by their mates, but while Manoah's wife is benign and helpful, Delilah is treacherous and deceitful. Father and son become aware of the threat to their lives too late, but Manoah only fears death in 13:22, while Samson embraces it in 16:28. Active and passive roles are shifted about, but the two remain essentially alike.[16]

It is clear, then, that the narrator intends Manoah to prefigure Samson; he anticipates the son's fatal lack of recognition with the father's near-fatal obtuseness about the angelic messenger, which itself is typified by Manoah's ignorance of the command about not cutting the boy's hair. Such prolepsis is not uncommon in biblical narrative; elsewhere in Judges, Gideon's rejection of kingship in 8:23 serves as a foil for his son Abimelech's claim to royal power in 9:1ff. But in the case of Samson the narrator uses the parallel of father and son not to contrast the goodness of one with the disobedience of the other, but to bring out on the individual level what the book of Judges says about Israel as a whole. The narrative framework of the book shows Israel involved in a cycle of apostasy, foreign oppression, calling out to God, and temporary deliverance by a divinely appointed judge, a cycle that is repeated in the episodes beginning in 2:11, 3:7, 3:12, 4:1, 6:1, 10:6, and 13:1. Israel is portrayed as unable to extend the successes of any one judge beyond his/her death. The people are trapped in a vicious cycle that condemns them to continuous oppression, even to the point of being driven from the land, because of their inability to remember (cf. 2:10b, 3:7) until the moment of need (cf. 6:13, 10:10). In the Samson stories we see the "hero" acting out this cycle in his own personal behavior: Samson's attraction to foreign women leads to his betrayal of God by revealing the secret in 16:17, which in turn results in his "oppression" by the Philistines. In 16:28 he calls out to God for help and "delivers" Israel by destroying the Dagon temple and, ironically, himself as well. Despite this, 18:1 testifies that Samson's victory was only temporary, as the continued Philistine presence forces the Danites to scout out a new location.[17]

This "personalization" of Israel's cyclical failure in Jud. 16 is also reflected in the narrator's presentation of two generations of one family—Manoah and Samson—as equally unperceptive and therefore unable, or unwilling, to change. As Manoah cannot seem to learn anything in chapter 13, so Samson does not learn that involvement with Philistine women in 14 and 16 leads only to destruction. While he still possesses his strength, and the secret of that strength in his Nazirite vow, he is momentarily better than his father. Once he reveals it, he becomes, like his father, "an ordinary man." The possibility of real salvation is lost once again to Israel, until the cycle is broken (again temporarily) by the institution of dynastic kingship in 1 Sam. 8.

In many of the quotations that the speaker uses for characterization in the Joseph story, the reader is affected in ways that support their effect upon the listener within the story. Reuben's attempt at self-vindication in Gen. 42:22 cannot but strike the brothers as well as the reader as a display of his weakness rather than his strength. Just as Jacob finds his sons' version of the events in Egypt unconvincing (42:36), so the reader is made aware of their shortcomings by the changes they introduce in the quotations in 42:31–34. The series of quotations by Judah and his brothers in Gen. 43:3, 5, 7 impress upon the reader and upon Jacob the extent of Joseph's power over them, and their inability to do anything other than what he demands. In Judah's long speech in 44:19–34 both Joseph and the reader are made to sympathize with Jacob and his fate to an extent heretofore unprecedented in the story. At the same time Judah himself becomes a much more attractive figure because of the responsibility he takes upon himself with regard to Benjamin and his father.

But on another level, the use of quoted direct speech in the story serves a different kind of characterizing function with respect to the extent of Joseph's knowledge. By first supporting the illusion of Joseph's omniscience and then revealing the limitations of his knowledge at a later point, the narrator allows the theme of divine providence to emerge in a unique way. The centrality of this concept to the whole of the Joseph story is expressed in a variety of ways, some explicit, others understated. Joseph stresses God's control each time he interprets a dream (40:8; 41:16, 25, 28, 32) and in his understanding of the events of his own life and the life of his family (45:5–12; 50:20). The narrator reflects this theme occasionally in direct comments about Joseph's success (39:23, 25) but more extensively in the organization of the plot (e.g., the extent of the famine) and in the timely intrusions of influential minor characters such as the "man" in 37:15–17 and the cupbearer in 41:9.[18] Moreover, providence is not presented as a wholly passive ideal, according to which humans lack all initiative and respond blindly to the gestures of a puppet master. Joseph's seizing the opportunity in 41:33–36 is an expression of the necessary human response to providence: success comes out of a combination of patience, proper understanding of the auspicious moment, and appropriate action such as dovetails with the larger divine plan.[19] Initially, Joseph's skills in dream interpretation and divination allow him perceptions of the future more accurate than those of any other character, and the fulfillment of his predictions in 41:47–49, 53–57 adds to the trustworthiness and authority of his words. This sense of Joseph's superior knowledge extends from his success with Pharaoh into his encounter with his brothers in chapters 42–44. Because he has been so correct in his behavior thus far, so accurate in his predictions, and so adamant about God being the source of all meaning, the reader is prepared to accept Joseph's actions in 42:7ff., strange as they may seem, as ultimately purposive and rooted in the will of the divine. The brothers, on the other hand, have captured none of the reader's sympathies for having thus far escaped retribution for the kidnapping of their brother, without so much as a word of reproof. When Joseph begins to deceive them in 42:7, the reader does not even lift an eyebrow but joins Joseph in the superior position he attains by masking his identity, and revels in the ironic reversals that he devises as punishment for their earlier crime.[20]

The role that quoted direct speech plays in this development in chapters 42 and 43 is to heighten the reader's appreciation of Joseph's power. In 42:14 Joseph uses his own words as "proof" of his accusation of spying, even though the brothers' account of their situation has given him little evidence for such a charge. The quotations in 43:3, 5, 7 emphasize by sheer weight of repetition that Joseph's demand to see Benjamin is the single factor that controls the fate of his family. But a more significant expression of this power is in the development of the reader's sense of Joseph's foresight; his accusations seem perfectly designed to evoke responses that betray the brothers' weaknesses—e.g., Reuben's self-exculpation in 42:22, the excuses they offer to their father in 42:31–34, and their lack of real concern for Simeon, whom they are in no great hurry to ransom. In chapter 37, when they were in control, they successfully deceived Jacob, but now that Joseph dominates, the appearance of the money in their saddlebags in 42:35 casts a dark shadow over their account of Simeon's fate. The rebuke they receive from their father in 42:36, 38 functions as that long-awaited and much-deserved condemnation that they did not receive in 37:33ff. By the end of chapter 42, it appears to the reader as if Joseph himself stands next to God in determining the fate of his brothers.

As the story progresses, however, Joseph's deception begins to wear thin. While he delights in the ruse about the divining cup (44:1ff.), the reader has become painfully aware of Jacob's frailty. Joseph's attempt to detain Benjamin becomes a cruel act, one that cannot be part of a divinely sponsored master plan but must be a reflection of Joseph's personal desire for revenge. Judah's speech in 44:19–34 is crucial at this point in the narrative, for it points out by means of quotations much that Joseph does not know: Jacob's deep fear that Benjamin, like Joseph, will never return (vv. 27–29), Judah's concern for his father's life (30–31, 34), and his assumption of responsibility for the boy (32–33). Even though it is clear that Judah does not know he is speaking to Joseph, the presence of these details in the speech creates an uncanny feeling that someone who knows more than Joseph or Judah has orchestrated this encounter.[21]

Joseph responds to Judah's challenge in 45:5–13 with an explanation that avows the authorial role of God in these events, an idea that has gained importance as Judah's speech has undermined Joseph's apparent omniscience. Because Joseph is shown to have known less than he seemed to know, controlled less than seemed to be in his hands, the reader's appreciation of God's providential direction is greatly enhanced. At the point when Joseph ceases "playing god" to his brothers (here one recalls the dreams of 37:5–11), God's real control of events far beyond Joseph's reach can be acknowledged.[22]

It is striking that divine providence figures so strongly in the two longest human speeches in the biblical narrative—Judah's in 44:19–34 and Abraham's servant's in Gen. 24:34–49—which are also the two most extensive cases of quoted direct speech in the Bible. The recapitulation by Abraham's servant may speak more directly about divine control, but Judah's discourse also leads to the appreciation of the providential by both the characters and the reader. Both are speeches by powerless individuals who are at the mercy of their listeners' decisions: The servant's speech aims at convincing Laban that he should release his daughter to the family YHWH has designated, and the purpose of Judah's words is to persuade Joseph to give up his control over their affairs (and return it to God). But while the characters can see only the inevitability of the argument as the speaker has framed it, the reader sees the quoter at work reconstructing history and is made to realize that neither the servant's nor Judah's helplessness is as complete as it is made to seem. As with Joseph's initiative in 41:33–36, both Judah and the servant display the art of the "interpreter" of the providential moment, speaking and quoting with a skill that is capable of turning opportunity into reality. Their speeches are essentially commentaries on the words of other speakers. The presentation of these other words in objectified quotations (which the reader can check for accuracy) is part of a strategy of self-effacement that is perfectly consonant with the idea of human obedience to divine authority, which is at the center of both speeches. At the same time, the artistry and subjective organization of these speeches bring out the necessity of the human will for taking advantage of the providential moment, without dramatizing the self to the point of obscuring the subtle workings of the deity.

Extending this insight to the discourse level penetrates to the heart of the relationship between the "omniscient" narrator and God. Unlike third-person omniscient narrators in modern fiction, the biblical narrator has a partner in his craft, who, while more powerful and at least equally omniscient, allows the narrator to portray him as a "character" in the story.[23] On a purely literary level, the narrator treats God like any other figure, describing his comings and goings, his perspective on creation ("And the Lord saw that it was good," Gen. 1:10), even God's private musings ("Now the Lord had said, 'Shall I hide from Abraham what I intend to do?'" Gen. 18:17). There is no particular vocabulary or syntactic features that are indicative of divine speech. But from an ideological or theological standpoint, God's status as a character is untenable. If the narrator posits an authoritative, omniscient, and exclusive deity, then he cannot presume to stand outside that creation. The narrator exists not because his advice is sought by God, but by reason of literary necessity. Since, for a variety of reasons, the God of Israel chooses not to relate his own story, it is left to another, or others, to tell the tale. The narrator is omniscient only because God grants him that perspective on the world.

It has been suggested that the relationship between God and the narrator be understood in terms of analogy: as God creates a populated universe, so, too, the narrator fashions his world. Both God and the narrator know what is in the hearts of their creatures, and both know what the future holds in store for them.[24] The posture of the character as narrator in Gen. 24 and 44 enables us to develop this idea further. We have seen how the narrator is absolutely authoritative within the confines of his literary construction, yet, at the same time, he is passive in terms of the theological universe that he describes. In order to get around this dilemma, the biblical narrator must efface his own presence by remaining anonymous and by presenting his material in a manner that is ostensibly neutral and objective.[25] But as we have seen, the narrator who appears merely to report the happenings of a divinely ordered cosmos does, in fact, comment upon that story with great subtlety. In an analogous way, the character who acts as narrator in these longer speeches embodies a similar tension between autonomy and dependence. A storyteller such as Abraham's servant is cast precisely in the mold of *his* maker, that equally anonymous, half-hidden, omniscient narrator who brings him to life in the story. Judah's vulnerability before Joseph, who nonetheless allows him to speak (and to quote him), mirrors the relationship between the narrator and God. And the reader, like his audience-counterpart in the story, is called upon to see through the veil of objectivity to the deeper purpose of the narrator's art: the appreciation of human ingenuity in the service of the divine, which takes place both in story and in discourse.[26]

In the story of Joseph and in Genesis 24, the emphasis upon divine providence is tied to the fact that the deity is not an active, or interactive, character. When God steps into the foreground to have contact with other figures in the story, the question of omniscience becomes significant for understanding the use of quoted direct speech in those narratives. In the following texts, divine omniscience is contrasted with the perceptions of the characters to point up the severe limitations of human knowledge and the ultimate control of YHWH.

God's exceptional status allows him knowledge of words that are spoken when his presence is not formally indicated, even when the words are not spoken aloud. The former situation is illustrated by 1 Kg. 20:28, where, in an oracle of judgment spoken by an anonymous prophet, YHWH quotes the private words of the servants of the king of Aram in 20:23. In this case, God's omniscience is impressed upon the reader and the king of Israel simultaneously, allowing both to appreciate the irony of the Arameans' futile attempts at military strategy. The privileged position of Ahab is contrasted with the lack of knowledge of Ben-hadad, reflecting the narrator's attitude toward the two kings throughout the first part of the chapter. Ben-hadad is the cruel besieger of Shomron, who whimsically changes his demands from day to day (vv. 3–5), brags about the size of his army (v. 10), and sits drinking with his officers in the face of the Israelite attack (vv. 12, 16). The king of Israel, on the other hand, is shown trying to reason with the enemy (vv. 4, 9), leading his own troops into battle despite vastly unequal odds (vv. 14–15), and, most important, trusting in God and in the advice of his prophet (vv. 13, 22, 28).[27]

But Ahab's superior knowledge in v. 28 is completely reversed in the episode of the disguised prophet that follows in vv. 35–43. Here the king is criticized for his disobedience toward the laws of *ḥerem;* instead of having killed Ben-hadad, Ahab enters into an alliance with him (20:34).[28] Once again, the king is addressed by a prophet using an oracle to drive his point home (v. 39), but now the king of Israel is the object of deception and condemnation. Here the reader knows more than the king (i.e., that the wounded man is a prophet in disguise) but is not aware of the prophet's intentions until the moment he denounces the king in v. 40. While the quotation in 20:28 granted the reader partial foreknowledge of the outcome, he is shut out from that perspective in 20:35–43. The reader's privilege is relative to the characters in the story, but omniscience is left to God alone.

In Num. 22:10–11 Balaam quotes information about his visitors in response to God's question in 22:9. The quotation is close enough to the wording of the original speech of Balak's messengers (vv. 5–6) that one cannot justly accuse Balaam of trying to deceive YHWH. Moreover, insofar as the narrative assumes God's omniscience, the repetition of these details serves little purpose on the story level, except as a possible test of Balaam's trustworthiness as a reliable quoter. But as is the case with Jud. 13:7, the significance of the quote in this text is to be found only on the level of discourse. In order to understand this, it is necessary to examine the motives behind God's question to Balaam in v. 9; why is Balaam asked to repeat what is already known to both God and the reader?

The question in 22:9 is similar in function to other interchanges in which the speaker asks a question whose answer he already knows, in order to test the listener's perception of both the question and the one who asks it. In other cases where such deceptive questions are asked, particularly when God is the speaker, the inadequacy of the listener's response to the query is immediately laid bare by means of a direct accusation. In Gen. 3:11 and 4:11, God quickly abandons his pretense of ignorance and reveals the extent of his knowledge of the wrongdoings of Adam and Cain, respectively.[29] But in Numbers 22, two unconventional things take place: Balaam answers the question with no deceit whatever, and God makes no accusation against Balaam at that point in the story. Instead, an attack on Balaam takes place later in the chapter on grounds that are not entirely clear. In 22:20 Balaam receives God's permission to travel to Balak, but in vv. 22ff. God's anger at Balaam breaks forth precisely for having undertaken the journey. Within the story itself it is difficult, if not impossible, to reconcile this contradiction. It is likely the result of an uneven editing process in the chapter, in which more than one original story in vv. 2–20 was combined with the more homogeneous episode of Balaam's ass in vv. 21–53.[30] But on a thematic level of discourse, there is an integral connection between the "unnecessary" repetition in quoted direct speech in 22:10–11, the changing attitudes of God regarding Balaam's journey to Moab, and the conflict between Balaam and his ass in 22:21–35.

It has been remarked that the story of Balaam and his ass in 22:21–35 serves to anticipate Balaam's relationship to Balak in 22:36–24:25. As Balaam becomes furious with the animal three times for injuring him or leading him astray, so Balak denounces Balaam for his thrice-repeated blessing of Israel.[31] The ass perceives God's presence, to which Balaam is blind, much the same as Balaam the visionary understands what is opaque to Balak throughout the rest of the story. No manner of divination can affect the oracles and blessings placed in Balaam's mouth by YHWH. Balaam is thus prepared for his task by being taught a lesson about obedience and vision by the God in whose name he is about to speak.

Balaam's reeducation begins in 22:21, but the reader has been shown the need for such learning by the very fact of Balaam's quotation in 22:10–11. While the prophet is willing to grant final authority to God, he does not seem to be aware of YHWH's omniscience. His response to the question of 22:9 is factually correct, but the reader must perceive the incongruity of YHWH seeking information from a diviner! As with the man in Gen. 3:9 and Cain in 4:9, God's deceptive question brings forth a response that reflects the listener's perception of him as a powerful, yet limited deity. But in Numbers 22 the narrator develops an ironic perspective from which the reader does not condemn Balaam so much as laugh at him for his benightedness. Toward this end, God's criticism of Balaam is held back until the end of the chapter, and the theme of Balaam's comprehension is brought to the fore only in his struggle with the ass. God's changes of opinion in vv. 20–22 underscore Balaam's lack of control over his circumstances and prepare the way for his complete bewilderment at the behavior of an animal of whom he is the supposed master. As the story progresses, God sports with Balaam, taking advantage of his ignorance relative to the level of understanding possessed by a mere beast of burden. Even though he does gain knowledge in 22:31–35, Balaam ultimately becomes nothing more than God's tool for deceiving Balak. After 22:35 Balaam ceases to develop as a character and acts only in the capacity of a messenger of YHWH.

In light of this theme of knowledge and ignorance on the part of both characters, an omission made by Balaam in his quote in 22:10–11 becomes meaningful at a later point in the story. Balaam does not mention

to God the flattery directed at him by Balak in 22:6: "kî yādaʿtî 'et 'ăšer
tĕbārēk mĕbōrāk wa'ăšer tā'ōr yû'ār" (For I know that whomever you
bless remains blessed, and whomever you curse is cursed), perhaps omitting the words for stylistic reasons such as shortening, or out of respect
for God. A reformulation of these words, *not* originally spoken by God,
yet now sponsored by him, comes forth out of Balaam's mouth in 24:9:
"mĕbārăkêkā bārûk wĕ'ōrărêkā 'ārûr" (Blessed be those who bless you,
and cursed be those who curse you)—but now it is descriptive of *Israel*.
The irony inherent in 24:9 functions on two levels: (a) The very people
whom Balak intended to curse are now blessed with Balak's own words,
and by a process set in motion by those words. (b) God reveals his omniscience in the story by quoting, through the agency of Balaam, words
that Balaam neglected to tell him in 22:10–11.

The Balaam story demonstrates well the exceptional nature of God as
a character in biblical narrative. As a rule, human protagonists remain
exclusively within the confines of the story, never addressing the reader
directly. The narrator, on the other hand, always stands outside the story
to address the reader and does not involve himself in the life of his
characters. Only God straddles both sides: Like a character, he is "controlled" by the narrator as he interacts with others, and his speech is
always placed within a narrative framework—even one so simple as
"God said."[32] Like the narrator, God displays omniscience, being capable
of discerning the inwardmost human emotions and possessed of the
ability to create and alter the situations within which the characters function. In Numbers 22 God is active on both levels of understanding. His
contact with Balaam takes place within the story as the two relate directly
to each other as characters. Yet God's presence in the text is also dis-
course-oriented in its revelation of God's omniscience directly to the
reader. The irony of Balaam's situation is shared not just by the narrator
and the reader as they look upon his blindness from some great height,
but by God as well.

Perhaps the most brilliant use of quoted direct speech to highlight
divine omniscience appears in Gen. 18:13, where God quotes Sarah's
unspoken words of v. 12 and alludes to her internal reaction to the
promise of a child in her old age: "lāmâ zeh ṣāḥăqâ śārâ" (Why did Sarah
laugh?). Earlier we noted the tone of rebuke present in God's speech,
and its relationship to the change in Sarah's language in v. 13. But the
quotation does more than accuse Sarah of disbelief; the publicizing of
her private words demonstrates to her (and to Abraham) who this exceptional speaker is and why his promise should be taken seriously. In 18:1–
8, the narrator gives no indication that Abraham's three visitors are
anything other than ordinary travelers, accepting the generous hospi-
tality of their host. The first hint of something unusual is their knowl-

edge of Sarah's name in 18:9. This is followed by a switch to the singular verb form *wayyō'mer* for the delivery of the promise in v. 10, but they still do not identify themselves or mention YHWH's name. In contrast to his depiction of Abraham's reaction to the promise in 17:17, the narrator turns our attention to Sarah, who has been silent and hidden thus far. The phrase "wĕśārâ šōmaʿat" (Now Sarah was listening . . .) in 18:10b signals a shift in point of view to her person, much the same as the phrase "wĕribqâ šōmaʿat" functions in Gen. 27:5. In 18:11 the dramatic flow of the narrative is broken in order to recall essential background information, in light of which the reader judges Sarah's reaction less harshly. From her vantage point, long past menopause, the suggestion of renewed fertility is understandably suspect, if not completely ridiculous—especially coming from an unknown visitor. In this context it is hardly surprising that she mocks the very possibility of such an event with her laughter and her words.[33]

God's response is ostensibly addressed to Abraham, but it is really directed at Sarah. He reveals himself first by his omniscience, quoting what has not been spoken to him. Sarah hears her silent thoughts pronounced aloud by another, spoken to her husband, no less, whom she had blamed in 18:12 ("waʾdōnî zāqēn," For my husband is old). God's reworking of her original language to read "waʾănî zāqantî" (For I am old) is a direct reproof of her denigration of her husband, but it is delivered on a level that Abraham himself is not aware of. All he can possibly understand is God's anger at Sarah's lack of belief in the God in whom he trusts. Human and divine "hearing" are thus contrasted for Sarah in a way that cannot but impress upon her the nature of the God who made the promise in 18:10. God's self-revelation goes further by drawing a connection between omniscience and omnipotence: He who can hear all can also contravene the laws of nature: "hăyippālēʾ mēYHWH dābār" (Is anything too wondrous for YHWH?) In the face of such an overwhelming demonstration of the limits of her knowledge (and her privacy), Sarah tries to hide her fear and embarrassment by denying her laughter in 18:14. But a deity who can discern hidden thoughts and mental states can easily detect so obvious a lie, and the final word in this dialogue rests with God in 18:15.

For the reader, the sudden appearance of God's omniscience in the quotation in v. 13 opens up the story in similar ways. The hidden identity of the messenger(s) becomes clear, and the series of closed, or enclosed figures is laid bare: Sarah, *within* the tent, speaks *within* herself. God's quote reveals the fact of her eavesdropping as well as the details of her private speech, and promises the emergence of a son from *within* her own body.[34] These themes are taken up again in the succeeding episodes: In 18:17–19 God deliberates whether or not to reveal to Abraham his hidden plans for the cities of the plain. In 19:12–13 the mysterious visitors make known their destructive intentions to Lot, but his family greets the prediction skeptically: "wayĕhî kimṣaḥēq bĕʿênēy ḥătānāyw" (But he appeared to his sons-in-law to be jesting, 19:14). In the end, God's omniscience is vindicated by the absence of even ten righteous people for whose sake the city might have been saved.[35]

2.

Quoted direct speech plays many roles in the development of the plot in biblical narrative. Most frequently it functions temporally; quotations behave like many other types of repetition in retarding the action of the story and focusing attention on the present moment.[36] In the extensive quotations of Gen. 24:34–39 and 44:19–34, time is not only stopped but actually relived through the long and detailed flashbacks provided by Abraham's servant and by Judah, respectively. Unverifiable quotations may fill in a gap in the story at a later point in the narrative, as does the speech of the mysterious man in Gen. 37:17, telling Joseph where his brothers have gone. Or a quotation may raise the question of whether or not a particular speech-act even took place, as with David's alleged oath in 1 Kg. 1:13, 17, 30.

In this section our primary interest lies in the relationship of the quotation to other types of repetition in the chapter, and in the incorporation of quoted direct speech into the formal structure of the narrative. One example of this structural role can be found in Numbers 11, where the quotation in 11:13 is part of a redactional effort aimed at joining together two different stories. In chapter 3 it was noted that Moses' quotation in Num. 11:13 appears in the middle of a speech (vv. 11–15) that, according to most critics, combines elements of two originally distinct narrative traditions within 11:4–34. Verses 4–10, 13, 18–24a, 31–34 tell of the people's demand for meat and of God's bringing of the quail to both satisfy and punish that urge. Verses 11–12, 14–17, 24b–30, on the other hand, tell a story of Moses' dissatisfaction with being solely responsible for the people's welfare, and the dispensing of the divine spirit upon the seventy elders who will share the burdens of leadership in some unspecified way.[37] Within the structure of Moses' speech in 11:11–15, v. 13 has a unifying role, recalling through quotation the events of the quail story (vv. 4–6) in the new context of Moses' complaint about his solitary situation.

In order to fully understand its function, we must examine the quotation in light of the structure of the whole of Moses' speech (see fig. 1). Moses begins and ends his argument with references to God's mistreatment of him, in v. 11 (hărēʾōtā) and v. 15 (bĕrāʿātekā).[38] He asks why he has not found favor with God ("lāmâ lōʾ-māṣātî ḥēn bĕʿênêkā") and finishes by

Fig. 1

Num. 11:11–15

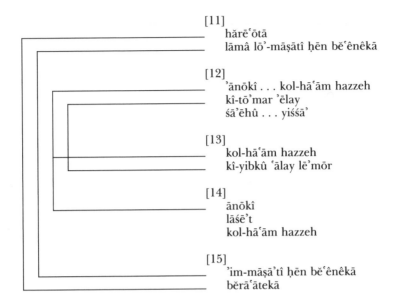

[11]
   hărē'ōtā
   lāmâ lō'-māṣātî ḥēn bĕ'ênêkā

[12]
   'ānōkî . . . kol-hā'ām hazzeh
   kî-tō'mar 'ēlay
   śā'ēhû . . . yiśśā'

[13]
   kol-hā'ām hazzeh
   kî-yibkû 'ālay lē'mōr

[14]
   ānōkî
   lāśē't
   kol-hā'ām hazzeh

[15]
   'im-māṣā'tî ḥēn bĕ'ênêkā
   bĕrā'ātekā

requesting that, if he has truly found favor in God's eyes ("'im-māṣā'tî ḥēn bĕ'ênêkā"), God should mercifully put him out of his misery. In v. 12 he complains that God has asked him to carry the people "like a nurse carries an infant" ("śā'ēhû . . . yiśśā'"), and in v. 14 he declares that he cannot bear the burden (*lāśē't*), for it has become too heavy for him. In both verses Moses refers to himself by means of the pronoun *'ānōkî*. At the center of the speech, in v. 13, Moses explains that he cannot sustain the people for the specific reason that he himself cannot produce the amount of food necessary to feed them. In 11:4–6 the people's complaint centers on the quality of the food they have—there is no meat, no variety. But in the context of Moses' speech the quotation takes on a quantitative aspect, implying that Moses cannot provide enough food by himself and cannot "carry" them as the ideal nourisher described in v. 12.[39] In addition to its role in synthesizing these two themes, v. 13 is also tied into the rest of the speech on a stylistic basis. In vv. 11, 12, 13, and 14, Moses describes the people as "kol-hā'ām hazzeh." Verses 11, 12, and 13 are all phrased as interrogatives, and in both 12 and 13 the question is followed with an explanatory clause beginning with *kî* and containing a quotation. In v. 12 Moses offers a hypothetical unverifiable quotation from God ("kî-tō'mar 'ēlay"), and in v. 13 he quotes the people's complaint first spoken in vv. 4–

6. Thus both in form and in content the quotation in v. 13 is well integrated into its present setting.

The attempt to bring the two stories together is not restricted to this short speech. A larger analogy can be drawn between the needs of Moses (assistance in leading) and those of the people (meat, other foods) under the rubric of diversification—of both leadership and diet.[40] The means by which the quail is brought (*rûaḥ*, 11:31), "wind," is also the term for essential "spirit" to be shared by the elders (vv. 17, 25, 26, 29). Both the manna and the spirit are gifts that descend from God (*Y-R-D*, vv. 9, 17, 25), and the use of the expression "hitqaddĕšû lĕmāḥār" (Sanctify yourselves for tomorrow, v. 18) in preparation for the arrival of the quail implies that this event, like the dispensing of the spirit, will be a holy one for the rest of the people (cf. Ex. 19:22; Josh. 3:5). In both stories the root '-S-P is used prominently, to indicate the fulfillment of the respective requests for meat and for assistance. The "riffraff" (*hā'asapsup*) who instigate trouble in v. 4 end up gathering quail in v. 32 (*wayya'aspû, 'āsap*). At God's command, Moses "gathers" the seventy elders (vv. 16, 24), who, after prophesying en masse, are rejoined with the rest of the people (*wayyē'āsēp*, v. 30), presumably to begin asserting their new authority. In the end, the composite nature of the narrative remains apparent to the critical eye, but the differences between the two traditions are partially overshadowed by their common concerns.

Quotation as a form of repetition and commentary is often a part of a larger, more elaborate plot structure, as was noted, for example, in the relationship of Judges 13 to the rest of the Samson cycle. In the next text to be discussed, quoted direct speech contributes to two different but complementary ways of schematizing the story. One is a synchronic, chiastic order, while the other is a diachronic reading with extensive parallelism between the first and second parts of the story. In this narrative in particular, both the fact of quotation and the theme and content of the quoted speech are of significance for understanding its discourse functions.

We noted earlier that the Shunammite woman quotes herself in 2 Kg. 4:28 to accuse Elisha of having deceived her and to persuade him to act on behalf of her child. Whatever fears she may have expressed in v. 16 seemed to have been allayed by the fulfillment of his promise in the following verse: "So the woman conceived and bore a son at the appointed time, as Elisha had declared to her." But as she expresses so forcefully in her quotation in v. 28, she sees the untimely death of her son in 4:20–21 as a betrayal of Elisha's word.

The quotation and her original speech in v. 16 are part of a chiastic enclosure at whose center are two deceptions:

A   "Don't deceive your handmaiden" (16)
  B   Deception of woman (death of child) (20)
  B'   Deception by woman (of husband) (22–23)
A'   "Didn't I say to you, 'Don't deceive me'?" (28)

While the woman is completely passive during the child's illness, the boy's death leads her to deceive her husband, brushing off his inquiry about her unexpected journey to Mt. Carmel with an evasive *šālôm* (v. 23).[41] As she has been deceived, so she must now practice deception in order to get to Elisha, which she does by denying that the death has really taken place. Instead of mourning the child, she places it in Elisha's room, where it will not be found. The careful closing of the door in 4:21 may have as much to do with preventing the life essence of the child from escaping as with maintaining secrecy.[42] In the same vein, the fact that she is unwilling to reveal the boy's condition to her husband and to Gehazi, and then does so only obliquely to Elisha in 4:28, may be related to this effort to forestall his death until Elisha can arrive to resuscitate him. Between vv. 16 and 28 a new side of the Shunammite woman emerges: strong, active on her own behalf, reinterpreting her earlier words to address the present moment of crisis.[43]

Verses 16–28 form the central section of a larger chiasm that embraces the entire story and sheds further light on the characterization of the woman (see fig. 2). Segments {A} and {A'} (vv. 8, 37) mark the perimeters of the story, recounting the initial and final encounters between Elisha and the Shunammite woman. The expressions describing her reactions to Elisha—"wattaḥăzeq-bô" (She prevailed upon him, v. 8) and "wattippōl ʿal-raglāyw" (She fell at his feet, v. 37)—are linked to each other by the description of her reaction in v. 27: "wattaḥazēq běraglāyw" (She caught hold of his feet). Only in this central encounter is there physical contact between these two characters; in the rest of the story they remain at arm's length. In v. 8, the verb *Ḥ-Z-Q* in the *hipʿil* has the unusual meaning of "to detain" or "to prevail upon," though it commonly connotes physical contact.[44] As such, the use of this particular root sets up the expectation of actual grasping that takes place in 4:27. At the end of the story the woman again refrains from contact, falling at his feet, but not holding fast to them. The use of the root *Ḥ-Z-Q* contributes to the depiction of the relationship between Elisha and the Shunammite. In the first part of the story (vv. 8–16), their behavior toward each other is very formal; she is summoned by Gehazi in v. 12 {C}, through whom Elisha speaks to her in v. 13, and in v. 15 she approaches no closer than the entrance to the room. After the promise of the child in v. 16 she deferentially refers to Elisha as "my lord," and to herself as "your handmaiden." In complete contrast to this for-

Fig. 2

2 Kg. 4:8–37—Chiastic Structure

{A}　Elisha and Woman; first meeting—"wattaḥāzeq-bô" (v. 8)
　{B}　Preparation of Elisha's room; "miṭṭâ; ʿ-L-H; Š-K-B" (10–11)
　　{C}　Elisha commands Gehazi: "qĕrāʾ laššûnammît hazzōʾt" (12)
　　　{D}　Gehazi speaks: "She has no child." (14)
　　　　{E}　Promise of Elisha: "kāʿēt ḥayyâ" (16a)
　　　　　{F}　Reaction of woman: "Don't deceive me." (16b)
　　　　　　{G}　Deception of woman (death of child); woman passive (20)
　　　　　　{G′}　Deception of husband (death of child); woman active (21–23)
　　　　　　{A″}　"wattaḥăzēq bĕraglāyw" (27)
　　　　　{F′}　Reaction of woman: "Don't deceive me" (quotation) (28)
　　　　{E′}　Oath of woman: "ḥay-YHWH wĕḥê-napšĕkā" (30)
　　　{D′}　Gehazi speaks: "The child has not awakened" (31)
　　{B′}　Use of Elisha's room; "miṭṭātô; ʿ-L-H; Š-K-B" (32–33)
　　{C′}　Elisha commands Gehazi: "qĕrāʾ ʾel-haššûnammît hazzōʾt" (36)
{A′}　Elisha and woman; final meeting—"wattippōl ʿal-raglāyw" (37)

mality is the close proximity and lack of decorum at their subsequent meeting in v. 27, where she pushes past Gehazi to confront Elisha directly.[45] She delivers the quotation in a physical and emotional posture so different from the context in which the original statement was spoken that the reader cannot fail to see the change in her personality. The structure of the chiasm also contrasts Elisha's promise of v. 16a {E} with the Shunammite's oath in v. 30 {E′}. Elisha promises life, "kāʿēt ḥayyâ," but after the death of the child, the woman swears by YHWH's "life" as well as by Elisha's ("ḥay-YHWH wĕḥê-napšĕkā") that she will not let go of him as he "abandons" her.[46] In her eyes, Gehazi is not a suitable substitute for Elisha, even though she accepted him as Elisha's emissary in 4:12–16. Only after Elisha himself restores the child can decorum also be restored; in v. 36 {C′} Elisha orders Gehazi to call the woman once more, and she again observes the distance between them.

This movement from formality to intimacy and back again aids in depicting the severity of the trauma experienced by the woman, contrasting her behavior at the moment of crisis with her more customary, formal manner before and after. This contrast, among other characterizing elements, is an essential part of a narrative strategy that tries to justify the woman's claim that Elisha is somehow liable in the death of the child (*years* after his original promise) and therefore responsible for doing everything in his power to revive him. In order to keep the focus on Elisha, the narrator has minimized the role of the husband. He seems to be powerless before his wife's requests (vv. 10, 23), and his involvement with the child is limited to three words in v. 19—"śāʾēhû ʾel-ʾimmô" (Carry him to his mother)—hardly expressive of deep concern. Correspondingly, the woman's reluctance to ask for anything from Elisha (v. 13) places the initiative for granting the child solely upon the man of God. Elisha's ignorance of what has transpired, stressed in 4:27, is contrasted with the woman's knowledge. As noted earlier, her words in 4:16 were most likely a nervous response to a startling prediction. But when she quotes those words in v. 28 she gives the impression of having had prescience; she knew something terrible would happen to the child and expressed her fears to Elisha even before its birth.[47] This makes Elisha's "blessing" seem like a rather reckless projection of his own assumptions about her desires. The granting of a child had no negative moral force in and of itself, but now the act of restoring the child to life carries with it a moral imperative that invests the story with meaning beyond the level of a simple miracle tale.[48]

The theme of deception highlighted by the quotation is developed further by another principle of organization in the narrative. In this schema the entire pericope of 4:8–37 can be read as two parallel series of events, the second duplicating the first but also building upon it in ways that change the nature of the story completely (see fig. 3). In {A} and {A′}, the Shunammite woman makes a request of her husband that she proceeds to act upon. In both cases these speeches are longer (and less cryptic) than all her other discourses. In section {B}, Elisha comes to the woman, but in {B′} she undertakes to travel to him, indicative of her aggressiveness in this part of the story. In {C} and {C′} Elisha orders Gehazi to speak to the woman on his behalf, both times asking after her general welfare.[49] Sections {D} and {D′} point out Elisha's limited perception; he is aware of some hidden problem but cannot determine its dimensions. While the woman's close-lipped response in v. 13 gives him no indication at all, her speech in v. 28 lets him know that something has happened to the child, even if Elisha does not know precisely what.[50] In sections {E} and {E′} Gehazi presents answers, both of which reflect a state of "childlessness" in the household—first, "She has no child" (v. 14), and then "The child has not awakened" (v. 31). In {F} and {F′} Elisha again commands Gehazi to call the woman, and in {G} and {G′} Elisha and the woman again face each other, initially for the promise of the birth of a child (which is fulfilled in v. 17), and finally for the gift of her revived son in v. 37. While the woman's response to the promise in v. 16 introduces a note of unease into the story, her silence in v. 37, coupled with her physical gestures of thanksgiving, bespeaks her complete satisfaction with the final outcome of that promise.[51]

Between these two longer consequences lies the account of the death of the child in vv. 18–21. In contrast to the rest of the story there is a minimal amount of dialogue; only the child's complaint, "My head, my head," and the father's command to bring him to his mother in v. 19

Fig. 3
2 Kg. 4:8–37—Parallel Structure

{A}   Woman and husband; request by woman involving Elisha (9–10)
 {B}   Elisha arrives at Shunem (11)
   {C}   Command to Gehazi: "qĕrā' laššûnammît hazzō't"
       (Elisha speaks through Gehazi) (12)
     {D}   Elisha and woman; hidden problem, Elisha ignorant (13)
       {E}   Gehazi speaks, answer given: no son (14)
         {F}   Command to Gehazi: "qĕrā'-lâ" (15)
           {G}   Elisha and woman: mother gains child (16–17)

Death of child (18–21) "wattisgōr ba'adô; miṭṭâ '-L-H; Š-K-B"	Servant carries child (*N-Ś-'*) mother leaves child (*wattēṣē'*)

{A'}   Woman and husband; request by woman involving Elisha (22–23)
 {B'}   Woman arrives at Mt. Carmel (25a)
   {C'}   Command to Gehazi: "hinnēh haššûnammît hallāz . . ."
       (Elisha speaks through Gehazi) ". . . rûṣ-nā' liqrā'tâ" (25b–26)
     {D'}   Elisha and woman: hidden problem, Elisha ignorant (27–30)
       {E'}   Gehazi speaks, answer given: child is dead (31)

	Resuscitation of child (32–35) "wayyisgōr . . . ba'ad šĕnêhem; miṭṭâ '-L-H; Š-K-B"	

       {F'}   Command to Gehazi: "qĕrā' 'el-haššûnammît hazzō't" (36a)
         {G'}   Elisha and woman: mother regains child:
                              mother carries child
                                    (*N-Ś-'*)
                              mother leaves with child
                              (*wattēṣē'*) (36b–37)

break the silence. Close attention to detail, particularly to the mother's actions, replaces the expected reporting of emotional reactions. As her language has been ambiguous, so her motives for bringing the child to Elisha's room are unclear. Is this an indication of her anger at Elisha for having deceived her, a statement of blame placed upon his bed? Or is it an expression of hope, that the man of God's miraculous power is somehow still contained in his room, in his bed?

The parallel structure draws attention to this central section and sheds light on the way the reader, too, is deceived by her words and by the story. According to the conventions of the annunciation story in the Bible, the reader expects the birth itself to appear either at the high point or at the denouement of the story.[52] But what happens in 2 Kg. 4:19–20 is a sudden and complete reversal of that expectation, in a way that appears to add a startling new conclusion to the story with the decease of the child. Yet the narrative continues, challenging even the finality of death. Verses 20–21 prove to be another deceptive ending, with a peripeteia so extreme that the reader is forced to reinterpret the nature of the story being told.[53] The birth of the child is no longer the essential miracle but merely a necessary precondition for the performance of Elisha's real feat, returning the child to life. The Shunammite's statement in v. 16—"Do not deceive your handmaiden"—anticipates the false ending of v. 17, just as her quotation in v. 28 anticipates Gehazi's lack of success in v. 31 (another false ending). Her reinterpretation of her own words also signals the reader to reevaluate her previous behavior in light of these new developments and to revise his judgment about Elisha's "good deed." But these deceptively temporary closures serve also to heighten the greatness of Elisha's achievement at the real end of the story. The actions and objects associated with the boy's death in vv. 20–21—ascending to the upper chamber, placing the child on Elisha's bed, closing the door—are all important elements of Elisha's efforts to revive him in vv. 32–35. Stylistically the two sections are similar, as once again no words are spoken, and the narrator presents a highly detailed, unemotional description of Elisha's ministrations. The remaining parallels involve the mother as well: As the dying child was carried to his mother at the father's command (v. 20, *śā'ēhû, wayyiśśā'ēhû*), she herself picks up her revived son at Elisha's request in vv. 36–37 (*śĕ'î, wattiśśā'*). In v. 21 she departed from the room without her son (*wattēṣē'*) in what proved to be a false ending to the story; at its true conclusion in v. 37 she again leaves the chamber (*wattēṣē'*), but with the child in her arms.[54]

In 2 Kg. 4:8–37 quoted direct speech functions on a number of different levels of discourse. It is an important part of a chiastic structure that focuses attention on deceptive activity within the plot. It is also a powerful means of dramatizing the change in the Shunammite woman's personality that develops as a result of Elisha's promise and the child's brush with death. On a thematic level, the idea of deception is not restricted to the woman's perceptions but extends to the use of false endings by which the reader is taken in as well. Most important, this analysis demonstrates how every aspect of the quotation—style, content, location, theme—is intimately tied to larger frameworks of composition that give shape and meaning to the narrative whole. Just as the Shunammite's quotation in 4:28 repeats and comments upon her own words, the repetition of the story pattern in vv. 22–37 is a reinterpretation of the prior account in 4:8–21 that sponsored it. Here quoted direct speech is a microcosmic paradigm of a text's ability to comment upon itself, to renew itself by transforming a birth story into a story of rebirth.

3.

In chapter 2 we commented briefly on a small number of quotations in which the narrator repeats words already spoken by a character, introduced with specific attribution to that character and with the verb '-*M-R*.[55] These are not true cases of quoted direct speech as we have defined it, since they are presented by the narrator only for the benefit of his implied audience and do not function on the level of story. On the other hand, they are explicit repetitions of attributed direct speech, as distinct from indirect speech or summary. Two of these instances, 1 Kg. 11:2 and 2 Kg. 14:6, quote legal traditions from Deuteronomy attributed to God as the bases for negative judgments against Solomon and Amaziah, respectively.[56] The considerable distance between source and quotation grants these repetitions something of a "reminding" or actualizing force for their audiences, allowing the repetition to function as the application of a legal precedent spoken long before.

Those texts in which a repeated speech occurs in the same pericope as its source are more complex and more interesting. There is no need to remind the reader of what was said for informational purposes, since the repetition follows immediately (1 Sam. 8:6; 1 Kg. 21:4) or soon after the original speech (Gen. 28:6; 1 Kg. 12:12). In each of these cases, the narrator's quotation shifts the point of view to that of the *listening* character, while at the same time commenting critically upon either the original speaker or the listener. This is most clearly illustrated in 1 Kg. 21:4, where, in a unique configuration, the narrator's quotation stands between the original speech of Naboth in v. 3 and its quotation by Ahab in v. 6. This medial position allows for the evaluation of three separate points of view—Naboth's, Ahab's, and the narrator's.

1 Kg. 21:2–3 (Naboth)	*21:4 (Narrator)*	*21:6 (Ahab)*
"Wayyō'mer nābôt 'el-'aḥ'āb:	"Wayyō'mer:	"Wayyō'mer:
ḥālîlâ lî mēYHWH mit-tittî	lō'-'ettēn lĕkā	lō'-'ettēn lĕkā
'et-naḥălat 'ăbōtay lāk"	'et-naḥălat'ăbôtāy"	'et-karmî"
(And Naboth said to Ahab: "God forbid that I sell you my patrimonial inheritance."	(And he said: "I will not sell you my patrimonial inheritance."	(And he said: "I will not sell you my vineyard."

The first part of the statement in v. 4, "lō'-'ettēn lĕkā," is repeated by Ahab in v. 6, while the second part, "'et-naḥălat 'ăbōtāy," preserves Naboth's original terminology from v. 3.

Although the narrator's presentation of the speech of his characters is generally reliable, there are not a few instances in which the narrator takes the liberty of presenting words that his character could never have said. David, in 1 Sam. 21:3, could not have persuaded Abimelech of the truth of his secret mission if he had not specified a location, but simply said, "'el-mĕqôm pĕlônî 'almônî" (to such-and-such a place). Here the narrator wishes to demonstrate that David is fabricating an excuse and that one place name would have been as good as the next.[57] Nor would an Israelite responding to Absalom in 2 Sam. 15:2 have said, "mē'aḥad šibṭê-yiśrā'ēl 'abdekā" (Your servant belongs to one of the tribes of Israel) without specifying which tribe, except that the narrator wants to emphasize the ongoing nature of Absalom's campaigning among people from a variety of tribes at the city gate.[58] In 1 Kg. 21:4 the narrator has also "tampered" with the speech of his character, conflating the actual speeches of two separate individuals. Verse 4 is interposed between the original speech (21:2–3) and the quoted direct speech in 21:6. As noted above, v. 6 reflects Ahab's point of view: His substitution of the word *kerem* in v. 6 and his omission of the oath formula "ḥālîlâ lî mēYHWH" reflect his bitterness over Naboth's refusal to sell him his vineyard. In v. 4, however, the quotation is told partly from the subjective perspective of the insulted Ahab and partly from the objective standpoint of the narrator. The quotation itself emphasizes on the one hand Ahab's feelings of personal humiliation by citing his reformulation in 21:6—"lō'-'ettēn lĕkā"—as the reason for his being "sullen and resentful." On the other hand, the narrator makes it very clear that Naboth's phrase "naḥălat 'ăbōtāy" is the official designation for the vineyard, as well as the principle of possession against which Ahab's reactions should have been judged. Ahab might be justifiably upset by Naboth's rejection of his offer—if it were only a matter of property, as he represents it in v. 6. But by stating that Ahab was perturbed by Naboth's refusal to sell his patrimonial inheritance, the narrator makes Ahab seem all the more childish and, in the end, all the more guilty.

In 1 Sam. 8:6 the narrator also repeats words just spoken in the previous verse, in a shortened, but otherwise accurate form:

1 Sam. 8:5	*1 Sam. 8:6*
"And they [the people] said to him: 'Behold, you have grown old, and your sons do not follow in your ways. Now appoint us a king to rule over us like all the nations.'"	"And Samuel was displeased that/when the people said:
	'Give us a king to rule over us.'"
("'attâ śîmâ-lānû melek lĕšopṭēnû kĕkol-haggôyim")	("tĕnâ-lānû melek lĕšopṭēnû")

The omissions, however, focus attention on the ambiguity of Samuel's reaction to the people's demand. Is he upset because God's leadership is being challenged, i.e., "give us a king (of flesh and blood) to rule us"? Or is his reaction more personal, resenting the rejection of his own leadership—"Give us a *king* to rule us (*lĕšopṭēnû*), not a *šôfēṭ*"?[59] Verse 6 represents Samuel's perceptions of what has just been said by the people, and the omission of the phrase *kĕkol-haggôyim* (like all the nations) suggests that the personal interpretation is more likely. Confirmation of this reading comes immediately in v. 7, as God rebukes Samuel for thinking that he, not God, is the rejected leader. As in 1 Kg. 21:4, the narrator's repetition here is an ostensibly objective version of the character's perceptions that is ultimately used to criticize his ideas as misperceptions.[60]

In Gen. 28:6, the narrator repeats Isaac's blessing of Jacob (28:1) as he depicts Esau's reaction to that blessing, in order to present his motivation for marrying an Ishmaelite woman. When taken as part of the pericope Gen. 27:46–28:9, the repetition carries with it no critical or ironic overtones. Jacob is blessed by his father and sent out to find a wife from his mother's side of the family; Esau naturally seeks out a mate from his paternal uncle. But when we read this section as part of a redacted whole that includes Gen. 27:1–45 as well, then Esau's behavior here seems more pathetic in light of his previous experience.[61] Esau has heard Jacob's words correctly, as shown by the narrator's literal repetition of the command "lō'-tiqqaḥ 'iššâ mibbĕnôt kĕnāʿan" (Do not marry a Canaanite woman) in 28:6. But just as he followed his father's instructions literally in the previous chapter and lost the blessing to his brother, Esau once again makes the wrong choice by taking a wife from the outcast Ishmaelite branch of the family. A further irony is that it was Esau's marriage to a Hittite woman in 26:34 that led to Jacob's being blessed and sent away; Esau is once again too late in trying to please his father.[62]

In the two remaining cases, the quotation is used by the narrator as an ironic comment on the speaker of the quote. In Jud. 21:18 the repetition of the oath sworn in 21:1 points up the pseudo-legality of the scheme to circumvent it and ridicules the "fight first, think later" mentality of the tribal alliance against the Benjaminites.[63] By reading the oath literally, wives are not "given" (*N-T-N*, v. 22), but rather "caught" (*Ḥ-Ṭ-P*, v. 21) or "stolen" (*G-Z-L*, v. 23). In 1 Kg. 12:12 the narrator repeats the command Rehoboam made to the people in 12:5 just prior to the king's announcement of policies stricter than those of his father. The quotation draws attention to the people's obedience as an ironic counterpoint to the king's fear that he can ensure their loyalty only by enforcing servitude.[64]

In summary, repetitions of direct speech by the narrator inform the reader of a shift in point of view, while also criticizing the limitations of that point of view. The closer in time and distance the narrator's repetition is to the original statement, the more likely it is meant to highlight the listener's understanding (1 Sam. 8:6; 1 Kg. 21:4). Conversely, the greater the distance between the two, the greater the emphasis upon the speaker of the quote (Jud. 21:18; 1 Kg. 12:12). As with other types of repetition, the narrator is not bound to repeat his source literally, though he may do so with effect (Gen. 28:6). The infrequency of quotations that show the internal reactions of the listener reflects a general tendency on the part of the narrator to summarize the thoughts of his characters rather than present them in direct speech.[65] The scarcity of repeated quotes that draw attention to the speaker is due to the fact that the narrator's citations are considered reliable and need no further verification—since the source of that verification could only be the narrator himself. As we noted above, some of these quotations seem to be needlessly repetitious, but the poetics of repetition in biblical narrative are not yet as clear as we would like, and different, conflicting aesthetics may be present even within the same text.

4.

Unverifiable quotations pose an interesting discourse problem in that they frequently present new information whose veracity the reader must evaluate without the assistance of an earlier locution. The question of the authenticity of such quotations is important because of the relatively high proportion of false unverifiable citations: Out of thirty-seven unverifiable quotations in thirty-two speeches, there are ten deliberate lies in seven speeches. By contrast, the corpus of ninety-four verifiable quotations contains only two cases of falsification (Gen. 3:1; Ex. 32:24), and even in these texts the quotation bears some resemblance to the original speech. This difference is the inevitable result of the absence of a specific prior speech against which the unverifiable quote can be measured. While verifiable quoted direct speech allows for a wide range of more or less accurate repetitions (with at least some degree of truth in most), unverifiable quotations tend to be either true or false with very little shading in between. In comparison with the subtlety of a deceptive verifiable quotation like Gen. 3:1, fabricated unverifiable quotes are usually obvious lies, as in Josh. 9:11; 1 Sam. 19:17, 21:3; and 2 Kg. 5:22.

On the level of discourse it could be said that all quoted direct speech is unverifiable, since, in both the original speech and the quotation, the reader has only the narrator's presentation of the character's words. But it is still essential for the reader to assess the authenticity of unverifiable quotations within the framework of the story. Most commonly, the narrator will confirm or deny the citation by means of the context. Abimelech's accusation that Sarah deceived him by claiming that she was Abraham's sister with the words "'āḥî hû'" (Gen. 20:5b) is rendered believable by the verifiability of Abraham's analogous quotation in the first half of 20:5—"'āḥôtî hî'" (She is my sister)—as well as by Abraham's own confession in v. 13.[66] By contrast, Gehazi's lie to Naaman in 2 Kg. 5:22 is set against the extended description of Elisha's refusal in 5:16, as well as the inside view of Gehazi's plan in 5:21.[67] The story is a paean to Elisha's powers of clairvoyance; Naaman hears the lie spoken but assumes it to be true, while Elisha recognizes its falseness, despite the fact that he was not present. The nature or role of the quoter can also be a significant factor. In Num. 11:20, the identity of the speaker—YHWH—renders the quotation believable, as is also the case with Moses' quote of God's words in Ex. 33:12b: "Yet you have said, 'I know you by name, and you have also found favor in my eyes.'" On the other hand, because prophets quoting oracles from YHWH are generally reliable, the narrator in 1 Kg. 13:18 must add the comment "kiḥēš lô" (He lied to him) in order to ensure the perceptibility of the lie. The quotation may also be proven false by being completely uncharacteristic of the speaker to whom it is assigned, as, for example, the harsh words Michal ascribes to David in 1 Sam. 19:17.

In his encounter with verifiable quotations, the reader has become accustomed to being in a privileged position, knowing at least as much as, and probably more than, the quoting character. This situation is reversed with unverifiable quotations, and the character has the upper hand. Since in most cases the narrator will indicate to the reader whether the quote is true or fictitious, there is no confusion of point of view. But in at least four instances the narrator does not provide complete clarification, and the reader is left with a more ambiguous perspective. For example, Joseph's brothers' quotation in Gen. 50:17 was likely an invention of their own devising, but the narrative leaves open the possibility that it may have actually taken place. In this text, the presence of ambiguity adds little, if anything, to the story. But the uncertainty that surrounds the remaining quotations, all of which occur in the Succession Narrative, is very much in keeping with the narrator's ambivalent presentation of many of his characters.[68] In 2 Sam. 15:8, when Absalom says to David, "For your servant swore when I lived in Geshur in Aram, saying, 'If YHWH will surely return me to Jerusalem, I will worship YHWH,'" are we to believe that Absalom actually swore such an oath, when his obvious intention in going to Hebron was to begin his uprising? While the excuse is apparently plausible to David, that he finds it acceptable may be a comment on the king's lack of awareness of Absalom's intentions. Although the truth of the quotation remains uncertain, its importance is quickly overshadowed by a far greater breach of confidence, Absalom's rebellion itself.

In 2 Sam. 16:3 and 19:27 there are two competing unverifiable quotations that offer mutually exclusive truth claims, neither of which is clearly confirmed by the narrator. In 16:3 Ziva, Mephiboshet's servant, accuses his master (in his absence) of going over to Absalom's side for the alleged purpose of regaining his father's throne. After the rebellion is put down, Mephiboshet claims that Ziva lied and that his sympathies lay entirely with David (19:27). On the one hand, Ziva's claims are accepted by David in 16:4, as he grants to the servant everything that belonged to the master. On the other, the narrator's comment in 19:25 about Mephiboshet's personal hygiene during the rebellion supports the idea that he was truly "in mourning" for David.[69] In addition, the excuse of his lameness is very reasonable, rendering unlikely Ziva's suggestion that his master was seeking after power. But again, David clearly has his doubts; the most he will do is to split the former royal estate between master and servant (19:30). The characters and the narrator know the truth of their claims, but the reader is never given enough information to be certain. In the final analysis both reveal their opportunism in the calculated way in which each approaches David—Ziva with gifts (16:1), and Mephiboshet unwashed and unchanged (19:25) and praising David to the heavens (19:31)—so that the ambiguity of their claims makes it somehow appropriate that they should end up as partners.[70]

The final case of a questionable unverifiable quotation revolves around David's alleged oath to Bathsheba promising Solomon's succession in 1 Kg. 1:17, 24, 30. We noted above how Nathan and Bathsheba "reminded" David of his oath, in order to compel him to act on Solomon's behalf.[71] The first part of the story makes enough of a point of the king's infirmity (1:1–4, 15) so that even David's own attestation of the validity of the oath in v. 30 remains suspect in the eyes of the reader. Whereas the characters in the previous example were aware of the truth or falsehood of their claims, we are left in doubt about the accuracy of David's memory and the degree to which he (and we) have been manipulated by Nathan and Bathsheba. In spite of the divine promise in 2 Samuel 7, one sees the extent to which human interests control the choice of the king. As David's power declines following Nathan's condemnation in 2 Sam. 12:7–14, it is fitting that Nathan figures strongly in the choice of his successor as well.[72]

The importance of ambiguity as a narrative strategy in the Bible is being studied more and more, as it becomes more apparent that the reader's knowledge seriously affects the way he interprets the text.[73] When the reader knows no more than the character (e.g., no more than

David in 2 Sam. 16:4), such ambiguity is manifested simultaneously on the level of story (what does David think of Ziva's claim?) and on the level of discourse (how does the reader respond to Ziva's quotation, and further, how does the reader evaluate David's response?). In each of the cases from the Succession Narrative the questionable unverifiable quotation is used to show a profound ambivalence about David's knowledge and judgment, for in each case he must act upon his evaluations. In 2 Sam. 15:8 his decision nearly costs him the throne; in 1 Kg. 1:30 his acceptance of Nathan's reminder preserves it for Solomon. Both acts raise serious questions about his ability to rule Israel.

CONCLUSIONS

As a form of dialogical expression, that is, as speech within speech, the quotation brings one set of words into contact and/or conflict with another. The speaker of the quote engages in a temporal dialogue between past and present, as well as in an interpersonal encounter with his fellow characters; his relationship to his audience in the story is revealed in the way he uses the quotation to evoke a response, verbal or otherwise. This relationship is not a simple one of true and false telling. While the presentation of lies is rare in quoted direct speech, neither do characters necessarily tell "the whole truth" when they quote prior speech, and, in fact, a high percentage of quotations fall within this gray area.

The reader's awareness of truth and half-truth is encouraged by the "repetitious" aspect of quotation as well. Verifiable quoted direct speech is a type of deliberate repetition whose identity as repeated speech allows the reader to compare its initial and subsequent formulations in a uniquely controlled environment. While we have frequently found similarity of language between the original statement and its quotation, we have also noted the power of context to transform the meaning of the quotation regardless of its fidelity to the original words. In this light, small variations in language and the omission of words or clauses may take on a significance far beyond their size in reshaping the meaning of the quotation.

This study has drawn attention to a particular mode of direct speech, as well as to the contrast between direct and indirect address. Direct speech must be approached as a type of discourse whose nature and usage are distinct from narration, but whose interaction with that narrative voice is of great significance for understanding the dynamics of the text.[1] The study of repetitive forms should strive to isolate distinct tropes such as quoted direct speech, in order to understand the effect of each mode of repetition upon the poetics of the whole. At the same time, it is essential to see such individual features against the background of the plenitude of repetitive styles in biblical narrative, in order to better understand the dynamic of the text as a whole.

Regarding the relationship between quotation and variation in repetition, it would be valuable for future studies to contrast the use of quoted direct speech in the texts we have studied with the conventions of postexilic biblical narrative and Intertestamental literature as well. Y. Hoffmann has suggested a historical connection with various levels of literalness in repetition. In his schema, verbatim repetition as found in the Ugaritic materials and in other ancient Near Eastern literary texts represents an early (eighteenth to fourteenth centuries B.C.E.) artistic norm from which biblical narrative liberates itself by introducing greater variation in repetition (tenth to seventh centuries B.C.E.) The final stage of this liberation process is the eventual disappearance of repetition in late biblical narrative, such as Esther and Jonah, though Hoffman himself admits that a text like Daniel is a problematic exception to his plan.[2] The temporal aspects of this thesis should be examined in conjunction with a full study of the types of repetition in Late Biblical Hebrew, with special attention to the conventions of repetition in Genesis–2 Kings. An examination of the use of quotations within this period (quoted direct speech and other types) would be a necessary concomitant.

In addition, greater attention should be paid to the types and functions of repetition in ancient Near Eastern literature. There seem to have been different standards for looser or stricter repetition in Old Babylonian and Assyrian recensions of the same literary text, and the resulting changes may produce very different meanings.[3] Here too, the study of the use of quotations may prove enlightening about the dynamics of that literature, as well as about its relationship to biblical narrative.

Our analysis of the functions of quoted direct speech on the complementary levels of story and discourse has revealed the overwhelming importance of different degrees of knowledge—of the narrator, the characters, and the reader—and the types of effects gained by exploiting the discrepancies and concinnities among the three points of view. The continuum of awareness displays at one end the overt contrast of truth to falsehood, as in Gen. 3:1, 3 or in Gen. 50:17 and other ambiguous unverifiable quotations. More commonly with verifiable quotations, there is a finely graded scale moving from repetition to reinterpretation, as in texts like Gen. 18:13, Num. 11:13, 1 Kg. 21:6, 2 Kg. 4:28, as well as quotations repeated by the narrator. The interplay of these various levels of cognition weaves together story and discourse as it pits the quoter against his audience in the text, and against the reader outside the story.

Because of the reader's access to both the original speech and its repetition, the whole notion of recontextualization is of great importance in quoted direct speech. Although the quoted words take on meaning ascribed to them by their new context, they still retain some autonomy as identifiable prior direct speech, which carries within it some of the sense of its original context. For example, the quotation of the women's song for David and Saul (1 Sam. 18:7) by the Philistines in 21:12 and 29:5 recontextualizes a song of praise and victory into a warning about its hero. Despite his valor (or perhaps because of it), David's faithfulness is called into question. Even in 18:8–9, Saul takes it as a threat to his own position, and it leads to David's being cast out, as he is again in 21:15–16 and 29:6–7. As repetition, each time the song is recalled the negative result for David is the same; as reinterpretation, however, the quotation reflects a change. Each recurrence shows David siding more with his enemy, first seeking asylum from Saul (21:11) and then preparing to fight against him (29:1–11). Or it might be argued that the quotation of the song in 29:5 is opposed to the contextual meaning of both 18:7 and 21:12. On the earlier occasions the song poses a threat to David's life. But ironically in 29:5, the quotation preserves David by being the excuse for his dismissal from the battlefield by the Philistines.[4] The meaning of the quotation is to be found somewhere between the original context and its quoted setting, drawing upon elements of both contexts, yet never fully aligned with either.[5]

It has long been recognized that one segment of the Bible may comment upon and reinterpret another, to the extent that one can speak about a process of inner-biblical *midrash*.[6] Legal traditions such as the Decalogue are taken up by Hosea and Jeremiah in the context of judgments against the people (Hos. 4:2; Jer. 7:9). The same two prophets also make use of the patriarchal traditions about Jacob for similar purposes (Hos. 12:3–5, 13–14; Jer. 9:3). Later prophets may reinterpret the words of their predecessors, as with Daniel's famous re-reckoning of Jeremiah's 70-year oracle (Jer. 25:9–12; 29:10) to cover a period of 70 "weeks of years," or sabbatical cycles, making a total of 490 years (Dan. 9:24).[7] N. M. Sarna has demonstrated how Psalm 89 is a commentary upon the promise of the Davidic covenant in 2 Sam. 7.[8] M. Fishbane sees these and other reworkings of older materials as signposts of an "exegetical consciousness" whose concern is the revitalization of revelation within the context of an ongoing tradition of interpretation. He distinguishes between three modes of aggadic exegesis.[9] In the first, the past is quoted in order to be repudiated and replaced by a new vision, as in Jeremiah's rejection of vicarious punishment in 31:28–29: "In those days they will no longer say, 'The fathers have eaten sour grapes, and the children's teeth are set on edge.'"[10] The second type interprets the events of the present hour as entirely congruent with, or as a continuation of, the salvific experience of the past. This is most often accomplished by means of analogy, e.g., the allusions to the Exodus in Is. 11:11–16 and Mic. 7:14–20, but quotations may also be employed, as in Jer. 16:14–15 //

23:7–8.[11] The most appropriate counterpart to this in the narrative literature we have discussed is the repeated quotations of the promise to the patriarchs.

The third type of transformation "is actually a reformulation of memory itself."[12] While Fishbane is referring to the kind of historical and theological rereading of the past done by the Chronicler, this mode is also appropriate for many of the examples of quoted direct speech that we have discussed. In a certain sense, quoted direct speech reflects a similar "exegetical consciousness" within earlier biblical narrative, though not necessarily fraught with the theological significance it has in legal and prophetic texts. For not only is quoted direct speech used to apply the words of one narrative text to another across a span of time (e.g., Jud. 11:17, 19), but a tradition of the reinterpretation of the spoken word exists *within the pericope itself* and directly affects the way we read these smaller units of narrative. A text such as 2 Kg. 4:8–37 demonstrates both the character's reinterpretation of her own words and the ability of the narrative to invest itself with new and different meanings in the course of its unfolding. If the earliest forms of midrash are found in the exegetical patterns of the prophets, the Deuteronomist, and the Chronicler,[13] the roots of the midrashic process itself are to be located in the self-conscious patterns of repetition and reinterpretation found in quoted direct speech and other forms of deliberate repetition in biblical narrative.

APPENDIX
Quoted Direct Speech in Deuteronomy

Deuteronomy contains some forty examples of quoted direct speech, nearly all of which are quoted by Moses within the series of long addresses that make up the bulk of the book.[1] The introductory *verba dicendi* for these quotations follow patterns described in chapter 2: One-half of the texts employ a finite form of the verb '-M-R; most of the remaining cases use another verb of introduction, such as *D-B-R* (1:6) or *Ṣ-W-H* (1:16), in conjunction with the infinitive *lēʾmōr*. Only rarely is finite '-M-R followed by *lēʾmōr* (1:9). These verbs appear in the *paʿal* form or the converted *yipʿal* form, denoting past speech. The breakdown of the different configurations of quoter, original speaker, and listener is roughly similar to that of quoted direct speech in other books: twenty-two quotations follow the pattern XYZ, twelve are XXY, and six are XYY. There are no narrator-sponsored quotations in Deuteronomy, primarily because Moses is so active as a narrator. In half the examples, Moses quotes God's words to the people—e.g., 1:6–8; 2:2–7; 3:2; etc.—and these account for the greatest number of XYZ quotations. The XYY quotations, such as 1:14, 22a, 27–28, 41, etc., repeat the words of the people whom Moses is addressing, and occur mostly within chapter 1. The XXY quotations show Moses quoting his own words to the people, either as part of a dialogue with them (1:9–13, 29–33) or with God (3:25; 9:26–29), or simply as a description of his own previous words and actions (1:16–17; 2:27–29; 3:18–20). There are also two instances of quotation within quoted direct speech. In 1:27–28, Moses quotes the people quoting the spies: "You complained in your tents, saying, ' . . . Our kinsmen have made our hearts melt, saying, "The people are greater and taller than we; the cities are great and fortified up to heaven; and moreover, we have seen the sons of the Anakim there." ' " In 1:39a, Moses quotes God quoting the people: " 'Moreover your little ones, about whom you said "They will become a prey." . . . ' " Deuteronomy also contains a large number of anticipatory "quotations," often spoken with a hypothetical or negative tone (e.g., 8:17; 9:4), but that fall outside our definition of quotation as prior speech.[2]

Most of the quotations in Deuteronomy occur in the course of Moses' retelling of Israel's life immediately after the Exodus, including the wanderings in the desert (1:6–3:29), his account of Israel at Sinai (4:9–5:28), and his version of the story of the golden calf and its aftermath in 9:8–10:11. In two of the above speeches, a series of quotations is followed by the term *ʿattâ* (4:1; 10:12) and the characteristic shift to the present moment of address, clarifying the rhetorical function of the citations: In 1:6–3:29 Moses uses quotation to set up his presentation of laws and rules in 4:1ff.; his recounting of Israel's apostasy in 9:8–10:11

serves as a preface to his exhorting the people in 10:12ff. to remain faithful to YHWH.

Occasionally, quoted direct speech is used in the presentation of legal material. In 17:16, an unverifiable quotation from YHWH, prohibiting Israel from returning to Egypt, is part of the injunction against a king's freedom to multiply horses.[3] Two quotations in 18:16–20 are used to explain the rationale behind the Deuteronomic idea of the prophetic office. In 19:7 Moses repeats his own words outlining the establishment of the cities of refuge (19:2), after explaining their purpose in the intervening verses. The most noteworthy example of a quotation of a legal text is Moses' rehearsal of the entire Decalogue in 5:6–18. Here the quotation is at once a reminder to the people of their obligations to God and a preface to Moses' delivery of "the teaching, the statutes and the ordinances which the Lord your God has commanded me to teach you," mentioned in 6:1 and developed in chapters 12–26. By means of the quotations immediately following the Decalogue in 5:21–28, Moses establishes his authority to impart such commandments.[4]

Quotations in Deuteronomy have a number of characteristics that are quite different from their counterparts in biblical narrative, and that reveal something of their literary functions. While verifiable quotations in narrative usually occur in the same pericope as the original speech, this holds true in only one case in Deuteronomy—19:7 quoting 19:2. Moreover, the status of this text is complicated by the fact that both the source and the quotation occur in the very same speech by Moses. The use of the participial introduction *měṣawwěkā* (which I command you) lends to the quotation more of a reiterative quality, rather than conveying a sense of words recovered from an earlier context. The "present tense" sense of the entire book of Deuteronomy adds background and depth to the use of the participle, as do the temporal aspects of the pericope in 19:2–7. While this law is future oriented, anticipating the occupation of the land (note also the participial form *nōtēn* in v. 2), the recapitulatory quote of the beginning of the law in 19:7 pulls the reader back into the present—"Because of what *will* transpire, I *now* command you. . . . " To the extent that this is really an instance of verifiable quoted direct speech, it lacks that tension between the original setting of the words and their recontextualized meaning which is characteristic of most quotations.

Equally rare are cases of quoted direct speech in which the original statement is found outside the pericope but within the boundaries of the book of Deuteronomy. In the context of prescribing the type of prophetic leadership that will be necessary after his death, Moses, in 18:16, quotes the people's expression of their fear of death in the face of the revelation at Sinai, as well as their request that Moses should converse with God in their stead (5:21–24). These references are followed in 18:17 by his quote of God's approval of the people's initiative (5:25), leading into the promise that God will continue to raise up such an intermediary to guide the people after their entry into the land (18:18–20). While it is not uncommon to find Deuteronomy (and other legal texts) referring to earlier narrated events, such as the Exodus, in legal motivation clauses,[5] only here is verifiable quoted direct speech used to provide a historical or situational justification for such a law. The speech in 18:16 is very similar in language to 5:22 and displays characteristic shortening by omitting 5:23–24 completely. The quotation in 18:17 shows a similar combination of abridgment of and fidelity to 5:25, but the continuation of God's speech in 18:18–20 is a striking addition to the original. Whereas in 5:25 God simply agreed to Moses' appointment as mediator, in 18:18–20 this agreement serves as a precedent, justifying the role of future leaders who will succeed Moses. The quotation begins with the past, referring to a time preceding Moses' present speech, but its concern is not truly with that present moment. It is ultimately directed at a post-Mosaic era, which itself will look back upon the words of Moses for direction.[6]

It must be remembered that the temporal relationship between chapters 5 and 18 is closer than might first be expected, because both are part of a continuous address to Israel by Moses, beginning in Deut. 1:6 and extending through nearly the entire book. The dependency of 18:16–20 on 5:20–25 is not truly a relationship of quotation to original speech; it is rather one of a quotation to an earlier quotation, the source of which lies outside the borders of Deuteronomy, perhaps in Ex. 20:16 or in a similar account that has not come down to us.[7] Moses requotes what he already quoted once as a theological rationale for the prophet who is to replicate Moses' own position as a go-between—a quoter—for God and Israel. Robert Polzin makes an even more sweeping narrative claim about the function of this quotation in relation to the narrative voice of the Deuteronomic History:

> The "prophet like Moses" is the narrator of the Deuteronomic History, and through him, the Deuteronomist himself. The Deuteronomist uses Moses to explain by a hortatory lawcode the wide-ranging implications of the Decalogue; this same author will soon be using the Deuteronomic narrator to explain in an exemplary history the wide-ranging implications of that lawcode.[8]

On a story level, Moses' quotation of the Decalogue in 5:6–18, of his appointment by the people and by God in 5:20–27, and of God's command in 5:28 ("But you remain here with me, and I will give you the entire Instruction"), establishes his authority to be a lawgiver in chapters 12–26. But on the level of discourse, the quotation in 18:16–20 sets the stage for the interpretation of history in light of that Instruction, which is developed in Joshua–2 Kings.

The only other instances in which a quotation in Deuteronomy might be verified by another text in that book are Moses' quotations of God's refusal to allow him to enter the land in Deut. 1:37; 3:26–28; 31:2. What is striking here is the fact that the original statements of this decree (32:48–52, 34:4) are located at a *later* point in the book than the quotations themselves. This reversal upsets our understanding of verifiable quoted direct speech as a reflection of the time-continuum of narrative, and raises the question of whether these quotations are meant to be verified at all, an issue to which we will shortly return.

The remaining quotations have no referents within Deuteronomy, and fall into three categories:

1. Quotations whose potential sources exist in similar language outside the book, usually in Exodus or Numbers. There are two cases of verbatim repetition: Deut. 1:39b quoting Num. 14:31, and Deut. 3:2 quoting Num. 21:34. But the majority show some variation in language without a radical change in meaning, e.g., Deut. 1:41 quoting Num. 14:40; Deut. 2:26 quoting Num. 2:21.[9] On the fringes of this category are quotations like Deut. 5:21–24 quoting Ex. 20:18, and Deut. 9:26–29 quoting Ex. 32:11–13, both of which paraphrase the Exodus accounts to a greater extent and include some different material as well.

2. Quotations whose possible sources in Exodus or Numbers use direct speech but with dissimilar language and frequently with different meaning. Deut. 1:9–13, for example, concerns itself with Moses' delegation of authority, but its language is very unlike that of Ex. 18:18ff. In Exodus, Jethro tells Moses himself to appoint such leaders, while in Deuteronomy Moses instructs the people to

perform the task. The ideas expressed in Deut. 1:35–36, 37–39—the death of the desert generation excluding Caleb and Joshua—are similar to those found in Num. 14:22–24, 28–34, and 32:11–12. But apart from an occasional word or phrase in common (and the above-mentioned quote of God's quotation of the people in 1:38b), the two versions are more divergent than nearly any two speeches we have compared in narrative quoted direct speech.[10] According to the canons of verifiability discussed above, quotations in this category are functionally unverifiable despite the existence of earlier formulations.

3. Quotations that have no counterpart in direct speech in Exodus or Numbers, i.e., unverifiable quotations as defined above. For example, Deut. 1:14 quotes a positive response by the people that is not to be found in either Ex. 18 or Num. 11. Moses' speech about passing through the land of the Edomites in 2:2–7 is at variance with Num. 20:14–21, and the traditions about the Moabites and the Ammonites in Deut. 2:9, 17–19 are not present in Numbers. Moses' investiture of Joshua in Num. 27:15–23 is accomplished without the direct speech quoted by Moses in Deut. 3:20–22. Further examples of such unverifiable quotations are found in Deut. 1:6–8, 22, 29–33; 2:13, 24–25, 31; 3:23–25; 4:10; 5:25; 9:23.

What is the significance of such a large concentration of unverifiable quotations in the narrative portions of Deuteronomy, and the concomitant scarcity of verifiable quotations here and in the rest of the book? It would appear that the idea of verifiability in Deuteronomy is different from that of other books, in which quotation and original statement are compared for accuracy. In this sense Deuteronomy is essentially self-referential, and the authenticity of its quotations depends *not* upon comparison with prior speech but upon the authoritative voice who quotes them, that is, Moses. While a third-person narrative voice frames the book in 1:1–5 and 34:1–12, and occasionally makes itself felt elsewhere as well,[11] it is Moses who speaks for both God and Israel throughout the book. Only twice are the voices of other human characters heard, and even then they are in unison with Moses: In 27:1–8 Moses and the elders speak to the people, and in 27:9–10 Moses and the levitical priests do the same. Throughout the first thirty chapters of Deuteronomy, God's words are heard only when quoted by Moses (1:6–8, 35–36, etc.). Only toward the end of the book, when God's ultimate control over Moses is expressed in speeches that announce Moses' death (31:14; 32:48–52; 34:4), does the privilege of quoting divine speech revert to the impersonal narrator.

Moses' narrative voice has such overwhelming authority in Deuteronomy that it is capable of authenticating all its quotations, regardless of the presence or absence of an earlier "verifying" speech act. His quotation of the Decalogue in 5:6–18 does not direct the reader to turn back to Ex. 20:1–14 to look for discrepancies that might show deliberate change on Moses' part, thereby revealing something about Moses' person. On the contrary, the quotation of God's voice enhances the authority of the speaker and establishes his credibility in preparation for his dictation of an additional set of commandments in chapters 12–26, to which only he was privy. The roles of "quoter" and lawgiver come together in Deuteronomy in such a unique way that from this perspective, too, the narrator affirms that "never again did there arise in Israel a prophet like Moses" (34:10).[12]

ABBREVIATIONS

ANET	*Ancient Near Eastern Texts Related to the Old Testament,* ed. James B. Pritchard
AV	*Authorized Version*
BDB	*A Hebrew and English Lexicon of the Old Testament,* ed. Frances Brown, Samuel R. Driver, Charles A. Briggs
BZAW	*Beihefte zur Zeitschrift für die alttestamentliche Wissenschaft*
CBQ	*Catholic Biblical Quarterly*
CBQMS	Catholic Biblical Quarterly Manuscript Series
GKC	*Gesenius' Hebrew Grammar,* ed. E. Kautsch, trans. A. E. Cowley
HUCA	*Hebrew Union College Annual*
ICC	International Critical Commentaries
JAAR	*Journal of the American Academy of Religion*
JAOS	*Journal of the American Oriental Society*
JBL	*Journal of Biblical Literature*
JCS	*Journal of Cuneiform Studies*
JJS	*Journal of Jewish Studies*
JPS	*The Holy Scriptures,* Jewish Publication Society, 1917
JQR	*Jewish Quarterly Review*
JSOT	*Journal for the Study of the Old Testament*
LXX	Septuagint
MT	Masoretic Text
NAB	*New American Bible*
NEB	*New English Bible*
NJPS	New Jewish Publication Society translation of *The Torah,* 2d ed., 1967; *The Prophets (Nevi'im),* 1978; and *The Writings (Kethuvim),* 1982
OTS	*Oudtestamentische Studien*
RSV	*Revised Standard Version*
SBL	Society of Biblical Literature
VT	*Vetus Testamentum*
VTSup	*Vetus Testamentum Supplements*
ZAW	*Zeitschrift für die alttestamentliche Wissenschaft*

NOTES

1. Repetition and Quotation in Biblical Narrative

1. Literally "dibběrâ tôrâ kilšôn běnē ʾādām," an exegetical principle associated with R. Yishmael in the Rabbinic period. While Ibn Ezra does not use precisely this language, the phrase reflects a tradition of interpretation about repetition that informed the discussions of Ibn Ezra, David Kimḥi, and other traditional Jewish exegetes. In an ongoing debate with the school of R. Akiba as to whether or not the repetition of a word imputes more than one meaning to a verse—e.g., rāʾōh tirʾeh (1 Sam. 1:11; Berakot 31b) or hikkārēt tikkārēt (Num. 15:31; Sanhedrin 64b)—R. Yishmael held that such repetitions were purely stylistic in nature. Cf. J. N. Epstein, *Mevoʾot Lassifrut Hattannaʾim* (Jerusalem, 1975), pp. 522ff.; A. J. Heschel, *Torah min Hashamayim Beʾaspeqlariyah shel Haddorot* (New York, 1957), pp. 3–12. While most cases deal with the repetition of the same word or root, there is also discussion of interchangeable synonyms in *Midrash Tehillim* 9:7; *Sifrei Bammidbar*, Nasoʾ, section 23.

2. Ibn Ezra on Ex. 20:1; compare his comments on Ex. 18:21; 32:9; Deut. 5:5; 24:16. See also his *Yesod Moraʾ*, chapter 1, *Kitvei Avraham Ibn Ezra*, vol. 2 (Jerusalem, 1970).

3. David Kimḥi on Gen. 24:39. Cf. also his note on 32:13.

4. Umberto Cassuto, "Biblical and Canaanite Literature," in *Biblical and Oriental Studies*, vol. 2 (Jerusalem, 1975), pp. 29–32. Cf. also "The Israelite Epic," pp. 77–79.

5. Nehama Leibowitz, *ʿIyyunim Ḥadashim Besefer Shemot* (Jerusalem, 1954), p. 72, n. 4.

6. Idem, *ʿIyyunim Besefer Bereshit* (Jerusalem, 1968), p. 295. See also her article "Keitsad Liqroʾ Pereq Battanakh," in *Nefesh Veshir* (Jerusalem, 1954), pp. 90–104.

7. See above, n. 1; Isaac Heinemann, *Darkei Haʾaggadah* (Jerusalem, 1954), pp. 12, 96–97.

8. See the now classic comparison of biblical and Homeric styles by Erich Auerbach, *Mimesis* (Princeton, 1953), pp. 3–23.

9. Meir Sternberg, "Mivneh Haḥazarah Bassippur Hammiqraʾi," *Hassifrut* 25 (1977): 109–50, esp. pp. 110–20. Sternberg has written extensively on the role of gaps and gap-filling in his studies of 2 Sam. 11 (Menahem Perry and Meir Sternberg, "Hammelek Bemabbaṭ ʾIroni," *Hassifrut* 1 [1968]:263–92) and Gen. 34 ("ʾIzzun ʿAdin Bassippur ʾOnes Dina," *Hassifrut* 4 [1973]:193–231). On the question of overt judgments by the narrator, see the debate between Perry and Sternberg on one hand, and Uriel Simon on the other: Uriel Simon, "Sippur Miqraʾi Betefisah ʾIronit," *Hassifrut* 2 (1970):598–607; Menahem Perry and Meir Sternberg, "Zehirut-Sifrut: Lebeʿayot Haʾinterpreṭatsiyah Vehappoʾeṭiqa shel Hassippur Hammiqraʾi," *Hassifrut* 2 (1970):608–63.

Sternberg's work is now available in English in *The Poetics of Biblical Narrative* (Bloomington, Ind., 1985), which contains, inter alia, the greatest part of his Hebrew articles on biblical narrative.

10. Yair Hoffmann, "Bein Qonventsiyah Le'estrategiyah," *Hassifrut* 28 (1979): 91–94; Sternberg, "Mivneh Haḥazarah," p. 121.

11. Sternberg, "Mivneh Haḥazarah," p. 133; Hoffmann, p. 92.

12. Sternberg's response to Hoffmann in *Poetics*, p. 536, n. 37, directs the reader to Robert Alter's defense of the practical exegetical value of many of Sternberg's readings:

> . . . very few literary conventions are treated by writers as invariable, and hence obligatory without exception. . . . It is by no means necessary to insist that every instance of a small variation in repeated phrases should yield a significance . . . to justify the inference that this was, in fact, an artful convention used by writers and recognized by their readers. (*The Art of Biblical Narrative* [New York, 1980], p. 103)

The question that remains is *how* one is to decide whether the variation is significant.

13. Cf. H. C. Brichto, *The Problem of Curse in the Hebrew Bible* (Philadelphia, 1963), p. 26.

14. For further examples of this type in Ibn Ezra's interpretation of legal texts, cf. E. Z. Melamed, *Mefarshei Hammiqra'* (Jerusalem, 1964), vol. 2, pp. 587–89.

15. Note also Kimḥi's comments on Gen. 3:1–5, 12:1, 21:12, 27:7; 1 Sam. 3:10; cf. further Melamed, *Mefarshei Hammiqra'*, vol. 2, pp. 831–35.

16. On Gen. 6:13, see *Minoaḥ Ve'ad Avraham* (Jerusalem, 1949), p. 38; Gen. 46:12 is discussed in "The Story of Judah and Tamar," in *Oriental and Biblical Studies*, trans. I. Abrahams, vol. 1 (Jerusalem, 1973), pp. 34–40; Ex. 32:24 is treated in Cassuto's *Perush 'al Sefer Shemot* (Jerusalem, 1952), p. 294.

17. On the use of *Leitwörter* in biblical narrative, cf. Martin Buber, "Über die Wortwahl in einer Verdeutschung der Schrift," *Werke*, vol. 2, *Schriften der Bibel* (Munich, 1964), pp. 1111–14; Alter, *Biblical Narrative*, pp. 92–94; Michael Fishbane, *Text and Texture* (New York, 1979), pp. 8, 19, 35, 50–54; Shimon Bar-Efrat, *Ha'itsuv Ha'omanuti shel Hassippur Bammiqra'* (Tel Aviv, 1979), pp. 22–26; James Muilenburg, "A Study in Hebrew Rhetoric," *VTSup* 1 (1953):97–111.

18. Sternberg, "Mivneh Haḥazarah," pp. 109, 149; Shlomith Rimmon-Kenan, "The Paradoxical Status of Repetition," *Poetics Today* 1 (1980):151–59, highlights the tension between change and sameness: "Repetition is present everywhere and nowhere, i.e., there is no repetition without difference, and no difference without repetition, and each can only be discussed in terms of the other." See also Bruce Kawin, *Telling it Again and Again* (Ithaca, 1972), pp. 9–70.

19. Sternberg, "Mivneh Haḥazarah," pp. 115–18.

20. Alter, *Biblical Narrative*, pp. 91, 112.

21. See above, n. 17, and Fishbane, *Text and Texture*, pp. 40–62; also J. P. Fokkelman, *Narrative Art in Genesis* (Assen and Amsterdam, 1975), pp. 85–236; idem, *Narrative Art and Poetry in the Books of Samuel*, vol. 1 (Assen, 1981).

22. E.g., Gen. 37:36 is repeated in 39:1, marking the inclusion of the story of Judah and Tamar; cf. Fishbane, *Text and Texture*, p. 60; idem, *Biblical Interpretation in Ancient Israel* (Oxford, 1985), pp. 85–86; C. Kuhl, "Die Wiederaufnahme—ein literarisches Prinzip?" *ZAW* 64 (1952):1–11; Shemaryahu Talmon, "The Presentation of Synchronicity and Simultaneity in Biblical Narrative," in *Studies in Hebrew Narrative Art Throughout the Ages*, ed. J. Heinemann, Scripta Hierosolymitana, vol. 27 (Jerusalem, 1978):9–26.

23. Robert Polzin, *Moses and the Deuteronomist* (New York, 1980), pp. 25–145; Moshe Weinfeld, *Deuteronomy and the Deuteronomic School* (Oxford, 1972), pp. 13ff.

24. Y. T. Raddai, "Chiasm in Kings," *Linguistica Biblica* 31 (1974):52–67. On Gen. 11:1–11, see Fokkelman, *Narrative Art*, pp. 13–59, esp. p. 22; Bar-Efrat, *Ha 'itsuv Ha'omanuti*, pp. 118–29; idem. "Some Observations on the Analysis of Structure in Biblical Narrative," *VT* 30 (1980):172. On Gen. 25–35, see above, n. 21.

25. David J. Clines, *The Theme of the Pentateuch, JSOT* Supplements 10 (Sheffield, 1978). See also Dennis T. Olson, *The Death of the Old and the Birth of the New: The Framework of the Book of Numbers and the Pentateuch* (Chico, Calif., 1985), pp. 186–91.

26. Cf. Klaus Koch, *The Growth of Biblical Narrative* (New York, 1969), pp. 132–48; Robert C. Culley, *Studies in the Structure of Hebrew Narrative* (Philadelphia, 1976), pp. 49–54. Both of these writers address the relationship of such doublets to oral tradition. Alter, *Biblical Narrative*, pp. 131–54, discusses the literary value of including these parallel accounts even when they may contradict one another on the plot level.

27. Alter, *Biblical Narrative*, pp. 47–62; Culley, *Hebrew Narrative*, pp. 41–43; 59–63; John Van Seters, *Abraham in History and Tradition* (New Haven, 1975), pp. 202–208.

28. Meir Sternberg's work on this issue ("Mivneh Haḥazarah") is extremely important, but in focusing his attention on broad issues he makes too few distinctions between the repetition of words, of phrases, of scenes, etc. The important exceptions to this are his discussions of parables (pp. 143–44), of the repetition of dialogue versus that of narration (pp. 128–32), and of repetition by a character as opposed to repetition by the narrator (pp. 138–40), the last of which will be taken up in greater detail below. Robert Alter, in his chapter entitled "The Techniques of Repetition" (*Biblical Narrative*, pp. 88–113), is somewhat more systematic in setting out five categories—*Leitwort*, motif, theme, sequence of actions, and type-scene—as a "scale of repetitive structuring running from the smallest and most unitary elements to the longest and most composite ones" (p. 95). The type of treatment we are suggesting requires much more detail, and much greater specificity in the definition of terms. Like Sternberg's work, Alter's schema moves the general discussion of repetition far beyond where it has been, and is highly suggestive for continued efforts in this area.

29. Hans Walter Wolff, "Das Zitat im Prophetenspruch," in *Gesammelte Studien zum Alten Testament* (Munich, 1964), pp. 36–129; cf. esp. pp. 38–41, 51–53, 87–90.

30. Ibid., pp. 56–58.

31. W. J. Horwitz, "Audience Reaction to Jeremiah," *CBQ* 32 (1970):555–64. For a different type of analysis of Jeremianic quotations, cf. G. V. Smith, "The Use of Quotations in Jeremiah XV 11–14," *VT* 29 (1979):229–31.

32. A. S. van der Woude, "Micah in Dispute with the False Prophets," *VT* 19 (1969):244–60; James Crenshaw, *Prophetic Conflict*, BZAW 123 (New York, 1971), pp. 23–38. Compare Walther Zimmerli, *Ezekiel*, vol. 1, trans. R. E. Clements (Philadelphia, 1979), p. 36; Moshe Greenberg, "Hammuva'ot Besefer Yeḥezkel Kereqa' Lannevu'ot," *Beth Miqra'* 50 (1972): 273–78.

33. Cf. Thomas W. Overholt, "Jeremiah 2 and the Problem of 'Audience Reaction,'" *CBQ* 41 (1979):262–73.

34. "Quotations in Wisdom Literature," *JQR* 30 (1943/40):123–47; idem, "Quotations as a Literary Usage in Biblical, Oriental, and Rabbinic Literature,"

HUCA 22 (1949):157–219, as well as Gordis's commentary *Koheleth: The Man and his World* (New York, 1968), pp. 95–108.

35. In the psalms, for example, many of the "enemy quotations" fall into this category—Pss. 2:2–3; 22:8–9; 52:8–9; 75:10–11; 95:7–8. On ancient Near Eastern literature, see Gordis, "Quotations as a Literary Usage," pp. 118–20, 133–34. Cf. also the Akkadian "Dialogue of Pessimism," trans. R. D. Biggs, in *Ancient Near Eastern Texts* (hereafter *ANET*), ed. James B. Pritchard, 3d ed. with Supplement (Princeton, 1969), p. 601.

36. Gordis, "Quotations as a Literary Usage," p. 109.

37. Michael V. Fox, "The Identification of Quotations in Biblical Literature," *ZAW* 93 (1981):416–31. Fox suggests a number of criteria that might be used to identify quotations more objectively: The presence of another speaker in the text; the use of a virtual verb of speaking or thinking (e.g., Pss. 22:8–9; 55:22–23); the use of certain stereotyped modes of expression such as naming formulas (Gen. 41:51–52; 1 Sam. 1:20). See also R. N. Whybray, "The Identification and Use of Quotations in Ecclesiastes," *VTSup* 32 (1980):435–51.

38. Cf. Herman Meyer, *The Poetics of Quotation in the European Novel* (Princeton, 1968); Jean Weisgerber, "The Use of Quotations in Recent Literature," *Comparative Literature* 22 (1970):36–45; Peter J. Rabinowitz, "'What's Hecuba to us?' The Audience's Experience of Literary Borrowing," in *The Reader in the Text*, ed. S. I. Suleiman and I. Crosman (Princeton, 1980), pp. 241–63; J. Hillis Miller, *Fiction and Repetition* (Cambridge, Mass., 1982), pp. 1–22; Mikhail Bakhtin, *Problems of Dostoevski's Poetics* (Ann Arbor, Mich., 1973).

39. Meir Weiss, "Weiteres über die Bauformen des Erzählens in der Bibel," *Biblica* 46 (1965):181–206; idem, "Mele'ket Hassippur Bammiqra'," *Molad* 20 (1962):404–406.

40. Jacob Licht, *Storytelling in the Bible* (Jerusalem, 1978), pp. 51–95.

41. Alter, *Biblical Narrative*, pp. 88–113, esp. p. 97. Alter does discuss the tension between direct and indirect discourse, as well as the primacy of direct speech in biblical narrative (pp. 63–87).

In her books on Genesis and Exodus, Nehama Leibowitz pays close attention to variations in retelling by characters, in keeping with her general statement quoted above (p. 3). But while she provides many interesting and valuable insights into those texts, she is not concerned with quotation per se, nor does she support her assumption that such variations are always significant by examining a larger sample of biblical narrative.

42. Brevard S. Childs, *The Book of Exodus* (Philadelphia, 1974), pp. 362–63.

43. Sternberg, "Mivneh Hahazarah," pp. 128, 131–32, 139–40; see also Sternberg's "Proteus in Quotation Land," *Poetics Today* 4 (1982):107–10.

44. On the distinction between "showing" and "telling," cf. Wayne Booth, *The Rhetoric of Fiction* (Chicago, 1961), pp. 3–8. On the functions of dialogue in biblical narrative, cf. Alter, *Biblical Narrative*, pp. 63–87, 114–30; Shemaryahu Talmon, *Darkei Hassippur Bammiqra'* (Jerusalem, 1965), pp. 41–49; Bar-Efrat, *Ha'itsuv Ha'omanuti*, pp. 89–99.

45. Kawin, *Telling it Again and Again*, pp. 34–70.

46. See V. N. Voloshinov, "Reported Speech," in *Readings in Russian Poetics*, ed. L. Matejka and K. Pomorska, Michigan Slavic Contributions 8 (Ann Arbor, 1978), pp. 153–76; idem, *Marxism and the Philosophy of Language* (New York, 1973). The very fact of quotation within a new context represents an attempt to undermine the meaning of the original quotation and to bend it to fit the requirements of its new location. This is not too distant from the ways in which quotations function as prooftexts in Midrash. See Michael Fishbane, "Revelation

and Tradition: Aspects of Inner-Biblical Exegesis," *JBL* 99 (1980): 343–61; idem, *Biblical Interpretation*, pp. 1–19.

47. Cf. J. L. Austin, *How to Do Things with Words* (Cambridge, Mass., 1962); John R. Searle, *Speech Acts* (Cambridge, 1969); Mary Louise Pratt, *Toward a Speech Act Theory of Literary Discourse* (Bloomington, Ind., 1977), pp. 79–99; Seymour Chatman, *Story and Discourse* (Ithaca, N.Y., 1978), pp. 161–66. On speech-act theory and biblical narrative, see G. Sheintuch and U. Mali, "Liqra't Nituaḥ 'Iloqutsiyoni shel Hassiḥah Bassippur Hammiqra'i," *Hassifrut* 30–31 (1981):70–75; E. A. Levenston, "The Speech-Acts of God," *Hebrew University Studies in Literature and the Arts* 12 (1984):129–45.

48. The terms "story" and "discourse" are common in structuralist criticism, though definitions differ from writer to writer. The expressions derive from Emile Benveniste's distinction between *histoire* and *discours*, event and narration respectively, as he saw them on a linguistic level, which in turn is indebted to the Sassurean bifurcation of *langue* and *parole;* cf. *Problems in General Linguistics*, trans. M. E. Meeks (Coral Gables, Fla., 1971). The adaptation of the terms by literary critics such as Tsvetan Todorov and Roland Barthes is described by Jonathan Culler, *Structuralist Poetics* (Ithaca, N.Y., 1975), pp. 197–200. Todorov recognizes their antecedents in the Russian formalist distinction between plot (*sjuzet*) and story (*fabula*); cf. *The Poetics of Prose* (Ithaca, N.Y., 1977), pp. 25–27. In our definition of these terms, and throughout this study, we acknowledge the influence of Chatman, *Story and Discourse*, esp. pp. 9–42.

49. These diagrams are intended to illustrate our use of the terms "story" and "discourse" and therefore omit other stages in the process of communication between author and reader, such as implied author, narratee, etc. A fuller discussion of this process can be found in Chatman, *Story and Discourse*, pp. 146ff.; see also Shlomith Rimmon-Kenan, *Narrative Fiction: Contemporary Poetics* (London and New York, 1983), pp. 86–105.

50. Cf. Meir Sternberg, "Bein Ha'emet Lekhol Ha'emet," *Hassifrut* 29 (1979): 110–46.

2. Formal Aspects of Quoted Direct Speech

1. See above, chapter 1, pp. 9–10, and notes 29–38.

2. For example, in 1 Kg. 22:15, is Micaiah consciously mocking the king by "quoting" (alluding to) the words of the prophets in vv. 6 and 12? (Cf. S. J. DeVries, *Prophet Against Prophet* [Grand Rapids, Mich., 1978], pp. 38–39). In Gen. 37:33, is Jacob quoting the words his sons planned to say in 37:20, or is this a conclusion he reaches on his own, without their suggestion? As these examples indicate, intention refers only to the character's discernible motivations in using quoted direct speech, and not to the author's "intentions" in composing the work.

3. See also Gen. 24:7, 32:10, 13, 48:4; Ex. 32:13, 33:1; Num. 10:29; Deut. 34:4. This category would also include the quotations of the announcement of Moses' death in Deut. 1:37, 3:26ff., 31:2.

4. We have also excluded the quotations of 2 Sam. 7:5ff. spoken by Solomon in 1 Kg. 8:16, 18–19, 25 (and by God in 1 Kg. 9:5), since neither Solomon's prayer nor his subsequent vision constitutes a true narrative context.

5. Gen. 24:37, 42:31–34, 44:19–34; Ex. 32:23–24; Num. 22:10–11, 24:12–13.

6. We refer here to the idea that the speaker, or quoter, has assumed the role

of narrator with respect to his audience within the story (Laban, Joseph). See G. Savran, "The Character as Narrator in Biblical Narrative," *Prooftexts* 5 (1985):1–17.

7. Cf. further Gen. 43:3–5; Ex. 33:12; Num. 11:18–20; 1 Kg. 18:11, 14.

8. Cf. Gen. 12:19, 24:49, 27:8, 31:30, 44:30, 33, 50:5, 50:17 (unverifiable); Ex. 5:18, 32:13; Num. 24:14; Josh. 14:10; Jud. 9:39, 11:23; 1 Sam. 10:20, 12:13, 21:4 (unverifiable), 29:9; 1 Kg. 1:17 (unverifiable), 2:9. The reverse order (*wěʿattâ* with a demand, followed by a quotation) is also attested in Num. 24:11; 2 Sam. 3:18 (unverifiable), 13:33. Occasionally *wěʿattâ* may also introduce an accusation, as in Josh. 9:23. The use of the term is hardly restricted to quoted direct speech; see the general discussions by A. Laurentin, "we ʿattah—kai nun," *Biblica* 45 (1964):171–97, and by H. A. Brongers, "Weʿattah im Alten Testament," *VT* 15 (1965):289–99. Its appearance in the message sent by Jephthah to the king of Ammon in Jud. 11:12ff. is characteristic of biblical epistolary style.

9. Note also Ex. 5:8, 17; Num. 11:13, 18; 1 Kg. 12:9, 10; and 1 Kg. 21:4, 6 (with the help of the narrator in v. 4).

10. Gen. 26:9a, 9b; 31:11–12, 29; 43:3–5, 7 (both unverifiable); 50:5, 17 (unverifiable); Ex. 5:8, 17; 33:12a, 12b (unverifiable); Num. 14:18, 31; 24:11, 12–13; Josh. 9:11 (unverifiable); 9:22; Jud. 11:17, 19; 1 Sam. 12:10, 12; 21:3 (unverifiable); 21:12; 29:5, 9; 1 Kg. 12:9, 10; 2 Kg. 5:13, 26 (unverifiable).

11. E.g., Rehoboam (1 Kg. 12:9, 10), Ahab (1 Kg. 20:5, 28; 21:6), and Jehu (2 Kg. 9:12).

12. *Contra* Wolff, "Das Zitat," p. 87.

13. The number of unverifiable quotations in each book is roughly proportional to the amount of quoted direct speech in that book:

	Verifiable		Unverifiable		Totals
	speeches	quotes	speeches	quotes	speeches/quotes
Gen.	16	35	7*	9	22/44
Ex.	5	7	2*	2	6/9
Num.	10	10	1*	1	10/11
Josh.	3	3	1	1	4/4
Jud.	5	6	1	1	6/7
1 Sam.	10	11	4	4	14/15
2 Sam.	4	4	6	9	10/13
1 Kg.	12	15	7*	7	18/22
2 Kg.	5	5	2	3	7/8

*Indicates a single speech containing both a verifiable and an unverifiable quotation.

14. Martin Noth, *A History of Pentateuchal Traditions*, trans. B. Anderson (Englewood Cliffs, N.J., 1972), pp. 17–19; S. McEvenue, *The Narrative Style of the Priestly Writer* (Rome, 1971), pp. 1–8, 19–21, 182, 189; Otto Eissfeldt, *The Old Testament: An Introduction* (New York, 1965), 188–89, 204–207. The single potential point of disagreement is Num. 14:31 quoting 14:3, which some critics assign to P. Cf. M. Noth, *Numbers* (Philadelphia, 1968), p. 101.

15. Twenty-three out of thirty-seven unverifiable quotes, as against fifty out of ninety-four verifiable quotes.

16. Gen. 3:1, 3; 31:29; Ex. 19:23; 33:12a, 12b (unverifiable); Num. 11:21; 14:18; 32:11–12; Josh. 1:13; 1 Sam. 15:18; 2 Sam. 3:18 (unverifiable); 1 Kg. 2:4 (unverifiable); 13:17; 13:18 (unverifiable); 2 Kg. 9:12, 36–37. Gen. 31:11–13 and Jud. 13:7 are attributed to angels.

17. In most cases God quotes not to inform but to bring a charge against an individual (Gen. 18:13) or to announce punishment (Gen. 3:17; 1 Kg. 20:28). The only exception to this is Ex. 32:8, but even here the quotation of the people's sin is brought in the service of a judgment against them.

18. Gen. 31:29, 42:22, 42:31; Josh. 9:11 (unverifiable); 1 Sam. 17:24; 2 Sam. 3:18 (unverifiable); 2 Kg. 9:12. This accords with the relative frequency of finite '-M-R + *lē'mōr* in all direct speech settings, quoted or unquoted, in Genesis–2 Kings. Of 543 occurrences of *lē'mōr*, in only 57 cases does it appear together with finite '-M-R. In Deuteronomy the proportion is even smaller; in 37 occurrences of *lē'mōr* it is preceded by finite '-M-R only twice.

19. Ex. 32:13; Num. 22:19; 1 Kg. 1:47 (unverifiable); 13:17, 22. When taken in comparison with the use of '-M-R as a direct speech marker in all speeches by characters and by the narrator (excluding etiologies but including legal material and divine speech), this is a relatively *frequent* divergence! In the thousands of occasions on which direct speech is introduced in these texts, only thirty-nine cases omit the verb '-M-R entirely. Interestingly, one-third of these thirty-nine cases are accounted for in only two chapters: 2 Kg. 1 uses *D-B-R* nine times to introduce direct speech, and 1 Kg. 13 employs it four times, including the two cases of quoted direct speech mentioned above. In both of these stories, the extensive preoccupation with the fulfillment of a *dĕbar YHWH* spoken by a prophet indicates that this is not a random stylistic variation in these two chapters, but a deliberate narrative substitution aimed at emphasizing the reliability of the true *dābār*.

20. S. R. Driver, *A Treatise on the Use of the Tenses in Hebrew* (Oxford, 1881), pp. 192–93.

21. Cf. *Gesenius' Hebrew Grammar,* ed. E. Kautsch, trans. A. E. Cowley (Oxford, 1910), #107f, h (hereafter *GKC*). Agreement on these passages is not unanimous, as the divergence in translations make clear. *AV, JPS,* and *NEB* render both instances in the past, while *NAB* and P. Kyle McCarter (*1 Samuel,* The Anchor Bible [Garden City, N.Y., 1981], pp. 354, 424) translate both as ongoing. The *RSV* has 21:12 in the past and 29:5 as repetitive, but *NJPS* reverses this order.

22. Cf. *GKC;* Ronald J. Williams, *Hebrew Syntax: An Outline,* 2d ed. (Toronto, 1967), #167.

23. Cf. Stanley Gevirtz, *Patterns in the Early Poetry of Israel* (Chicago, 1963), pp. 15–24.

24. Cf. Culley, *Hebrew Narrative,* pp. 27–41; Van Seters, *Abraham in History,* pp. 167–83.

25. The following examples are intended to be illustrative, not exhaustive. For a more complete description, see G. Savran, "Stylistic Aspects and Literary Functions of Quoted Direct Speech" (Ph.D. diss., Brandeis University, 1982), pp. 53–61.

26. This is particularly true of Ugaritic epic, where long sections are frequently reproduced verbatim, e.g., in the story of King Krt, the extensive set of instructions given to Krt by El in lines 62–153 is reproduced in lines 155–299, with no essential abridgment of the original. Cf. Cyrus Gordon, *Ugaritic Textbook* (Rome, 1965), pp. 250–53. Quoted direct speech appears very rarely, if at all, in the Ugaritic material. In a number of texts, the messenger is charged with a message, sometimes of considerable length, which he then delivers verbatim in the name of his master (e.g., Krt lines 137–53 are repeated in 282–97, and lines 250–61 are delivered in 269–81). This type of "anticipatory" quotation is the dominant style of quotation found in the Ugaritic epics, with two possible exceptions: Text

68 (III AB A), lines 8–10, and Text 51 (II AB), VII:17–18, 25–27 (compare the translations of C. H. Gordon, *Ugarit and Minoan Crete* [New York, 1960], pp. 46, 72, and H. L. Ginzberg, "Poems about Baal and 'Anat," *ANET*, pp. 130, 135). The ambiguity of these cases results from the absence of a clear formal means for indicating quoted direct speech in Ugaritic, as well as the apparent unpopularity of quotations in this literature. A survey of literary-critical issues in the Ugaritic epics is presented by Jack M. Sasson, "Literary Criticism, Folklore Scholarship, and Ugaritic Literature," in *Ugarit in Perspective,* ed. G. D. Young (Winona Lake, Ind., 1981), pp. 81–98.

27. Cf. also Gen. 31:11–13; 42:31; Num. 14:18; Jud. 9:38; 1 Kg. 12:9; 21:6.

28. *Contra, NJPS Torah* translates: "and the Lord proclaimed, 'The Lord! a God compassionate, etc.'" But cf. below, chap. 3, n. 67; note also the interchangeable use of *YHWH* and *'ĕlōhîm* in the quotations in Ex. 5:8, 17.

29. Y. Muffs, "'Iyyunim Battefillah Hannevu'it," *Eretz Israel* 14 (1978):48–54.

30. Cf. below, chap. 4, pp. 83–85.

31. Cf. Booth, *The Rhetoric of Fiction,* pp. 112–22. On the use and misuse of literary conventions, cf. Alter, *Biblical Narrative,* pp. 47–62.

32. In only ten shortened quotations are the quoted elements left unchanged: Gen. 3:17; 24:46, 47; 42:14; Ex. 5:8, 17; Num. 14:18, 24:11; Jud. 9:38, 18:24. One lengthened quotation is otherwise repeated verbatim (1 Kg. 13:17). Only minor types of morphological change occur in Jud. 11:17, 19; 1 Kg. 13:22; 2 Kg. 5:13.

33. An example of this uncertainty can be found in 1 Sam. 11:12, ostensibly quoting 10:27. For some examples of paraphrasis, look at Gen. 24:40 quoting 24:7; Gen. 42:31 quoting 42:11, 13; Num. 11:18 quoting 11:4–6; 1 Kg. 2:42 quoting 2:37–39.

On word order in clauses, cf. *GKC* #141–42; Williams, *Hebrew Syntax,* pp. 96–98; C. Brockelmann, *Hebräische Syntax* (Neukirchen, 1956), pp. 118–21. On word order in the Joseph story, see D. B. Redford, *A Study of the Biblical Story of Joseph, VTSup* 20 (Leiden, 1970), pp. 32ff.

34. Cf. below, chap. 3, pp. 63–64.

3. The Function of the Quotation: Story Analysis

1. Those texts in which the narrator quotes (or repeats) the direct speech of a character will be set aside till the next chapter, since these quotations are directed exclusively at the reader.

2. On criteria for determining irony, see Wayne Booth, *The Rhetoric of Irony* (Chicago, 1974).

3. Chatman, *Story and Discourse,* p. 62, calls these two "discourse time" (the time it takes to tell the story), and "story time" (the passage of time for the actants within the narrative). See his discussion of Genette's distinctions between order, duration, and frequency, pp. 62–84. In biblical literature, cf. Weiss, "Weiteres über die Bauformen," pp. 181–206; idem, "Mele'ket Hassippur Bammiqra'," pp. 402–406.

4. Cf. Alter, *Biblical Narrative,* p. 9, on the emphasis upon the difference between *zônâ* and *qĕdēšâ.*

5. Apparently there were overlapping claims to this land by the Israelites and the Ammonites. Although Chemosh is described as the Moabite national god in the Mesha Inscription, it is suggested that Chemosh was adopted by the Am-

monites, at least over the territory that was formerly under Moabite control. Cf. Robert Boling, *Judges,* The Anchor Bible (Garden City, N.Y., 1975), pp. 201–204; Roland deVaux, *The Early History of Israel* (Philadelphia, 1978), p. 821, 851.

6. In each of these texts, the extent of the listener's knowledge is indeterminate. In 2 Sam. 4 it is uncertain whether or not Baanah and Rechab were aware of David's response to the Amalekite in 2 Sam. 1; the story assumes either their ignorance or their stupidity, probably the latter. Similarly, it is not at all implausible that Achish had heard this song about David long before he met him in 1 Sam. 21. This ambiguity may force the reader to appeal to a "reminding" function for quotations that span longer periods of time, a concept that will be developed below.

7. Cf. Weiss, "Weiteres über die Bauformen," pp. 196f.; Sternberg, "Mivneh Hahazarah," pp. 131, 139f.

8. While this is an element of the narrator's discourse, we mention it here as a brief example of the way in which story and discourse are combined to produce a certain effect. The use of the participle contributes to the narrator's attempt to show the synchronicity of the scenes between Isaac and Esau (vv. 1–4) and Rebecca and Jacob (vv. 5ff.). We are meant to hear Rebecca's words as an echo of Isaac's, but also to judge her edited version of the speech. Cf. Talmon, "Synchronicity," pp. 9–26. On the structure of the speeches in the chapter, see Fishbane, *Text and Texture,* pp. 49–51.

9. Cf. also Ps. 132:15; Job 38:41; Neh. 13:15. A connection to the more widely used form *ṣēdâ* ("food" or "provisions") is further suggested by the Ketib *ṣydh* in 27:3. Cf. Gen. 42:25; Ex. 12:39; Josh. 9:11; Jud. 20:10; 1 Sam. 22:10; Ps. 78:25.

10. The use of the introductory *vayyo'mer* (he said) without a change in speakers has been suggested as a criterion for such pauses. Cf. Meir Shiloah, "Vayyo'mer . . . Vayyo'mer," *Sefer Korngrin,* ed. B. Z. Luria and A. Weiser (Jerusalem, 1964), pp. 251–67; Eric Lowenthal, *The Joseph Narrative in Genesis* (New York, 1973), p. 25, with reference to Reuben's speech in Gen. 37:21–22; Benno Jacob, *Das erste Buch der Tora: Genesis* (Berlin, 1934), p. 761, who suggests pauses at Gen. 9:25–26; 15:5; 16:9; 19:9; 20:9; 30:27–28; 41:38; 42:1–2. See also the discussion of Hushai's speech in 2 Sam. 17:7ff. in Bar-Efrat, *Ha'itsuv Ha'omanuti,* p. 33.

11. The remarkable contrast between Moses' defense of Israel before God (Ex. 32:8–14) and his subsequent anger at the people (32:15ff.) is reworked in Deuteronomy in a manner that reflects the importance of the quotation in 32:8 as proof to Moses of the people's apostasy. In Deut. 9:12–14, God tells Moses the same things about the rebellion as in Exodus, minus the direct quote from the people. As a result, Moses must actually descend the mountain and see the calf with his own eyes (9:15–16) in order to be convinced. Only then (after breaking the tablets and reascending) does he intercede on Israel's behalf, in language very similar to Ex. 32:10ff.

12. Cf. Ramban on 47:31, who attributes Jacob's insistence on swearing to his foresight.

13. Cf. Leibowitz, *Bereshit,* p. 381.

14. Alter, *Biblical Narrative,* p. 169, notes the reversal in the order of reference to Benjamin and to Joseph in v. 32 (compare v. 13). He suggests that this may indicate the brothers' desire to show Jacob that "they divulged this precious fact of Benjamin's existence only grudgingly."

15. On this meaning for *S-H-R,* cf. T. L. Thompson, *The Historicity of the Patriarchal Narratives,* BZAW 133 (Berlin, 1974), pp. 172–84.

16. The question of the unity of Gen. 42–44 centers on three issues:
(a) The discovery of the money in the brothers' sacks in 42:27–28 would seem to deflate the surprise of finding it in 42:35.
(b) The brothers fail to return to Egypt immediately to redeem Simeon in 43:1, indeed make no mention of him at all in 43:1–10.
(c) The questions attributed to Joseph by the brothers (43:7) and by Judah alone (43:3–5, 44:19) do not coincide with the version of Joseph's words reported in 42:9ff. Source critics have generally assigned 42:1–26, 29–38 to E, and 42:27–28, 43:1–44:34 to J (cf. Redford, *Story of Joseph*, pp. 149–58 for a full bibliography).

These difficulties can be harmonized without undue strain on the logic of the story:
(a) In 42:27–28, only one brother discovers the money, the rest imagining it to be a fluke of some kind. Upon returning home, they all open their bags (42:35) and realize that this is not the case.
(b) The brothers' abandonment of Simeon is, as Coats says, "an exegetical problem, not a literary-critical one." The exegesis leads to a negative assessment of the brothers' attitude toward Simeon, which is consistent with the kind of brotherly love they showed toward Joseph (G. W. Coats, *From Canaan to Egypt*, CBQMS 4 [Washington, D.C., 1976], p. 67).
(c) The quotations in 43:3, 5, 7 and 44:19–34 can be treated either as extensive paraphrases of the earlier material or as unverifiable quotations, which are close enough in meaning to the events of 42:9ff. to make their authenticity very likely.

Even if one holds that some of these cases are doublets, this does not justify source-critical divisions that ignore the wholeness of the redacted story. Doublets and doubling are frequent in the Joseph story in places where there is no question of multiple sources, e.g., dreams: Joseph in 37:5–11; the butler and the baker in 40:1–23; Pharaoh in 41:1–8. The use of doublets should be treated as a legitimate literary convention in this narrative, as it is elsewhere in the Bible. Cf. James S. Ackerman, "Joseph, Judah, and Jacob," in *Literary Interpretations of Biblical Narratives*, vol. 2, ed. K. R. R. Gros Louis (Nashville, 1982), pp. 85–113. Coats, *From Canaan to Egypt*, p. 63, suggests that speeches are purposefully doubled "at crucial turning points in the story's plot." Cf. Redford, *Story of Joseph*, pp. 75–76.

17. It is noteworthy that in both cases the brothers use a similar rhetorical technique. They present the "facts"—in chapter 37, the bloody tunic, in chapter 42, Joseph's demand—and let Jacob draw the conclusion himself.

18. Cf. *Genesis Rabbah*, 91:9; Rashi on 42:36.

19. Alter, *Biblical Narrative*, p. 170; Ackerman, "Joseph, Judah, and Jacob," p. 102.

20. On the theme of divine providence in the story, cf. R. M. Hals, *The Theology of the Book of Ruth* (Philadelphia, 1969), pp. 44–47; W. M. Roth, "The Wooing of Rebecca," *CBQ* 34 (1972):177–87. Both writers bring out wisdom elements in connection with this theme.

21. Cf. Culley, *Hebrew Narrative*, pp. 41–43; R. Melugin, "Muilenburg, Form Criticism, and Theological Exegesis," in *Encounter with the Text*, ed. M. Buss (Philadelphia, 1979), pp. 96–99. Alter, *Biblical Narrative*, pp. 53–54, emphasizes the absence of Isaac but does not go into the dynamics of the surrogate role assigned to the servant. This role took on an interesting sexual dimension in later midrashim; cf. Y. Zakovitch and A. Shinan, "Vattippol Meʿal Haggamal (Gen. 24:64)," *Hassifrut* 29 (1979):104–109.

22. Verse 30 indicates that Laban already knows some of what had transpired from Rebecca's own mouth. However, this could include little more than the knowledge that the man worships YHWH and is a servant of Abraham (provided the servant's prayer was audible), and that Rebecca has received some gifts from his hand. Laban's foreknowledge of these few details does not affect the argument presented here. Even Rebecca, who was present at the well, cannot have too much awareness of what this is all about. For similar speculations, cf. Abarbanal on Gen. 24:30.

23. See Rashi on Gen. 24:7; Ibn Ezra on 24:4. The terms *'ereṣ* and *môledet* occur together with the sense of "place" in Gen. 32:10 and Num. 10:30. In Gen. 12:1, *môledet* is intermediate between *'ereṣ* and *bêt 'āb;* Ramban suggests that it may refer to the city of Abraham's family. These three terms, while definitely referring to consanguineous entities, are not used with precision in the Bible and sometimes occur interchangeably, as in Ex. 6:14 and Num. 3:23–24. Cf. *Encyclopedia Biblia,* s.v. "Mishpaḥah," J. Liver, vol. 5, col. 582–88; Norman K. Gottwald, *The Tribes of YHWH* (Maryknoll, N.Y., 1979), pp. 287–88.

24. There is possibly some significance in the servant's change in the order of names in Rebecca's pedigree, emphasizing Nahor over Milcah in 24:47 to please Laban. Bethuel's absence from the story is noticeable, as is the designation of Laban in Gen. 29:5 as *ben-nāḥôr.* Rebecca, on the other hand, emphasized Milcah in 24:24 and runs to her *mother's* house with the news in 24:28.

25. In 24:43 he omits the reference to *běnôt 'anšê hā'îr* and changes the verb *Y-Ṣ-'* from plural to singular. If traditional Jewish commentators are correct in seeing a character test for Rebecca in the servant's omen, then the servant's subsequent omission of any possible reference to a trial is essential, in order to increase the dependence upon providence in Laban's eyes. Cf. Leibowitz, *Bereshit,* pp. 157–59, 172–73.

We should also note here the servant's introduction of the phrase *hiṣlîaḥ derek,* first into Abraham's mouth (v. 40), and then in his own words to describe his posture at the well (v. 42), to underscore further his sense of divine guidance. Later on, when Laban wishes to delay the departure, the servant uses the same, now-proven expression to gain his release (v. 56). For wisdom traditions associated with the phrase, cf. Roth, "The Wooing of Rebecca," pp. 186–87.

26. Arnold B. Ehrlich, *Miqra' Kifshuto,* 2d ed. (New York, 1969), ad loc.; Samuel R. Driver, *Genesis* (London, 1904), ad loc.; S. D. Luzzato, *Perush 'al Ḥamishah Ḥummeshei Torah,* 2d ed. (Tel Aviv, 1965), ad loc.

27. Gen. 29:25 and 37:4 are defined by M. Weiss as examples of *erlebte Rede,* or "free indirect speech," a technique of interior depiction not uncommon in the Bible. By taking advantage of an ambiguity as to whether a certain statement reflects the point of view of the narrator or of the character, *erlebte Rede* can present the thoughts and feelings of the character while maintaining a balance between the authoritative "telling" of the narrator and the more dramatic "showing" of the character's own inner world. On *erlebte Rede* in general literature, cf. Robert Scholes and Robert Kellogg, *The Nature of Narrative* (New York, 1966), pp. 177–204; Roy Pascal, *The Dual Voice* (Manchester, 1977), pp. 2–36. In biblical literature, cf. M. Weiss, "Einiges über die Bauformen des Erzählens in der Bibel," *VT* 13 (1963):456–75; idem, "Mele'ket Hassippur Bammiqra'," pp. 402–406; Sternberg, "Bein Ha'emet," pp. 110–46; idem, "Leshon, 'Olam, Uperspeqṭivah Be'omanut Hammiqra'," *Hassifrut* 32 (1982):88–131.

28. Cf. Gen. 17:17, 21:16, 28:17, 38:11b, and other examples discussed by Sternberg, "Bein Ha'emet," pp. 133–46.

29. Scholes and Kellogg, *The Nature of Narrative,* speak of "the ancient ten-

dency to think of thought simply as speech minus the sound" (p. 180), referring largely to Homer. It is questionable, however, whether this generalization should be extended to the Bible, given the infrequency of internal monologue relative to the narrator's presentation of internal states. Cf. Sternberg, "Bein Ha'emet," pp. 114, 133; Alter, *Biblical Narrative*, p. 68.

30. Sternberg, "Bein Ha'emet," pp. 110–14, points out that, in addition to the relative scarcity of interior speech, the repertoire of language, style, and function in interior monologue in the Bible is rather limited. He attributes this to a basic dynamic of all biblical narrative: The narrator reveals the inner thoughts of his characters ("the truth") but does so only partially, preventing the reader from knowing "the whole truth" about their motivations and feelings. This contributes significantly to an intentional ambiguity, creating a montage of perspectives upon a given character, none of which are definitive. Cf. Alter's aptly titled chapter "Characterization and the Art of Reticence," *Biblical Narrative*, pp. 114–30.

31. A similar appeal is made to these tribes in Num. 32:20ff., which is ascribed to JE by Noth and others. But the different content of that chapter—the tribes' demands, Moses' reluctance, the threat of sin—as well as the close relationship between Joshua and Deuteronomy make it most likely that the writer in Joshua is drawing upon the Deuteronomic version. Cf. Polzin, *Moses*, pp. 77–80.

32. On the problem of Hebron's conquest, cf. J. H. Hayes and J. M. Miller, eds., *Israelite and Judean History* (Philadelphia, 1977), pp. 222ff.; DeVaux, *Early History*, pp. 523–26, 534–40.

33. See the discussion and examples in Weinfeld, *Deuteronomic School*, pp. 1–27. In 2 Kg. 9:25–26 and 9:36–37 the deaths of Joram and Jezebel are interpreted by quoting Elijah's oracle against Ahab in 1 Kg. 21:19, 20b–26. Weinfeld (pp. 19–20) suggests that the quote in 9:26 attempts to "fulfill" Elijah's prophecy that Ahab would die in Naboth's vineyard (which he did not) by having Ahab's *son* Joram die in that very place. See further Polzin, *Moses*, pp. 9–24.

34. If the two versions are compared, nearly every omitted phrase has a synonymous counterpart that is retained:

Omitted (cf. Ex. 34:6–7)		*Remaining* (in Num. 14:18)
'ēl raḥûm wěḥannûn	/ /	'erek 'appayîm wěrab-ḥesed
'emet	/ /	ḥesed
ḥaṭṭā'â	/ /	pāšaʿ
ʿal běnē bānîm	/ /	ʿal-šillēšîm wěʿal-ribbēʿîm

Given this consistent pattern of deleting synonyms in the quotation, it is difficult to use the single Tetragrammaton in Num. 14:18 as a proof for Ibn Ezra's suggestion that Ex. 34:6 should read, "and the Lord proclaimed 'The Lord, a God compassionate . . . '" (cf. *NJPS Torah*, ad loc.).

In the case of the omitted phrase *nōṣēr ḥesed lāʾălāpîm*, which has no remaining parallel, an argument can be made for Moses' deliberate omission of it on the grounds of its irrelevancy to the situation in Num. 14. Cf. J. Scharbert, "Formgeschichte und Exegese von Ex. 34:6f. und seiner Parallelen," *Biblica* 38 (1957):132; Y. Muffs, "'Iyyunim Battefillah," pp. 48–54.

35. Cf. Muffs, "'Iyyunim Battefillah," p. 49.

36. Clines, *Theme of the Pentateuch*, pp. 51–52; Leibowitz, *Shemot*, p. 413. Note how Moses uses the root *G-D-L* in his response in each text: to describe God's strength in delivering Israel (Ex. 32:11), to emphasize how God's power will

strengthen by continuing to deliver them (Num. 14:17), and to remind God of his great *ḥesed* (Num. 14:19).

37. Gen. 12:7; 13:14b; 13:17; 15:7; 15:18; 17:8; 22:17; 26:2ff.; 28:4; 28:13, 15; 35:12; 50:24; see also Ex. 13:5, 11; Num. 11:12; 14:16, 23; 32:11; and nineteen times in Deuteronomy (cf. Clines, *Theme of the Pentateuch,* pp. 40–43). On the promise of the land, cf. Gerhard von Rad, "The Promised Land and Yahweh's Land in the Hexateuch," in *The Problem of the Hexateuch and Other Essays* (New York, 1966), pp. 79–93; Claus Westermann, *The Promises to the Fathers* (Philadelphia, 1980), pp. 21–27, 143–49; Noth, *Pentateuchal Traditions,* pp. 51–58. W. Brueggemann, *The Land* (Philadelphia, 1980), pp. 1–27, sees the whole question of the relationship to the land as a major organizing principle of biblical theology. On the ancient Near Eastern background to the promise, cf. M. Weinfeld, "The Covenant Grant in the Old Testament and in the Ancient Near East," *JAOS* 90 (1970):184–203; S. Loewenstamm, "The Divine Grant of Land to the Patriarchs," *JAOS* 91 (1971):509–10.

In most cases the notion of progeny is at least implicit in the promise. Clines, *Theme of the Pentateuch,* also includes the element of blessing, or relationship: "The triple elements are unintelligible one without the other, never strongly differentiated one from another in their manifestation in the text" (p. 31). However, efforts at such differentiation have been made by Westermann, *Promises to the Fathers,* pp. 2–30, 95–163, esp. pp. 128–29. Clines provides a useful list of allusions to the promise throughout the Pentateuch on pp. 37–43.

38. Cf. Kawin, *Telling it Again and Again,* p. 4: "Repetitious: When a word, precept, or experience is repeated with less impact at each recurrence, repeated to no particular end, out of a failure of invention or sloppiness of thought. Repetitive: When a word, precept, or experience is repeated with equal or greater force at each occurrence."

39. Sternberg, "Mivneh Haḥazarah," pp. 136–38; Savran, "The Character as Narrator," p. 11.

40. E.g., 1 Sam. 8:7; 13:1ff.; 15:1ff.; see McCarter, *I Samuel,* p. 215; D. M. Gunn, *The Fate of King Saul,* (Sheffield, 1980), pp. 33–61, 64.

41. Cf. 2 Sam. 1:14–16. In the same vein, it is very possible that the messenger who brought David the news of Uriah's death in 2 Sam. 11:23–25 changed Joab's message for fear of a violent response. In 2 Sam. 18:20 Joab's refusal to allow Ahimaaz to bring David the news of Absalom's death may stem from similar fears. See Perry and Sternberg, "Hammelek Bemabbaṭ 'Ironi," pp. 279–80.

42. R. A. Carlson, *David, The Chosen King* (Uppsala, 1969), p. 51, notes that both murders are perpetrated by non-Israelites. David does not refer to Ishbosheth here as "the anointed of the Lord" (1 Sam. 24:6, 10; 26:9, 16; 2 Sam. 1:14, 16). The crime is the murder of a "righteous man" (4:11)—worthy of punishment, but not of martyrdom.

43. David M. Gunn, *The Story of King David* (Sheffield, 1978), p. 95. See also P. K. McCarter, "The Apology of David," *JBL* 99 (1980):499–502; idem, *II Samuel,* Anchor Bible Commentary (Garden City, N.Y., 1984), pp. 64–65, 120–121; Charles Mabee, "David's Judicial Exoneration," *ZAW* 92 (1980):98–107.

44. Compare Gunn, *King Saul,* pp. 106ff.; McCarter, *I Samuel,* p. 427; H. W. Hertzberg, *I and II Samuel* (Philadelphia, 1964), p. 223; M. Segal, *Sifrei Shemu'el* (Jerusalem, 1968), pp. 209, 222.

45. On the basis of the threefold repetition of Amnon's death (vv. 32, 33, 39), Walter Brueggemann draws an interesting parallel with the death of the child in 2 Sam. 12: "Life and Death in Tenth Century Israel," *JAAR* 40 (1972):105.

46. The only variation is the interchange of the synonyms *hiqšâ* and *hikbîd;* cf. Ex. 7:3; 8:28; 9:34; 13:15.

47. Cf. Gray, *I and II Kings*, p. 304; Abraham Malamat, "The Organs of Statecraft in the Israelite Monarchy," in *Biblical Archaeologist Reader*, vol. 3, ed. E. F. Campbell and D. N. Freedman (Garden City, N.Y., 1970), pp. 195–96. For Mesopotamian parallels (the *mešarum* act), cf. J. J. Finkelstein, "Ammiṣadduqa's Edict and the Babylonian Law Codes," *JCS* 15 (1961):91–104.

48. Malamat, "The Organs of Statecraft," p. 176; Baruch Halpern, "Sectionalism and the Schism," *JBL* 93 (1974):527. Robert Cohn explains the interaction differently; Rehoboam designs his quotation in v. 9 to evoke a negative response from the *yĕlādîm*. See "Literary Technique in the Jeroboam Narrative," *ZAW* 97 (1985):28–29.

49. Note the use of the verb ʿ-*B*-*D* (to serve)—12:4: "We will *serve* you," and 12:7: "If you will be a *servant* to this people today and *serve* them . . . they will be your *servants* forever."

50. Compare the assessments by Halpern, "Sectionalism," pp. 530–32; J. Bright, *A History of Israel*, 2d ed. (Philadelphia, 1972), pp. 226–27; S. Herrmann, *A History of Israel in Old Testament Times* (Philadelphia, 1980), pp. 189–90.

51. On 44:19, see Redford, *Story of Joseph*, pp. 152–58; on 44:27–29, see Leibowitz, *Bereshit*, pp. 346ff.

52. So Speiser, *Genesis*, pp. 318–35; Gerhard von Rad, *Genesis*, rev. ed. (Philadelphia, 1972), p. 385; Redford, *Story of Joseph*, pp. 178ff.

53. Cf. above, n. 16, and the readings of the entire story by Alter, *Biblical Narrative*, pp. 159–77, and by Ackerman, "Joseph, Judah, and Jacob," pp. 86–113. Cf. also the reading of Gen. 37 by E. L. Greenstein, "An Equivocal Reading of the Sale of Joseph," in *Literary Interpretations of Biblical Narrative*, vol. 2, ed. K. R. R. Gros Louis (Nashville, 1982), pp. 114–25.

54. Redford, *Story of Joseph*, pp. 152–57, suggests various reasons for the discrepancies between 44:19 and 42:10: a desire to paraphrase, a psychological defensiveness by Judah carried over from 43:7, or even a failure of memory. Yet he is unwilling to admit to any such failure of memory on Joseph's part. But the point is not that Joseph necessarily "forgot" what went on in chapter 42 and so was "reminded" by Judah (though such a reconstruction is entirely reasonable), for this is a minor detail in his speech. Rather, Judah is granted a unique type of narrative authority to retell the past. As with Abraham's servant in Gen. 24, this exceptional status as an extensive "quoter" allows him to bypass the boundaries of verisimilitude common to most cases of quoted direct speech.

It is more than coincidental that Judah's discourse and that of Abraham's servant are the only two cases of longer speeches containing more than two verifiable quotations, and both reflect the powerlessness of their speakers in style as well as content. For further discussion of the relationship between the length of a speech and the authority of its speaker, see Savran, "The Character as Narrator," pp. 10–14.

55. The phrase "wĕ'āśîmâ ʿênî ʿālāyw" can imply favorable or unfavorable attention; cf. Jer. 24:6, 39:12, 40:4; Amos 9:4. Either way the stress is laid upon *Joseph's* intentions.

56. Judah's omission of Simeon's imprisonment is equally strategic, for its inclusion would undercut Judah's claim about the family's sense of commitment to one another.

57. See Ackerman, "Joseph, Judah, and Jacob," pp. 105–107; Ackerman points out the use of ʿ*ērābôn* in Gen. 38 as that which compels Judah to live up to his familial obligations.

58. Cf. Coats, *From Canaan to Egypt*, p. 43.

59. "The way the shadow of Joseph, who no longer lives but is present, lies

across the speech, and is revealed more and more as the really troubling factor, is particularly moving" (von Rad, *Genesis*, p. 394).

60. Verse 34 is the only line in the speech that omits courtly language. Note also that Judah's final word is *'ābî*.

61. We agree with Ackerman, "Joseph, Judah, and Jacob," pp. 87–88, that Joseph's plan was not entirely worked out in advance. While the chain of events in chapters 42–44 does compel the brothers to take greater responsibility, Joseph seems to be improvising along the way, and there is more than a little vengefulness and arrogance in his character. Judah's speech comes as an important corrective to a Joseph who has become carried away with this deception and has lost sight of its human consequences.

62. Cf. Ackerman, "Joseph, Judah, and Jacob," pp. 106–107.

63. Alter, *Biblical Narrative*, p. 175.

64. Cf. Phyllis Trible, *God and the Rhetoric of Sexuality* (Philadelphia, 1978), p. 109; Joel Rosenberg, "Kinship vs. Kingship: Political Allegory in the Bible" (Ph.D. diss., University of California at Santa Cruz, 1978), p. 115.

Speiser, *Genesis*, p. 21, does not treat *'ap kî-'āmar* as interrogative and translates, "Even though God told you not to eat from the tree . . ." on the strength of the meaning "although" for *gam kî* in Ps. 23:4. Rosenberg observes, however, that the expression *'ap kî-'āmar* is used consistently in the second half of an argument *a fortiori*, e.g., 1 Sam. 14:30; 2 Sam. 4:11. Given the absence of any putative prior statement by the serpent (cf. Rosenberg, p. 116; Ibn Ezra, ad loc.), the context of the speech argues for the conventional question: "Did God really say . . . ?" For further discussion of the phrase, cf. Rosenberg, p. 114; M. D. Cassuto, *Perush 'al Sefer Bereshit*, 5th ed. (Jerusalem, 1969), p. 95; Leibowitz, *Bereshit*, p. 23.

65. Cf. Cassuto, *Bereshit*, p. 96; Trible, *Rhetoric of Sexuality*, pp. 109–10. B. Jacob (*Genesis*, pp. 103–104) sees the shift from Ṣ-W-H (to command) to '-M-R (to say) to be one of the more significant changes wrought by the serpent, moving the woman's understanding of the prohibition away from the very idea of commandment. The woman's subsequent use of '-M-R in 3:3 indicates the success of this strategy.

66. The fictitiousness of the oath is held by Gray, *I and II Kings*, p. 88, and D. M. Gunn, *King David*, pp. 105–106, esp. n. 24. A more equivocal position is taken by J. A. Montgomery and H. S. Gehman, *A Critical and Expositional Commentary on the Books of Kings*, ICC (Edinburgh, 1951), pp. 74–75; Alter, *Biblical Narrative*, p. 98; and Fokkelman, *King David*, pp. 353–54. On the other hand, Kimḥi, ad loc., and Leibowitz, *Bereshit*, p. 177, hold that the quotation is genuine, but offer no supporting evidence.

67. Alter, *Biblical Narrative*, p. 98; Leibowitz, *Bereshit*, p. 177, notes a similar ploy in Rebecca's addition of the phrase *lipnê YHWH* in her quotation of Isaac's words to Jacob in Gen. 27:7.

68. Alter, *Biblical Narrative*, pp. 99–100.

69. On the range of meanings of *hălô'*, cf. H. A. Brongers, "Some Remarks on the Biblical Particle *hălô'*," *OTS* 21 (1981):177–89.

70. Boling, *Judges*, p. 265, adduces the *LXX* as evidence for a fuller quotation of the Danites' words by Micah. Evidence of this sort must be evaluated in light of the tendency of the Septuagint to repeat in literal fashion what the *MT* preserves with some variation. A classic example is the difference between the *LXX* and the *MT* versions of the messenger's speech to David in 2 Sam. 11 as dictated by Joab (vv. 19–21) and as actually delivered (vv. 23–24). The variations in the two speeches as found in the *MT* are harmonized by the *LXX*, destroying the irony

intended by Joab. Cf. Uriel Simon, "The Poor Man's Ewe Lamb," *Biblica* 48 (1967):218ff.; idem, "Samuel's Call to Prophecy," *Prooftexts* 1 (1981):125, 131, n. 10.

71. This analysis is indebted to Muffs, "'Iyyunim Battefillah," p. 50. See also Childs, *Exodus*, p. 594; James Muilenburg, "The Intercession of the Covenant Mediator," in *Words and Meanings: Essays Presented to David Winton Thomas*, ed. P. R. Ackroyd and B. Lindars (Cambridge, 1968), pp. 170–79; Muilenburg stresses the importance of the root *Y-D-ʿ* (six times in vv. 12–17) as it defines the covenant relationship between God, Moses, and Israel.

72. David Jobling, *The Sense of Biblical Narrative* (Sheffield, 1978), p. 26, with some reservations about v. 10. Noth, *Numbers*, p. 83, refrains from assigning J and E sources to the various sections, while George Coats, *Rebellion in the Wilderness* (Nashville, 1968), pp. 96ff., compares it with the P narrative, which he isolates in Ex. 16. The two stories share key words and themes that will be discussed below, chap. 4, pp. 94–96.

73. Jobling, *The Sense of Biblical Narrative*, p. 30; cf. also N. Leibowitz, *Studies in Bamidbar* (Jerusalem, 1980), pp. 110–11.

74. Part of the confusion results from the active presence of *three* parties with separate interests—Moses, God, and the Israelites. In other stories of mediation in the desert Moses generally indentifies himself either with the people (Ex. 33:12–17; Num. 14:13–19) or with God (Ex. 16:11–30). The extent of Moses' self-interest is exceptional in Num. 11, only paralleled perhaps by Ex. 17:1–7 and Num. 21:4–9, though neither of these is entirely clear. In Ex. 16:2–8, the people complain against Moses, but he tells them that their argument is not with him and Aaron but with God directly. When Aaron and Miriam challenge Moses' authority in Num. 12, and in the rebellion of Korah in Num. 16–17, God immediately sides with Moses, so that only two parties are striving with each other. The epic "law" of "two-to-a-scene" holds for the great majority of biblical stories. See Axel Olrik, "Epic Laws of Folk Narrative," in *The Study of Folklore*, ed. Alan Dundes (New York, 1965), pp. 129–41.

75. In v. 16 the woman uses the verb *K-Z-B*, meaning "to deceive," as in Num. 23:19; Micah 2:11; Prov. 14:5, or "to disappoint, fail," as in Is. 58:11 and Hab. 2:3; cf. M. A. Klopfenstein, *Die Lüge nach dem Alten Testament* (Zurich and Frankfort, 1964), pp. 176–210, esp. p. 187. This is replaced by the *hapax legomenon tašleh* in 4:28, whose root (*Š-L-W* or *Š-L-H*) has the sense "to be at ease" or "to be prosperous," as in Jer. 12:1 and Job 3:26. *BDB*, p. 1017, suggests an extension of this meaning to "to be careless" or "to neglect," as in 2 Chron. 29:11 (*tiššālû*). D. F. Burney, *Notes on the Hebrew Text of the Book of Kings* (Oxford, 1903), pp. 275–76, relates the root to *Š-G-G* or *Š-G-H*, meaning "to err," on the basis of its Targumic equivalent in Ps. 119:10, 67 and Job 12:16. Both Burney and *BDB* treat *tašleh* as causative—"to cause to neglect" or "to cause to err"—hence "to deceive." Gray, *I and II Kings*, p. 498, suggests "to cause to be at ease," i.e., "to lull into complacency."

76. Hermann Gunkel, *Geschichten von Elisa* (Berlin, 1924), pp. 20–21. On the phrase *kāʿēt ḥayyâ* (next year), found only here and in Gen. 18:10, cf. R. Yaron, "Ka ʿeth Ḥayyah and Kōh Lĕḥay," *VT* 12 (1962):500–501; O. Loretz, "K ʿt ḥyh— 'wie jetzt ums Jahr', Gen. 18:10," *Biblica* 43 (1962):75–78. On the relationship of this narrative to other birth stories, see Robert Alter, "How Convention Helps Us Read: The Case of the Bible's Annunciation Type-Scene," *Prooftexts* 3 (1983):115–30.

77. For examples of this type of unverifiable quotation, see Is. 37:24; Jer. 36:29; Hos. 2:5–7; Amos 7:16. Cf. Wolff, "Das Zitat," pp. 48, 85–87; and Claus

Westermann, *Basic Forms of Prophetic Speech* (Philadelphia, 1967), pp. 129–209. In the "Covenant Lawsuit," or *rîb* pattern, heaven and earth may be invoked as witnesses against Israel: Deut. 32:1; Is. 1:2; Jer. 2:12; Micah 6:2; Ps. 50:4. Cf. H. Huffmon, "The Covenant Lawsuit in the Prophets," *JBL* 78 (1959):285–95; J. Limburg, "The Root *rîb* and the Prophetic Lawsuit Speeches," *JBL* 88 (1969):291–304.

78. P. Kyle McCarter, "The Apology of David," pp. 500–501. J. C. Vanderkam, "Davidic Complicity in the Deaths of Abner and Eshbaal," *JBL* 99 (1980):521–39, bases his argument on (1) the achievements of David's band in 1 Sam. 22–30; (2) the support of Jonathan (23:16–18) and Abiathar (22:20–23); (3) David's rise to power in Hebron; (4) David's behavior in 2 Sam. 1. Cf. also Ehrlich, *Miqra' Kifshuto*, vol. 2, p. 181.

79. See the discussion by M. Greenberg, *Understanding Exodus*, pp. 124–28; Childs, *Exodus*, pp. 106–107. On a discourse level the narrator has underscored this reversal with the repetition of the root *P-G-'*, referring to the dangers of disobeying God in v. 3, and to the overseers' "encounter" with Moses in v. 20. The word *nēlĕkâ*, so full of promise in v. 3, is the verb used to describe the Israelites' return to their labors in vv. 4, 11, 18. Similarly, the frequent use of the verb *'-B-D*, referring to slavery or to loyalty to Pharaoh (vv. 9, 11, 15, 16, 18, 21), is a rebuff to God's command that Israel be sent forth "so that they may serve me" (4:23).

80. For a summary of older views, cf. Bruce C. Birch, *The Rise of the Israelite Monarchy* (Missoula, Mont., 1976), pp. 42–43; McCarter, *I Samuel*, pp. 12–14. The source-critical distinction between 10:20–21a and 21b–24 derives from Otto Eissfeldt, *Die Komposition der Samuelis Bücher* (Leipzig, 1931), p. 7. The neutral character of the material is stressed by Birch (pp. 47, 53) and by McCarter (p. 195).

81. Birch, *Israelite Monarchy*, pp. 48–51, develops this framework, building on categories laid out by Westermann, *Basic Forms*, pp. 129ff.

82. McCarter, *I Samuel*, pp. 195–96, points out that while lot-casting is used for various purposes in the Bible (e.g., Num. 26:55; Josh. 14:2; 1 Chron. 24:5, 25:8), the only other detailed accounts of its implementation occur in highly pejorative contexts: Achan in Josh. 7:10ff. and Jonathan in 1 Sam. 14:38–44.

83. Cf. Sternberg, "Mivneh Haḥazarah," pp. 136–38; Alter, *Biblical Narrative*, pp. 155–58.

4. The Function of the Quotation: Discourse Analysis

1. Alter, *Biblical Narrative*, pp. 65–70.

2. When speaking of the implied audience, we follow Wayne Booth's definition of the "implied reader" as the ideal reader or interpreter envisioned by the "implied author." As the actual writer stands apart from the implied author, so the implied reader is distant from the actual reader. Both "actual" figures are separated by time and space, but their implied counterparts are united in their mutual relation to the unique world of the particular text they share. "The author creates, in short, an image of himself and another image of the reader; he makes his reader as he makes his second self, and the most successful reading is the one in which the created selves, [implied] author and reader, can find complete agreement" (*Rhetoric of Fiction*, p. 138). Cf. also Chatman, *Story and Discourse*, pp. 147–51. For a range of perspectives that are more reader-oriented,

see the essays by Crosman, Culler, Iser, Prince, and Todorov in *The Reader in the Text*, ed. Susan R. Suleiman and Inge Crosman (Princeton, 1980).

3. Cf. below, pp. 85–87.

4. Cf., for example, Scholes and Kellogg, *The Nature of Narrative*, pp. 160ff.; René Wellek and Austin Warren, *Theory of Literature* (New York, 1970), pp. 216–25. Chatman, *Story and Discourse*, pp. 19–42, prefers the term "events" to include plot elements, actions, and happenings, and the terms "existents" to cover both characters and setting, in order to distinguish between the active and passive aspects of each category.

5. On double perspective in discourse, cf. Sternberg, "Bein Ha'emet," pp. 110–12; Voloshinov, "Reported Speech," pp. 155–60; Polzin, *Moses*, pp. 22–24.

6. Cf. Talmon, *Darkei Hassippur Bammiqra'*, pp. 32ff.; Alter, *Biblical Narrative*, pp. 114–30; Bar-Efrat, *Ha'itsuv Ha'omanuti*, pp. 73ff.; Licht, *Storytelling in the Bible*, pp. 31–33.

7. Cf. in particular the discussion by Crenshaw, *Prophetic Conflict*, pp. 39–62. Karl Barth (*Exegese von I Könige 13*, Biblische Studien, Heft 10 [Neukirchen, 1955], pp. 12–56) noted the importance of the exchange of roles by the two prophets but connected them to the inappropriate categories of election and rejection. For other interpretations of the story, cf. Alexander Rofé, "Classes in the Prophetic Stories," *VTSup* 26 (1974):158–63; Simon, "I Kings 13," pp. 106–17.

8. 2 Sam. 16:5; 19:7; cf. Gray, *I and II Kings*, p. 111.

9. Sternberg, "Mivneh Haḥazarah," p. 147; Yair Zakovitch, "The Tale of Naboth's Vineyard," in Meir Weiss, *The Bible from Within* (Jerusalem, 1984), pp. 387–88. On the concept *naḥălat 'ăbōtāy*, see Benjamin Uffenheimer, *Hannevu'ah Haqqedumah Beyisra'el* (Jerusalem, 1973), pp. 218–21; Francis I. Anderson, "The Socio-Juridical Background of the Naboth Incident," *JBL* 85 (1966):46–47.

10. Uffenheimer, *Hannevu'ah*, p. 221. Sternberg, "Mivneh Haḥazarah," p. 147, argues that Ahab's intentions are left deliberately unclear and suggests that as good a case can be made for Ahab's active involvement as for his being the unwitting beneficiary of Jezebel's crimes. See further Zakovitch, "Naboth's Vineyard," pp. 395–96. On the narrative strategy of Ahab's passivity, cf. G. Savran, "1 and 2 Kings," *The Literary Guide to the Bible*, ed. F. Kermode and R. Alter (Cambridge, 1987), pp. 146–64.

11. Leibowitz, *Bereshit*, pp. 403ff.; cf. also Rashi, Shadal, ad loc., and *Bereshit Rabbah* 100:9. *Contra*, cf. von Rad, *Genesis*, p. 432; Jacob, *Genesis*, pp. 938f.

12. *Contra*, cf. Samuel Lowenstamm, "The Making and Destruction of the Golden Calf," *Biblica* 38 (1967):481–90, who attempts to justify Aaron's claim on the basis of Ugaritic literature.

13. Childs, *Exodus*, p. 570. In 32:25, it is not clear if the phrase "kî pĕrā'ô 'aḥărôn" (for Aaron let them get out of control) is attributed to Moses (*NEB, NAB*) or to the narrator alone (*RSV*). *AV, JPS*, and *NJPS Torah* let the ambiguity stand, giving the reader a glimpse of Moses' reaction to Aaron's excuse by means of free indirect speech. In v. 22, the Samaritan Pentateuch reads *pāra'* in place of MT *bĕra'*, making Aaron's description of the people read "kî pāra' hû'" (they were out of control). Moses' subsequent use of the same phrase in v. 25, followed by the evaluation of Aaron as the *active* cause of their wildness, would effectively condemn Aaron with his own words.

14. J. Cheryl Exum ("Promise and Fulfillment: Narrative Art in Judges 13," *JBL* 99 [1980]:49) and Alter (*Biblical Narrative*, p. 101) both point to the mention of the boy's death as an ominous indication of Samson's ultimate failure.

15. Exum, "Judges 13," pp. 57–59, notes that the messenger declines to reveal his name, not at all unlike Jacob's adversary in Gen. 32:29. Cf. also Polzin, *Moses,* p. 183.

16. In addition to the obvious connections between Samson's hair and the revealing of his secret, note the use of sacrifices in both chapters (to YHWH in 13:20; to Dagon in 16:23), the foreshadowing of Samson's death (13:7; 16:16), the mention of Zorah and Eshtaol (13:25; 16:31), and the punning use of the root *P-ʿ-M* in 13:25; 16:20, 28. Cf. further, Edward Greenstein, "The Riddle of Samson," *Prooftexts* 1 (1981):243–47.

On the relationship of Samson's strength to the Nazirite vow, cf. Joseph Blenkinsopp, "Structure and Style in Judges 13–16," *JBL* 82 (1963):65–69; Exum, "Judges 13," p. 49; Boling, *Judges,* pp. 219–21. The root *P-L-ʾ* (13:18–19) occurs in connection with the Nazirite vow in Num. 6:2, as well as other oath-taking contexts such as Lev. 27:2 and Num. 15:3–8. Also, the root *ʾ-S-R* is used extensively in Jud. 15 and 16 (twelve times) with reference to physical binding, but its range of meaning extends to binding obligations (*ʾissār*) such as oaths and vows in Num. 30:3ff. There the expression *leʾsōr ʾissār* occurs in direct parallelism with the more common *lindōr neder,* which is the phrase used for swearing a Nazirite vow in Num. 6:2. These parallels enhance the likelihood that the conditions of the Nazirite vow are intrinsic to the plot.

17. Cf. Jud. 1:34; DeVaux, *Early History,* pp. 776–83. The anarchic situation in Jud. 17–21 is exemplified by the repetition of the formula "In those days there was no king in Israel; every man did what was right in his own eyes" (17:6; 21:25; cf. 18:1; 19:1). This phrase is anticipated by Samson's justfication of his love for the Philistine woman in 14:3 with the words "kî-hîʾ yāšěrâ běʿênāy" (for she is right in my own eyes). The relationship between Samson and Israel is developed in a somewhat different direction by Greenstein, "The Riddle of Samson," pp. 247–55.

18. A popular midrashic understanding is that the man is a divine messenger, sent to ensure that Joseph would meet up with his brothers. Cf. *Bereshit Rabbah* 75:4; 84:14, and Ramban, ad loc.

19. Cf. G. von Rad, "The Joseph Narrative and Ancient Wisdom," in *The Problem of the Hexateuch and Other Essays* (New York, 1966), pp. 292–300; Shemaryahu Talmon, "'Wisdom' in the Book of Esther," *VT* 13 (1963):454–55; Moshe Gan, "Megillat Esther Beʾor Sippur Yosef Bemitsrayim," *Tarbitz* 31 (1962):144–49.

20. Cf. Ackerman, "Joseph, Judah, and Jacob," pp. 88–89; Alter, *Biblical Narrative,* pp. 163–66.

21. Cf. Mary Savage, "A Rhetorical Analysis of the Joseph Narrative," in *Scripture in Context: Essays on the Comparative Method,* ed. C. D. Evans, W. H. Hallo, J. B. White (Pittsburgh, 1980), p. 95. Judah's use of an unverifiable quotation of Joseph's own words in 44:19 further undercuts Joseph's omniscience, suggesting to the reader that Joseph does not remember what he said and therefore does not correct Judah. Here the unverifiable quotation subverts the reliability of the listener, rather than that of the speaker.

22. Savage, "Joseph Narrative," pp. 95–96. Ackerman, "Joseph, Judah, and Jacob," p. 87, posits that the fulfillment of these earlier dreams is the motivation behind Joseph's deception in 42:7ff.: " . . . from Joseph's point of view, the dreams may not yet have been *completely* fulfilled. . . . All the brothers' sheaves had bowed to Joseph's sheaf, and Benjamin is still in Canaan."

23. On this relationship, see Sternberg, "Mivneh Haḥazarah," pp. 136–38; idem, "Bein Haʾemet," pp. 121–22; Alter, *Biblical Narrative,* p. 175; Bar-Efrat, *Haʿitsuv Haʾomanuti,* pp. 48–50; Hugh C. White, "Direct and Third Person Dis-

course in the Narrative of the 'Fall,'" in *Society for Biblical Literature Seminar Papers*, vol. 1, ed. Paul. J. Achtmeier (Missoula, Mont., 1978), p. 136.

24. Bar-Efrat, *Ha'itsuv Ha'omanuti*, p. 48.

25. Alter, *Biblical Narrative*, p. 157.

26. I am indebted to Robert Polzin for helping me clarify the nature of this relationship.

27. Uffenheimer, *Hannevu'ah*, pp. 177–78.

28. Uffenheimer, op. cit., p. 179, points out the connective use of the root *N-K-H* as a *Leitwort* in the chapter (vv. 20, 29, 35, 36, 37): the prophet is "struck" (vv. 35–37) as a sign of the king's failure to "strike" Ben-hadad.

29. Similarly, cf. Elisha in 2 Kg. 5:25ff. Note also Joseph's use of the question in Gen. 42:7. In addition to the deceptive questions in Gen. 3:1 and 3:9, Num. 22 has some striking similarities with the garden story. Only in these two narratives does an animal communicate in human speech. In both cases the animals know more than their human masters and reveal this knowledge in the course of "educating" their masters, albeit in different ways: The snake speaks on his own initiative, asking a deceptive question with the intent of deceiving the woman. The results of his efforts are the institution of mortality and the placing of an angel with a fiery sword to block the path to the garden and the tree of life (Gen. 3:24). The ass, on the other hand, has its mouth opened by YHWH, asks a straightforward rhetorical question (Num. 22:30) with no deception intended, and acts to save its master from an angel with a sword who stands in its way (22:32ff.).

30. In addition to the contradiction between vv. 20 and 22, scholars have suggested the presence of conflicting or unnecessary doublets in vv. 3a and 3b, v. 5 (the location of Balaam's home), and the repetition of the details of the envoy to Balaam in quoted direct speech in vv. 5–6 and 10–11. Cf. Noth, *Numbers*, pp. 171–78; Gray, *Numbers*, pp. 308–313; A. Rofe, *Sefer Bil'am* (Jerusalem, 1979), pp. 7–26, 37–45. For attempts at harmonizing some of these difficulties, cf. Rashi, Ibn Ezra, Ramban, Abarbanel, on Num. 22:30; Ehrlich, *Miqra' Kifshuto*, vol. 1, p. 283.

31. Cf. Alter, *Biblical Narrative*, p. 106.

22:28: "zeh šālōš rĕgālîm"
24:10: "zeh šālōš pĕ'āmîm"
22:28: "meh 'āśîtî lĕkā"
23:11: "meh 'āśîtā lî"

Just as the ass defends himself on the basis of his past good behavior (22:30), Balaam himself justifies his performance by appealing to his original promise to speak only what YHWH told him to say (23:12, 17; 24:12–13).

32. Even the book of Deuteronomy, while spoken primarily in direct address, is introduced by a third-person narrator (1:1–5) and closed by him as well (34:1–12), in order to define the immediate audience of Moses' words as existing within the text. Cf. Bar-Efrat, *Ha'itsuv Ha'omanuti*, pp. 54ff.; Sternberg, "Bein Ha'emet," pp. 111–13; Polzin, *Moses*, pp. 25–36.

33. Note also the skeptical reaction of the Shunammite woman in 2 Kg. 4:16, immediately after Elisha promises her a child. Cf. Van Seters, *Abraham in History*, pp. 204–205. It is conceivable that the text is making a subtle distinction between visual and aural comprehension: Is Abraham silent because, having seen the three men, he is somehow aware of their nature, and is Sarah's perception limited because she has only heard them?

34. For a similar use of multiple levels of concealment and disclosure, cf. the discussion of the story of Ehud ben Gera (Jud. 3:15–30) in Alter, *Biblical Narrative*, pp. 37–41.

35. For further connections between chapters 18 and 19, cf. Van Seters, *Abraham in History*, pp. 215–16; Talia Rozen-Ubarsky, *Me'elonei Mamre' ad Sedom* (Jerusalem, 1982), pp. 16–47, 140–42.

36. Cf. Weiss, "Weiteres über die Bauformen," pp. 194–206; idem, *Mele'ket Hassippur Bammiqra'*, pp. 405–406.

37. Cf. above, chapter 3, pp. 68–69.

38. This reading is a *tiqqûn sopĕrîm*, or "correction of the scribes," in place of MT *bĕrā'ātî*, changed for euphemistic reasons. See Saul Lieberman, *Hellenism in Jewish Palestine* (New York, 1962), pp. 28–37.

39. This connotation is supported and developed further by Moses' complaint to God in 11:22, in which he again addresses the difficulty of providing such a large quantity of food.

40. Cf. Jobling, *The Sense of Biblical Narrative*, pp. 35ff. Jobling also develops this theme in the adjacent story of Num. 12:1–16.

41. Her response to Gehazi's overture on behalf of his master in 4:26 is an identical *šālôm*. These two terse dismissals set the stage for her emotional outburst before Elisha in 4:28.

42. Cf. Gray, *I and II Kings*, pp. 496–97; Gunkel, *Geschichten von Elisa*, p. 23. Note also the closing of doors as a magical action in 2 Kg. 4:4.

43. Cf. A. Rofé, "The Classification of the Prophetical Stories," *JBL* 89 (1970):433–34.

44. Commonly, the verb *Ḥ-Z-Q* in the *hip'il* with the *bet* of object means "to grasp" (Deut. 22:25, 25:11), "to maintain contact" (Ex. 9:2; Is. 56:2; Job 2:3), or "to support" (2 Kg. 15:9; Is. 44:1, 51:18). The meaning "to detain" or "to prevail upon" is otherwise attested only in Jud. 19:4, but the subsequent usage of the verb denotes physical contact in Jud. 19:25, 29 (*RSV* translates 19:4 as "he made him stay"). Cf. also Is. 4:1.

45. In 4:25b–26 Elisha plans a formal reception, using the same expression he used in {C} and {C'} ("haššûnammît hallāz"), ordering Gehazi to act as his go-between ("we'ĕmor-lâ").

46. Only in 4:30 is she identified as "'ēm hanna'ar" by the narrator, as opposed to the more neutral epithet "hā'iššâ" used throughout the story. The woman's words in 4:30 are certainly somewhat cryptic, but they evoke the memory of Elisha's use of this precise oath three times in 2 Kg. 2:2, 4, and 6. The narrator suggests by analogy that, as Elisha would not forsake his master on the day of Elijah's ascent to heaven, the Shunammite will not allow Elisha to shirk his responsibility to her on the day of her son's death.

47. Some traditional Jewish commentators attributed foreknowledge to the woman in 4:16, e.g., Rashi: "Give me only a child who will be viable [*ben šel qaymā'*]." Cf. also Kimḥi, Gersonides, ad loc.

48. Cf. Rofé, "Classification of the Prophetical Stories," p. 434; Alter, "Annunciation," pp. 125–26.

49. Note the similarity of language in these commands, as well as those in vv. 15 and 36a ({F} and {F'}). In each case the root *Q-R-'* is used, and the woman is described alternately as "haššûnammît hazzō't" (vv. 12, 36a) or as "haššûnammît hallāz" (v. 25b).

50. It is entirely possible that Elisha does not know that the child has died until v. 32, when he sees him with his own eyes. Cf. R. Meir Leibush (Malbim) on 2 Kg. 4:29:

> At first Elisha thought that the child was merely unconscious, and that placing the staff on the child by his emissary would suffice. . . . When Gehazi said "The child has not awakened" he thought that the child was simply unconscious. . . .

Only [in v. 32] when Elisha entered the house did he see that "behold, the child was dead", and that the child had been dead when he was placed upon the prophet's bed.

Nothing in the text prior to v. 32 indicates that Elisha knew that the child was already dead. This reading has the advantage of explaining why Elisha sent Gehazi on ahead with his staff; unaware of the gravity of the situation, he assumed that a cure could be effected by the use of his rod alone. The extent of Gehazi's own cognizance is not clear from v. 31, as the verb *Q-Y-Ṣ* in the *hipʿil* can indicate either waking from sleep (1 Sam. 26:2; Is. 29:8) or reawakening from death (Is. 26:19; Jer. 51:39; Job 14:12; Dan. 12:2).

51. While one must be cautious about hypothesizing the existence of conventions from very few examples, some comparisons with the similar story of Elijah's resuscitation of the child in 1 Kg. 17:17–24 are called for. That story emphasizes a vocal aspect that may have been primary to stories of this type: In 1 Kg. 17:20–21 Elijah's prayers are recorded in direct speech, and in 17:24 the boy's mother voices aloud her praise of the man of God at the end of the tale—"ʿattâ zeh yādaʿtî kî ʾîš ʾĕlōhîm ʾāttâ." 2 Kg. 4:8–37, on the other hand, presents a variation on this theme in which the Shunammite woman acknowledges Elisha's greatness at the very *beginning* of the story: "yādaʿtî kî ʾîš ʾĕlōhîm qādōš hûʾ." Elisha's prayer to God in 4:33 is narrated, not spoken, and the Shunammite's response to the miracle in v. 37 is silent thanksgiving. But it is not at all certain which story precedes the other, or which represents the convention and which the variation. Cf. Rofé, "Classes in the Prophetic Stories," pp. 148–50; Culley, *Hebrew Narrative*, pp. 46–49; Gray, *I and II Kings*, p. 467; Uffenheimer, *Hannevuʾah*, pp. 269–72.

52. E.g., Jud. 13:24; 1 Sam. 1:20; and Gen. 18:1–15, whose conclusion is to be found in Gen. 21:1–2. Cf. Van Seters, *Abraham in History*, pp. 204–206; Alter, "Annunciation," pp. 119–26.

53. Cf. Frank Kermode, *The Sense of an Ending* (London, 1967), p. 18:

> The more daring the peripeteia, the more we may feel that the work respects our sense of reality; and the more certain we shall feel that the fiction under consideration is one of those which, by upsetting the ordinary balance of our naive expectations, is finding something out for us, something *real*. The falsification of an expectation can be terrible, as in the death of Cordelia; it is a way of finding something out that we should, on our more conventional way to the end, have closed our eyes to. Obviously it could not work if there were not a certain rigidity in the set of our expectations.

54. The strict parallelism between the two halves of the story is broken by the placement of the revival of the child in vv. 32–35 before elements {F′} and {G′}. This assymetry results from the fact that the story is concerned not simply with Elisha's power to perform miracles but with his relationship to the Shunammite woman as well; the true climax of the story is the mother's retrieval of her son at Elisha's command.

55. Gen. 28:6; Jud. 21:18; 1 Sam. 8:6; 1 Kg. 11:2, 12:12, 21:4; 2 Kg. 14:6.

56. While 2 Kg. 14:6 is a nearly literal quotation of Deut. 24:16, 1 Kg. 11:2 loosely paraphrases Deut. 7:3–4 (cf. also Deut. 23:4, 8–9). Note also that 2 Kg. 14:6 explicitly cites a written tradition.

57. Alter, *Biblical Narrative*, pp. 70–71, refers to this phenomenon as a "bias of

stylization" toward the use of direct speech. Cf. his comment on 2 Sam. 2:1 (p. 69).

58. Sternberg, "Bein Ha'emet," pp. 134–35; cf. also Jud. 18:4, *kāzōh wĕkāzeh*.

59. On Samuel's place in the tradition of the judges, cf. Uffenheimer, *Hannevu'ah*, pp. 141–45; DeVaux, *Early History*, pp. 751–55, 763–66; E. A. Speiser, "The Manner of the King," in *World History of the Jewish People, Vol. 3: Judges*, ed. B. Mazar (Givatayim, 1971), pp. 280–87.

60. In chap. 5 of *Problems of Dostoevski's Poetics*, Mikhail Bakhtin describes this type of narrative discourse as "double-directed" or "double-voiced" words (cf. esp. pp. 153, 163–64). The narrator's comment is at once an "objectivized" presentation of the character's speech as well as a dialogical response to those words, be it ironic, satirical, or critical in some other way.

61. Gen. 27:46–28:9 is assigned by most critics to P, which contains no other cases of quoted direct speech. Cf. von Rad, *Genesis*, pp. 281–82; Speiser, *Genesis*, pp. 214–16; Noth, *Pentateuchal Traditions*, p. 17. On viewing Gen. 27:1–28:9 as a unified redacted unit, cf. Fishbane, *Text and Texture*, pp. 48–51; Fokkelman, *Narrative Art in Genesis*, pp. 97–106.

62. Cf. also the suggestion about Esau's perceptions made by Weiss, "Einiges über die Bauformen," p. 470.

63. Cf. Boling, *Judges*, p. 294.

64. I owe this suggestion to James Ackerman; cf. above, chapter 3, pp. 56–58.

65. E.g., Jud. 15:2; 1 Sam. 15:11; 2 Sam. 4:1; cf. Sternberg, "Ben Ha'emet," p. 141. While instances of interior monologue do occur (e.g., Gen. 17:17, 21:16, 38:11; 1 Sam. 18:21), they appear more rarely than summaries in indirect speech.

66. By extension, the similarities between Gen. 12:10–20, 20:1–18, and 26:1–13 tend to confirm the reliability of the unverifiable quotations in 12:19 and 20:13 as well. Other unverifiable quotations rendered believable by their contexts include Gen. 37:17; 43:3–5, 7; 1 Sam. 9:23; 1 Kg. 1:48; 2 Kg. 6:28–29.

67. The following unverifiable quotations are also contradicted by their contexts: Josh. 9:11; 1 Sam. 21:3; 2 Sam. 1:7–9.

68. Cf. Gunn, *King David*, pp. 25, 58, 95–115; Gros Louis, "The Difficulty of Ruling Well," pp. 15–23; Charles Conroy, *Absalom, Absalom* (Rome, 1978), pp. 111–12.

69. Hertzberg, *I and II Samuel*, p. 366; Fokkelman, *King David*, pp. 32–33.

70. For a summary of divided scholarly opinion, cf. Conroy, *Absalom*, p. 106, n. 37; Gunn, *King David*, pp. 97, 138, nn. 6–7. Conroy suggests that the ambiguity grows out of a desire to condemn both Ziva and Mephiboshet, since both are related to the House of Saul.

71. Cf. above, chapter 3, pp. 64–65.

72. Ironically, it is *Yonatan* who brings to Adonijah the news that he will not become king (1:42–48); note also the use of the root *N-T-N* in v. 48: " 'ăšer nātan hayyôm yōšēb 'al-kis'î wĕ'ênay rō'ōt."

73. Cf., for example, Alter, *Biblical Narrative*, pp. 155–77; Adele Berlin, *Poetics and Interpretation of Biblical Narrative* (Sheffield, 1983), pp. 43–82, esp. pp. 50–52; Greenstein, "The Sale of Joseph," pp. 114–25; Gunn, *King David*, pp. 95–111; idem, *King Saul*, pp. 33–75, 115–31; Jonathan Magonet, *Form and Meaning: Studies in Literary Techniques in the Book of Jonah* (Bern and Frankfort, 1976); Perry and Sternberg, "Hammelek Bemabbaṭ 'Ironi," pp. 286–92; Sternberg, "Bein Ha'emet," pp. 143–46.

Conclusions

1. Cf. Alter, *Biblical Narrative*, pp. 63–87; Sternberg, "Mivneh Haḥazarah," pp. 116–17; 133–38.

2. Hoffmann, "Bein Qonventsiyah," pp. 96–99. Hoffmann suggests that geography may have played a part in this development, moving from the highly repetitive literature of Mesopotamia and Ugarit to the north and east, to the absence of any such repetition in the literature of Egypt to the south. Israel's medial position enabled her to be influenced from both directions.

3. Jerrold S. Cooper, "Symmetry and Repetition in Akkadian Narrative," *JAOS* 97 (1977):508–12; idem, "Gilgamesh Dreams of Enkidu: The Evolution and Dilution of Narrative," in *Essays on the Ancient Near East in Honor of J. J. Finkelstein*, ed. Maria De Jong Ellis (Hamden, Conn., 1977), pp. 19–34; cf. also Jeffrey H. Tigay, *The Evolution of the Gilgamesh Epic* (Philadelphia, 1982), pp. 54–109 and passim.

4. J. S. Ackerman, private communication.

5. "It may be further stated that an exegetical consciousness is, simultaneously, a constructive and deconstructive consciousness; for it both asserts and denies the authority of the text in question. The very cognition of the insufficiency of a textual authority—i.e., its lack, failure, or irrelevance to a present moment—is profoundly and dialectically bound up with a reassertion of its sufficiency, insofar as the revision is not presented as self-validating but rather finds its authority in the text-unit which elicited the exegetical response in the first place." (Fishbane, "Revelation and Tradition," p. 361.)

6. Cf. Fishbane, "Revelation and Tradition," pp. 343–61; idem, "Torah and Tradition," in *Tradition and Theology in the Old Testament*, ed. Douglas V. Knight (Philadelphia, 1977), pp. 275–300.

7. Fishbane, "Revelation and Tradition," pp. 356–59; idem, *Biblical Interpretation*, pp. 482–85.

8. Nahum M. Sarna, "Psalm 89: A Study in Inner-Biblical Exegesis," in *Biblical and Other Studies*, ed. Alexander Altmann (Cambridge, Mass., 1963), pp. 29–46.

9. Fishbane, "Revelation and Tradition," p. 360; idem. *Biblical Interpretation*, pp. 412–13.

10. Cf. also Ezek. 14:12–23; 18:2–20; 33:12–20; M. Weinfeld, "Jeremiah and the Spiritual Metamorphosis of Israel," *ZAW* 88 (1976):35–39. For an example from biblical narrative, cf. 2 Sam. 14:32–33.

11. Weinfeld, "Spiritual Metamorphosis," pp. 39–52.

12. Fishbane, *Biblical Interpretation*, p. 413.

13. For recent discussions of the Chronicler's exegesis, see Fishbane, *Biblical Interpretation*, pp. 380–407; Sara Japhet, *ʾEmunot Vedeʿot Besefer Divrei Hayyamim* (Jerusalem, 1977).

Appendix

1. The single exception is Deut. 34:3, where God quotes his own words to Moses.

2. Cf. 4:6; 7:17; 8:17; 9:4, 28; 12:20; 13:3, 7, 14; 15:9, 16; 17:14; 28:67; 29:18; 30:12–13. Note also the use of question and answer formulae in 6:20–25; 18:21; 29:23–27. The forms of direct speech in Deuteronomy deserve a more thorough rhetorical and literary analysis; cf. Polzin, *Moses*, pp. 25–72; Weinfeld, *Deuteronomic School*, pp. 171–78.

3. On this connection, cf. Simon, "I Kings 13," pp. 90–91; Weinfeld, *Deuteronomic School*, p. 369.

4. Cf. Polzin, *Moses*, pp. 50–51; Gerhard von Rad, *Deuteronomy* (Philadelphia, 1966), p. 60.

5. E.g., the use of creation in Ex. 20:11; of slavery in Egypt and the Exodus in Ex. 22:20, 23:9; Lev. 19:34; Deut. 5:15; 15:15; 16:1, 12; 23:8; 24:18, 22; of references to events in the wilderness period in Lev. 23:43; Deut. 23:5, 24:9, 25:17ff. On motivation clauses in general, cf. Berend Gemser, "The Importance of the Motive Clause in Old Testament Law," *VTSup* 1 (1953):50–66; Rifat Sonsino, *Motive Clauses in Hebrew Law* (Missoula, Mont., 1980).

6. Cf. Polzin, *Moses*, p. 58.

7. For a discussion of the relationship between the Sinai accounts in Exodus and in Deuteronomy, cf. Arie Toeg, *Mattan Torah Besinai* (Jerusalem, 1977), pp. 117–44; Weinfeld, *Deuteronomic School*, pp. 206–208.

8. Polzin, *Moses*, p. 61, and pp. 53–65 in general; von Rad, *Deuteronomy*, pp. 122–25.

9. Cf. also Deut. 1:42 quoting Num. 14:41–42; Deut. 5:6–18 quoting Ex. 20:1–14; Deut. 9:12 quoting Ex. 32:7–8; Deut. 9:13 quoting Ex. 33:11–13.

10. Cf. further Deut. 1:16–17 = Ex. 18:22; Deut. 1:20–21 = Num. 13:2; Deut. 3:18–20 = Num. 32:24; Deut. 3:26–28 = Num. 27:12–14; Deut. 10:11 = Ex. 32:24, 33:1–3.

11. The narrator's intrusions are very occasional in chapters 1–11, occurring in 4:41–51a and 10:6–7, 9; cf. also 2:10–12, 20–23; 3:9, 11, 13b–14. Toward the end of the book, as Moses' importance wanes, the narrator becomes more prominent in introducing direct speech: 27:1a, 9a, 11; 28:69; 29:1a; 31:1–2a, 7a, 9–10a, 14a, 14c–16a, 22–23a, 24–25, 30; 32:44–45, 48; 33:1, 2a, 7a, 8a, 12a, 13a, 18a, 20a, 22a, 23a, 24a; 34:1–4a, 5–12. The more frequent appearance of the narrator tends to confirm Polzin's idea that the Deuteronomic narrator assumes the "prophetic" role after Moses' death; cf. *Moses*, p. 61.

12. For further reflections on the uniqueness of the Mosaic voice, cf. Fishbane, *Biblical Interpretation*, pp. 439–40.

SOURCES CONSULTED

Ackerman, James S. "Joseph, Judah, and Jacob." In *Literary Interpretations of Biblical Narratives*, vol. 2, edited by Kenneth R. R. Gros Louis. Nashville: Abingdon, 1981, pp. 85–113.

Alonso-Schökel, Luis. "Sapiential and Covenant Themes in Genesis 2–3." In *Studies in Ancient Israelite Wisdom*, edited by James L. Crenshaw, pp. 468–80. New York: Ktav Press, 1976.

Alter, Robert. *The Art of Biblical Narrative*. New York: Basic Books, 1981.

———. "How Convention Helps us Read: The Case of the Bible's Annunciation Type-Scene." *Prooftexts* 3 (1983):115–30.

Anderson, Frances I. "The Socio-Juridical Background of the Naboth Incident." *JBL* 85 (1966):46–57.

Arpali, Boaz, "Zehirut! Sippur Miqra'i." *Hassifrut* 2 (1970):580–97.

Auerbach, Erich. *Mimesis*. Princeton: Princeton University Press, 1953.

Austin, J. L. *How to Do Things with Words*. Cambridge, Mass. Harvard University Press, 1962.

Bakhtin, Mikhail. *The Dialogic Imagination*. Translated by C. Emerson and M. Holquist. Austin: University of Texas Press, 1981.

———. *Problems of Dostoevsky's Poetics*. Translated by R. W. Rotsel. Ann Arbor, Mich.: Ardis, 1973.

Bar-Efrat, Shimon. *Ha'itsuv Ha'omanuti Shel Hassippur Bammiqra'*. Tel Aviv: Sifriat Poalim, 1979.

———. "Some Observations on the Analysis of Structure in Biblical Narrative." *VT* 30 (1980):154–73.

Barth, Karl. *Exegese von 1 Könige 13*. Biblische Studien, Schriftenreihe, Heft 10. Neukirchen: Neukirchener Verlag, 1955.

Benveniste, Emile. *Problems in General Linguistics*. Translated by M. E. Meeks. Coral Gables, Fla.: University of Miami Press, 1971.

Berlin, Adele. *Poetics and Interpretation of Biblical Narrative*. Sheffield: Almond Press, 1983.

Birch, Bruce C. *The Rise of the Israelite Monarchy: The Growth and Development of I Samuel 7–15*. SBL Dissertation Series, no. 28. Missoula, Mont.: Scholars Press, 1976.

Blenkinsopp, Joseph. "Structure and Style in Judges 13–16." *JBL* 82 (1963):65–76.

Booth, Wayne. *The Rhetoric of Fiction*. Chicago: University of Chicago Press, 1961.

———. *The Rhetoric of Irony*. Chicago: University of Chicago Press, 1974.

Brichto, Herbert C. *The Problem of Curse in the Hebrew Bible*. Philadelphia: Society for Biblical Literature, 1963.

Bright, John. *A History of Israel*. 2d ed. Philadelphia: Westminster Press, 1972.

Brockelmann, Carl. *Hebräische Syntax*. Neukirchen: Neukirchener Verlag, 1956.

Brongers, H. A. "Some Remarks on the Biblical Particle *halo'*." *OTS* 21 (1981): 177–89.

———. *"we'attah* im Alten Testament." *VT* 15 (1965):289–99.

Brown, Francis; Driver, Samuel R.; and Briggs, Charles A. *A Hebrew and English Lexicon of the Old Testament.* Oxford: Oxford University Press, 1907; reprinted 1953.

Brueggemann, Walter. *The Land.* Philadelphia: Fortress Press, 1977.

———. "Life and Death in Tenth Century Israel." *JAAR* 40 (1972):96–109.

Buber, Martin. *On the Bible: 18 Studies.* New York: Schocken Books, 1968.

———. "Über die Wortwahl in einer Verdeutschung der Schrift." In *Werke,* vol. 2, *Schriften der Bibel,* pp. 1111–74. Munich: Kosel Verlag, 1964.

Burney, C. F. *Notes on the Hebrew Text of the Book of Kings.* Oxford: Clarendon Press, 1903; reprint ed., New York: Ktav Press, 1956.

Carlson, R. A. *David, the Chosen King.* Uppsala: Almqvist and Wiksell, 1969.

Cassuto, Umberto. *Biblical and Oriental Studies.* 2 vols. Translated by Israel Abrahams. Jerusalem: Magnes Press, 1973–75.

———. *Minoah Ve'ad Abraham.* Jerusalem: Magnes Press, 1949.

———. *Perush 'al Sefer Bereshit.* 5th ed. Jerusalem: Magnes Press, 1969.

———. *Perush 'al Sefer Shemot.* Jerusalem: Magnes Press, 1952.

Chatman, Seymour. *Story and Discourse.* Ithaca, N.Y.: Cornell University Press, 1978.

Childs, Brevard S. *The Book of Exodus.* Philadelphia: Westminster Press, 1974.

Clines, D. J. *The Theme of the Pentateuch.* Sheffield: Journal for the Study of the Old Testament, 1978.

Coats, George W. *From Canaan to Egypt.* CBQMS 4. Washington, D.C.: Catholic Biblical Association of America. 1976.

———. *Rebellion in the Wilderness.* Nashville: Abingdon Press, 1968.

Cohn, Gabriel. *Das Buch Jona im Licht der biblischen Erzählkunst.* Assen: Van Gorcum, 1969.

Cohn, Robert L. "Literary Technique in the Jeroboam Narrative." *ZAW* 97 (1985):23–35.

Conroy, Charles. *Absalom, Absalom.* Rome: Biblical Institute Press, 1978.

Cooper, Jerrold S. "Gilgamesh Dreams of Enkidu: The Evolution and Dilution of Narrative." In *Essays on the Ancient Near East in Memory of Jacob Joel Finkelstein,* edited by Maria deJong Ellis, pp. 39–44. Memoirs of the Connecticut Academy of Arts and Sciences, vol. 19. Hamden, Conn.: Archon Books, 1978.

———. "Symmetry and Repetition in Akkadian Narrative." *JAOS* 97 (1977):508–12.

Crenshaw, James L. *Prophetic Conflict.* BZAW 124. Berlin and New York: Walter de Gruyter, 1971.

Cross, Frank Moore, *Canaanite Myth and Hebrew Epic.* Cambridge, Mass.: Harvard University Press, 1975.

Culler, Jonathan. *Structuralist Poetics.* Ithaca, N.Y.: Cornell University Press, 1975.

Culley, Robert C. *Studies in the Structure of Hebrew Narrative.* Philadelphia: Fortress Press, 1976.

Deem, Ariella. "The Great Woman of Shunem." In *Proceedings of the Eighth World Congress of Jewish Studies,* Division A, pp. 21–25. Jerusalem: World Union of Jewish Studies, 1982.

DeVaux, Roland. *Ancient Israel.* New York: McGraw-Hill, Inc., 1961.

———. The Early History of Israel. Philadelphia: Westminster Press, 1978.

DeVries, Simon J. *Prophet Against Prophet.* Grand Rapids, Mich.: William B. Eerdmans, 1978.

Driver, Samuel R. *Genesis.* Westminster Commentaries. London: Methuen, 1904.

———. *Notes on the Hebrew Text of the Book of Samuel.* Oxford: Oxford University Press, 1890.

———. *A Treatise on the Use of the Tenses in Hebrew.* Oxford: Oxford University Press, 1881.

Ehrlich, Arnold. *Miqra' Kifshuto.* 3 vols. 2d ed. New York: Ktav Press, 1969.

Eissfeldt, Otto. *Die Komposition der Samuelis Bücher.* Leipzig: J. C. Hinrichs, 1931.

———. *The Old Testament: An Introduction.* 3d ed. New York: Harper and Row, 1965.

Epstein, Jacob. *Mevo'ot Lassifrut Hattana'im.* Jerusalem: Magnes Press, 1957.

Exum, J. Cheryl. "Promise and Fulfillment: Narrative Art in Judges 13." *JBL* 99 (1980):43–59.

Fenik, Bernard, ed. *Homer: Tradition and Invention.* Leiden: E. J. Brill, 1978.

Finkelstein, Jacob J. "Ammiṣaduqa's Edict and the Babylonian Law Codes." *JCS* 15 (1961):91–104.

Fishbane, Michael. *Biblical Interpretation in Ancient Israel.* Oxford: Clarendon Press, 1985.

———. "Composition and Structure in the Jacob Cycle." *JJS* 26 (1975):15–38.

———. "Revelation and Tradition: Aspects of Inner-Biblical Exegesis." *JBL* 99 (1980):343–61.

———. "Torah and Tradition." In *Tradition and Theology in the Old Testament,* edited by Douglas V. Knight, pp. 275–300. Philadelphia: Fortress Press, 1977.

Fokkelman, J. P. *Narrative Art and Poetry in the Books of Samuel. Volume I: King David.* Assen: Van Gorcum, 1981.

———. *Narrative Art in Genesis: Specimens of Stylistic and Structural Analysis.* Assen: Van Gorcum, 1975.

Fox, Michael V. "The Identification of Quotations in Biblical Literature." *ZAW* 93 (1981):416–31.

Gan, Moshe. "Megillat 'Esther Be'or Sippur Yosef Bemitsrayim." *Tarbitz* 31 (1962):144–49.

Gemser, Berend. "The Importance of the Motive Clause in Old Testament Law." *VTSup* 1 (1953):50–66.

Gevirtz, Stanley. *Patterns in the Early Poetry of Israel.* Chicago: University of Chicago Press, 1963.

Good, Edwin. *Irony in The Old Testament.* Philadelphia: Westminster Press, 1965.

Gordis, Robert. *Koheleth: The Man and His World.* New York: Schocken Books, 1968.

———. *Poets, Prophets, and Sages.* Bloomington, Ind.: Indiana University Press, 1971.

———. "Quotations as a Literary Usage in Biblical, Oriental, and Rabbinic Literature." *HUCA* 22 (1949):157–219.

Gordon, Cyrus. *Ugarit and Minoan Crete.* New York: W. W. Norton and Company, 1960.

———. *Ugaritic Textbook.* Rome: Biblical Pontifical Institute, 1965.

Gottwald, Norman K. *The Tribes of Yahweh.* Maryknoll, New York: Orbis Books, 1979.

Gray, George B. *A Critical and Exegetical Commentary on the Book of Numbers.* ICC. Edinburgh: T. and T. Clark, 1903.

Gray, John. *I and II Kings.* 2d ed. Philadelphia: Westminster Press, 1970.

Greenberg, Moshe. "Hammuva'ot Besefer Yehezkel Kereqa' Lannevu'ot," *Beth Miqra'* 50 (1972):273–78.

―――. *Understanding Exodus.* New York: Behrman House, Inc., 1969.

Greenstein, Edward. "An Equivocal Reading of the Sale of Joseph." In *Literary Interpretations of Biblical Narratives,* vol. II, edited by K. R. R. Gros Louis, pp. 114–25. Nashville: Abingdon Press, 1982.

―――. "The Riddle of Samson." *Prooftexts* 1 (1981):237–60.

Gros Louis, Kenneth R. R. "The Difficulty of Ruling Well: King David of Israel." *Semeia* 8 (1977):15–33.

―――, ed. *Literary Interpretations of Biblical Narratives,* vol. 1. Nashville: Abingdon Press, 1974.

―――. *Literary Interpretations of Biblical Narratives,* vol. II. Nashville: Abingdon Press, 1982.

Gunkel, Hermann. *Meisterwerke Hebräischen Erzählungskunst, I: Geschichten von Elisa.* Berlin: n.p., 1924; reprint ed., Jerusalem: Hebrew University, 1973.

Gunn, David M. *The Fate of King Saul.* Sheffield: Journal for the Study of the Old Testament, 1980.

―――. *The Story of King David.* Sheffield: Journal for the Study of the Old Testament, 1978.

Halpern, Baruch. "Sectionalism and the Schism." *JBL* 93 (1974):519–32.

Hals, R. M. *The Theology of the Book of Ruth.* Philadelphia: Fortress Press, 1976.

Hayes, John H., and Miller, J. Maxwell, eds. *Israelite and Judaean History.* Philadelphia: Westminster Press, 1977.

Heinemann, Isaac. *Darkei Ha'aggadah.* Jerusalem: Magnes Press, 1964.

Herrmann, Siegfried. *A History of Israel in Old Testament Times.* Translated by. J. Bowden. Philadelphia: Fortress Press, 1981.

Hertzberg, H. W. *I and II Samuel.* Philadelphia: Westminster Press, 1964.

Heschel, Abraham Joshua. *Torah min Hashamayim Be'aspeqlariyah shel Haddorot.* New York: Soncino Press, 1962.

Hoffmann, Yair. "Bein Qonventsiyah Le'estrategiyah." *Hassifrut* 28 (1979):89–99.

Horwitz, W. J. "Audience Reaction to Jeremiah." *CBQ* 32 (1970):555–64.

Huffmon, Herbert. "The Covenant Lawsuit in the Prophets." *JBL* 78 (1959):285–95.

Hurvitz, Avi. *Bein Lashon Lelashon.* Jerusalem: Mosad Bialik, 1972.

Iser, Wolfgang. *The Act of Reading.* Baltimore: Johns Hopkins Press, 1978.

―――. "Indeterminacy and the Reader's Response." In *Aspects of Narrative,* edited by J. Hillis Miller, pp. 1–45. New York: Columbia University Press, 1971.

Jackson, Jared T., and Kessler, Martin, eds. *Rhetorical Criticism: Studies in Honor of James Muilenburg.* Pittsburgh: Pickwick Press, 1974.

Jacob, Benno. *Das Erste Buch der Tora: Genesis.* Berlin: Schocken Verlag, 1934.

Japhet, Sara. *'Emunot Vede'ot Besefer Divrei Hayyamim.* Jerusalem: Mosad Bialik, 1977.

Jobling, David. "Saul's Fall and Jonathan's Rise: Tradition and Redaction in I Sam. 14:1–46." *JBL* 95 (1976):367–76.

―――. *The Sense of Biblical Narrative.* Sheffield: Journal for the Study of the Old Testament, 1978.

Kautsch, E., ed. *Gesenius' Hebrew Grammar.* Translated by A. E. Cowley. Oxford: Oxford University Press, 1910.

Kawin, Bruce. *Telling It Again and Again: Repetition in Literature and Film.* Ithaca, N.Y.: Cornell University Press, 1972.

Kermode, Frank. *The Genesis of Secrecy.* Cambridge, Mass.: Harvard University Press, 1979.

―――. *The Sense of an Ending.* London and New York: Oxford University Press, 1967.

Klopfenstein, Martin A. *Die Lüge nach dem Alten Testament.* Zurich and Frankfort: Gotthelf Verlag, 1964.

Koch, Klaus. *The Growth of Biblical Narrative.* New York: Charles Scribner's Sons, 1969.

Kuhl, C. "Die Wideraufnähme—ein literarisches Prinzip?" *ZAW* 64 (1952):1–11.

LaPointe, Roger. *Dialogues Bibliques et Dialectique Impersonelle.* Paris: Desclée, 1971.

Laurentin, A. *"weʿattah—kai nun."* *Biblica* 45 (1964):171–97.

Lieberman, Saul. *Hellenism in Jewish Palestine.* New York: The Jewish Theological Seminary of America, 1962.

Leibowitz, Nehama. *ʿIyyunim Besefer Bereshit.* Jerusalem: World Zionist Federation, 1968.

————. *ʿIyyunim Ḥadashim Besefer Shemot.* Jerusalem: World Zionist Federation, 1969.

————. "Keitsad Liqroʾ Pereq Battanakh." In *Nefesh Veshir,* pp. 90–104. Jerusalem: Department of Youth Immigration, 1954.

————. *Studies in Bamidbar.* Jerusalem: World Zionist Organization, 1980.

Levenston, E. A. "The Speech-Acts of God." *Hebrew University Studies in Literature and the Arts* 12 (1984):129–45.

Licht, Jacob. *Storytelling in the Bible.* Jerusalem: Magnes Press, 1978.

Limburg, James. "The Root *rîb* and the Prophetic Lawsuit Speeches." *JBL* 88 (1969):291–304.

Liver, Jacob. "Mishpaḥah." *Encyclopedia Biblica,* vol. 5, cols. 582–88. Jerusalem: Mosad Bialik, 1968.

Loewenstamm, Samuel. "The Divine Grant of Land to the Patriarchs." *JAOS* 91 (1971):509–10.

————. "The Making and Destruction of the Golden Calf." *Biblica* 48 (1967): 481–90.

Lord, Albert Bates. *A Singer of Tales.* Cambridge, Mass: Harvard University Press, 1960.

Loretz, Oswald. "Kʿt ḥyh—'wie jetzt ums Jahr', Gen. 18:10." *Biblica* 43 (1962): 75–78.

Lowenthal, Eric. *The Joseph Narrative in Genesis.* New York: Ktav Press, 1973.

Luzzato, S. D. *Perush ʿal Ḥamishah Ḥummeshei Torah.* 2d ed. Tel Aviv: Dvir, 1965.

Mabee, Charles. "David's Judicial Exoneration." *ZAW* 92 (1980):89–107.

McCarter, P. Kyle. *The Anchor Bible: I Samuel.* Garden City, N.Y.: Doubleday and Company, 1980.

————. *The Anchor Bible: II Samuel.* Garden City, N.Y.: Doubleday and Company, 1984.

————. "The Apology of David." *JBL* 99 (1980):489–504.

McEvenue, Sean E. *The Narrative Style of the Priestly Writer.* Rome: Biblical Institute Press, 1971.

Magonet, Jonathan. *Form and Meaning: Studies in the Book of Jonah.* Beitrage zur biblischen Exegese und Theologie, no. 2. Bern and Frankfort: H. and P. Lang, 1976.

Malamat, Abraham. "The Organs of Statecraft in the Israelite Monarchy." In *Biblical Archaeologist Reader,* vol. 3, edited by E. F. Campbell and D. N. Freedman, pp. 163–98. Garden City, N.Y.: Doubleday and Company, 1970.

Melamed, Ezra Zion. "Breakup of Stereotyped Phrases as an Artistic Device in Biblical Poetry." *Scripta Hierosolymitana* 8 (1961):115–53.

————. *Mefarshei Hammiqraʾ.* Jerusalem: Magnes Press, 1964.

Melugin, Roy F. "Muilenburg, Form Criticism, and Theological Exegesis." In

Encounter with the Text, edited by Martin J. Buss, pp. 91–100. Philadelphia: Fortress Press, 1979.

Meyer, Herman. *The Poetics of Quotation in the European Novel.* Princeton: Princeton University Press, 1968.

Miller, J. Hillis. *Fiction and Repetition.* Cambridge, Mass.: Harvard University Press, 1982.

Miqra'ot Gedolot 'im Malbim. Jerusalem: 1964.

Montgomery, James A., and Gehman, Henry S. *A Critical and Exegetical Commentary on the Books of Kings.* Edinburgh: T. and T. Clark, 1951.

Muffs, Yohanan. "'Iyyunim Battefillah Hannevu'it." *Eretz Israel* 14 (1978):48–54.

Muilenburg, James. "The Form and Structure of the Covenantal Formulations." *VT* 9 (1959):347–65.

———. "The Intercession of the Covenant Mediator." In *Words and Meanings: Essays Presented to David Winton Thomas,* edited by P. R. Ackroyd and B. Lindars, pp. 159–81. Cambridge: Cambridge University Press, 1968.

———. "A Study in Hebrew Rhetoric: Repetition and Style." *VTSup* 1 (1953):97–111.

Nicholson, E. W. *Preaching to the Exiles.* Oxford: Oxford University Press, 1970.

Nielsen, Eduard. *Oral Tradition.* London: SCM Press, 1961.

Noth, Martin. *A History of Pentateuchal Traditions.* Translated by Bernhard Anderson. Englewood Cliffs, N.J.: Prentice-Hall, 1972.

———. *Numbers.* Philadelphia: Westminster Press, 1968.

Olrik, Axel. "Epic Laws of Folk Narrative." In *The Study of Folklore,* edited by Alan Dundes, pp. 129–41. Englewood Cliffs, N.J.: Prentice-Hall, 1965.

Olsen, Dennis T. *The Death of the Old and the Birth of the New: The Framework of the Book of Numbers and the Pentateuch.* Chico, Calif.: Scholars Press, 1985.

Overholt, Thomas W. "Jeremiah 2 and the Problem of 'Audience Reaction.'" *CBQ* 41 (1979):262–73.

———. *The Threat of Falsehood.* Napierville, Ill.: Alec R. Allenson, 1970.

Pascal, Roy. *The Dual Voice.* Manchester: Manchester University Press, 1977.

Pederson, Johs. *Israel: Its Life and Culture, I–II.* London: Oxford University Press, 1926.

Perry, Menahem, and Sternberg, Meir. "Hammelek Bemabbaṭ 'Ironi." *Hassifrut* 1 (1968):263–92.

———. "'Zehirut—Sifrut!' Leba'ayot Ha'inṭerpreṭatsiyah Vehappo'eṭiqah shel Hassippur Bammiqra'." *Hassifrut* 2 (1969):608–63.

Polzin, Robert. "'The Ancestress of Israel in Danger' in Danger." *Semeia* 3 (1975):81–98.

———. *Moses and the Deuteronomist.* New York: Seabury Press, 1980.

Pratt, Mary Louise. *Toward a Speech Act Theory of Literary Discourse.* Bloomington, Ind.: Indiana University Press, 1977.

Pritchard, James B., ed. *Ancient Near Eastern Texts Relating to the Old Testament.* 3rd ed. with supplement. Princeton: Princeton University Press, 1969.

Propp, Vladimir. *Morphology of the Folktale.* Translated by Laurence Scott. 2d ed. Austin, Texas: University of Texas Press, 1968.

von Rad, Gerhard. *Deuteronomy.* Philadelphia: Westminster Press, 1966.

———. *Genesis.* Rev. ed. Philadelphia: Westminster Press, 1972.

———. *The Problem of the Hexateuch and Other Essays.* New York: McGraw-Hill, Inc., 1966.

Rabinowitz, Peter J. "'What's Hecuba to us?' The Audience's Experience of

Literary Borrowing." In *The Reader in the Text,* edited by S. I. Suleiman and I. Crosman, pp. 241–63. Princeton: Princeton University Press, 1980.

Radday, Y. T. "Chiasm in Kings." *Linguistica Biblica* 31 (1974):52–67.

Redford, Donald B. *A Study of the Biblical Story of Joseph. VTSup* 20. Leiden: E. J. Brill, 1970.

Rimmon-Kenan, Shlomith. *Narrative Fiction: Contemporary Poetics.* London and New York: Methuen, 1983.

———. "The Paradoxical Status of Repetition." *Poetics Today* 1 (1980):151–59.

Rofé, Alexander. "Classes in the Prophetic Stories: Didactic Legenda and Parables." *VTSup* 26 (1974): 143–64.

———. "The Classification of the Prophetical Stories." *JBL* 89 (1970):427–44.

———. *Sefer Bil'am.* Jerusalem: Simor, 1982.

———. *Sippurei Hannevi'im.* Jerusalem: Magnes Press, 1982.

Rosenberg, Joel. "Kinship vs. Kingship: Political Allegory in the Bible." Ph.D. diss., University of California at Santa Cruz, 1978.

Roth, Wolfgang M. "The Wooing of Rebecca." *CBQ* 34 (1972):177–87.

Rozen-Ubarsky, Talia. *Me'elonei Mamre' 'ad Sedom.* Jerusalem: Simor, 1982.

Sarna, Nahum M. "Epic Substratum in the Prose of Job." *JBL* 76 (1957):13–25.

———. "Psalm 89: A Study in Inner-Biblical Exegesis." In *Biblical and Other Studies,* edited by A. Altmann, pp. 29–46. Cambridge, Mass.: Harvard University Press, 1963.

———. "The Psalm for the Sabbath Day." *JBL* 81 (1962):155–68.

Sasson, Jack. "Literary Criticism, Folklore Scholarship, and Ugaritic Literature." In *Ugarit in Perspective,* edited by G. D. Young, pp. 81–98. Winona Lake, Ind.: Eisenbraun's, 1981.

Savage, Mary. "A Rhetorical Analysis of the Joseph Narrative." In *Scripture and Context: Essays on the Comparative Method,* edited by C. D. Evans, W. H. Hallo, and J. B. White, pp. 79–100. Pittsburgh: Pickwick Press, 1980.

Savran, George. "The Character as Narrator in Biblical Narrative." *Prooftexts* 5 (1985):1–17.

———. "1 and 2 Kings." In *The Literary Guide to the Bible,* edited by F. Kermode and R. Alter, pp. 146–64. Cambridge, Mass.: Harvard University Press, 1987.

———. "Stylistic Aspects and Literary Functions of Quoted Direct Speech." Ph.D diss., Brandeis University, 1982.

Scharbert, Joseph. "Formgeschichte und Exegese von Ex. 34,6f. und seiner Parallelen." *Biblica* 38 (1957):130–50.

Schneidau, Herbert N. *Sacred Discontent: The Bible and Western Literary Tradition.* Baton Rouge, La.: Louisiana State University Press, 1976.

Scholes, Robert, and Kellogg, Robert. *The Nature of Narrative.* New York: Oxford University Press, 1966.

Searle, John R. *Speech Acts.* Cambridge: Cambridge University Press, 1969.

Segal, M. Z. *Sifrei Shemu'el.* Jerusalem: Kiryat Sefer, 1968.

Sheintuch, Gloria, and Mali, Uzziel. "Liqra' t Nituah 'Iloqutsiyoni shel Haśśihah Bassippur Hammiqra'i." *Hassifrut* 30–31 (1981):70–75.

Shiloah, Meir. "Vayyo'mer . . . Vayyo'mer." In *Sefer Korngrin,* edited by A. Weiser and B. Z. Luria, pp. 251–67. Jerusalem: Niv, 1964.

Simon, Uriel. "I Kings 13: A Prophetic Sign—Denial and Persistence." *HUCA* 47 (1976):81–117.

———. "The Poor Man's Ewe-Lamb." *Biblica* 48 (1967):207–42.

———. "Samuel's Call to Prophecy." *Prooftexts* 1 (1981):119–32.

———. "Sippur Miqra'i Betefisah 'Ironit." *Hassifrut* 2 (1970):598–607.

Smith, G. V. "The Use of Quotations in Jeremiah XV 11–14." *VT* 19 (1969):229–31.

Sonsino, Rifat. *Motive Clauses in Hebrew Law.* Missoula, Mont.: Scholars Press, 1980.

Speiser, Ephraim, A. *The Anchor Bible: Genesis.* Garden City, N.Y.: Doubleday and Company, 1964.

———. "The Manner of the King." In *World History of the Jewish People. Volume 3: Judges,* edited by Benjamin Mazar, pp. 280–87. Givatayim: Rutgers University Press, 1971.

Sternberg, Meir. "Bein Ha'emet Lekhol Ha'emet." *Hassifrut* 29 (1979):110–46.

———. "'Izzun 'Adin Besippur 'Ones Dinah." *Hassifrut* 4 (1973):193–231.

———. "Leshon, 'Olam, Uperspeqtivah Be'omanut Hammiqra'." *Hassifrut* 32 (1982):88–131.

———. "Mivneh Hahazarah Bassippur Hammiqra'i." *Hassifrut* 25 (1977):109–50.

———. *The Poetics of Biblical Narrative.* Bloomington, Ind.: Indiana University Press, 1985.

———. "Proteus in Quotation Land." *Poetics Today* 4 (1982):107–56.

Suleiman, Susan R., and Crosman, Inge, eds. *The Reader in the Text.* Princeton: Princeton University Press, 1980.

Talmon, Shemaryahu. *Darkei Hassippur Hammiqra'i.* Jerusalem: Hebrew University, 1965.

———. "The Presentation of Synchroneity and Simultaneity in Biblical Narrative." *Scripta Hierosolymitana* 27 (1978):9–26.

———. "Synonymous Readings in the Textual Traditions of the Old Testament." *Scripta Hierosolymitana* 8 (1961):335–83.

———. "'Wisdom' in the Book of Esther." *VT* 13 (1963):419–55.

Thompson, Thomas L. *The Historicity of the Patriarchal Narratives.* BZAW 133. Berlin: Walter de Gruyter, 1974.

Tigay, Jeffrey H. *The Evolution of the Gilgamesh Epic.* Philadelphia: University of Pennsylvania Press, 1982.

Todorov, Tzvetan. *The Poetics of Prose.* Ithaca, N.Y.: Cornell University Press, 1977.

Toeg, Arie. *Mattan Torah Besinai.* Jerusalem: Magnes Press, 1977.

Trible, Phyllis. *God and the Rhetoric of Sexuality.* Philadelphia: Fortress Press, 1978.

Uffenheimer, Benjamin. *Hannevu'ah Haqqedumah Beyisra'el.* Jerusalem: Magnes Press, 1973.

Uspensky, Boris A. *A Poetics of Composition.* Translated by V. Zavarin and S. Wittig. Berkeley: University of California Press, 1973.

Vanderkam, James C. "Davidic Complicity in the Deaths of Abner and Eshbaal." *JBL* 99 (1980):521–39.

Van Seters, John. *Abraham in History and Tradition.* New Haven and London: Yale University Press, 1975.

Voloshinov, V. N. *Marxism and The Philosophy of Language.* New York: Seminar Press, 1973.

———. "Reported Speech." In *Readings in Russian Poetics,* edited by L. Matejka and K. Pomorska, pp. 153–76. Michigan Slavics Contributions, no. 8. Ann Arbor, Mich.: 1978.

Weinfeld, Moshe. "The Covenant of Grant in the Old Testament and in the Ancient Near East." *JAOS* 90 (1970):184–203.

———. *Deuteronomy and the Deuteronomic School.* Oxford: Clarendon Press, 1972.

———. "Jeremiah and the Spiritual Metamorphosis of Israel." *ZAW* 88 (1976): 17–55.

Weisgerber, Jean. "The Use of Quotations in Recent Literature." *Comparative Literature* 22 (1970):36–45.

Weiss, Meir. *The Bible from Within.* Jerusalem: Magnes Press, 1984.

———. "Einiges über die Bauformen des Erzählens in der Bibel." *VT* 13 (1963): 456–75.

———. *Hammiqra' Kidemuto.* Jerusalem: Mosad Bialik, 1967.

———. "Mele'ket Hassippur Bammiqra'." *Molad* 20 (1962):402–406.

———. "Weiteres über die Bauformen des Erzählens in der Bibel." *Biblica* 46 (1965):181–206.

Wellek, René, and Warren, Austin. *Theory of Literature.* 3d ed. New York: Harcourt, Brace, 1956.

Westermann, Claus. *Basic Forms of Prophetic Speech.* Translated by Hugh C. White. Philadelphia: Westminster Press, 1967.

———. *The Promises to the Fathers.* Philadelphia: Fortress Press, 1980.

White, Hugh C. "Direct and Third Person Discourse in the Narrative of the 'Fall.'" In *Society for Biblical Literature Seminar Papers,* vol. 1, edited by Paul J. Achtmeier, pp. 121–40. Missoula, Mont.: Scholars Press, 1978.

Whybray, Roger N. "The Identification and Use of Quotations in Ecclesiastes," *VTSup* 32 (1980):435–51.

———. *The Succession Narrative.* London: SCM Press, 1968.

Williams, Ronald J. *Hebrew Syntax: An Outline.* 2d ed. Toronto: University of Toronto Press, 1970.

Wolff, Hans Walter. *Das Zitat im Prophetenspruch.* Evangelische Theologie Beiheft 4. Munich: Chr. Kaiser Verlag, 1937. Reprinted in *Gesammelte Studien zum Alten Testament,* pp. 36–129. Munich: Chr. Kaiser Verlag, 1964.

van der Woude, A. S. "Micah in Dispute with the False Prophets." *VT* 19 (1969):244–60.

Yaron, Reuven. "Ka'eth Ḥayyah and Koh Leḥay." *VT* 12 (1962):500–501.

Zakovitch, Yair. "The Story of Naboth's Vineyard." In Meir Weiss, *The Bible From Within,* pp. 379–405. Jerusalem: Magnes Press, 1984.

Zakovitch, Yair, and Shinan, Avigdor. "Vattippol Me'al Haggamal (Gen. 24:64)." *Hassifrut* 29 (1979):104–109.

Zimmerli, Walther. *Ezekiel I.* Translated by R. E. Clements. Philadelphia: Fortress Press, 1979.

GENERAL INDEX

INDEX OF
BIBLICAL PASSAGES

156